VISION

The Scholarly Contributions of Mark Searle to Liturgical Renewal

Anne Y. Koester
and
Barbara Searle
Editors

LITURGICAL PRESS
Collegeville, Minnesota

www.litpress.org

Cover design by David Manahan, O.S.B. Photo courtesy of Anne Searle.

1   2   3   4   5   6   7   8

Library of Congress Cataloging-in-Publication Data

Vision : the scholarly contributions of Mark Searle to liturgical
    renewal / Anne Y. Koester and Barbara Searle, editors.
        p. cm.
    Includes bibliographical references and index.
    ISBN 0-8146-2943-1 (alk. paper)
    1. Catholic Church—Liturgy.   2. Church renewal—Catholic Church.   I.
Searle, Mark, 1941–   II. Koester, Anne Y.   III. Searle, Barbara Schmich.
BX1970.V545 2004
264'.02—dc22   2003018927

To

the Order of Friars Minor, English Province,
who prayed with and supported Mark Searle in the spirit of St. Francis,
who educated him in the spirit of St. Bonaventure,
and who freed him for service to the wider Church

Contents

Foreword

The plans for this collection were drawn up at the dining room table in the Searle home in 2001. At the time, Barbara Searle was nearly finished assembling all of the published works of her late husband, Dr. Mark Searle. Her labors resulted in the comprehensive bibliography that is included in this volume. Barbara was also anticipating the tenth anniversary of Mark's death on August 16, 2002, and discerning with various people how the occasion could be kept. We wholeheartedly agreed that the time was right to honor Mark in some way for the remarkable contributions he made to the life of the Church. Our desire to honor Mark, however, was coupled with the conviction that his dreams for the liturgical life of the Church are yet unrealized and that the wisdom reflected in his work remains immensely valuable to liturgical scholarship and practice.

Our conversations led to the idea of publishing ten of Mark's scholarly essays in one volume and inviting current scholars in the field to introduce each of the essays. The articles selected demonstrate the tremendous breadth of Mark's interests and the depth of his contributions. Mark was known as a masterful and passionate teacher, and our hope is that through this collection, present and future generations will continue to learn from him.

The eleven individuals who contributed introductory essays accepted without hesitation the invitation to write for the book because of their sincere respect for and appreciation of Mark Searle as a scholar, colleague, and friend.

I did not have the privilege of knowing Mark personally but, like many others, I have come to know him through his work and to be inspired and guided by his vision.

Anne Y. Koester

Lawrence A. Hoffman

Appreciation

Mark Searle was a man of multiple gifts. Visionary yet practical, he was driven to discover the truths of things, and to apply them in a world that ached for the soft touch of the spirit. He was a brilliant scholar, but an ordinary man, sustained in his passion by the love of those whom he loved equally in return. His piercing dedication left its mark on all who met him, and when he died his friends, colleagues and students gathered with the certain knowledge that the world had lost a servant of God. His family lost more, for as much as he was a scholar, Mark was even more a devoted husband and father. It would have taken a book three times the size of this one to chronicle his love for Barbara, Anna, Matthew, and Justin. That book, indelibly inscribed already in Barbara's heart, will be passed along as family memories inevitably are, story by story, to children too young to remember their father in all that he was. This book, some of Mark's essays, celebrates Mark's public presence. Those who knew him will not be able to read Mark's words without recalling their author's gentle but urgent voice as he once spoke them. Some voices are never stilled.

Mark possessed a mind uniquely attuned to ultimates, and a resolve that focused them on life's everyday existence. He combined theory with practice, imagining what might be, but measuring his ideals against the world's harsh realities. Like the inhabitants of Plato's cave, he rose regularly above the shadows to behold the ideas on which the world depends. He preferred the cave to the ivory tower, however, and that is where he lived: among the people, lighting up the shadows with what his mind had seen beyond. He never sacrificed honesty to expedience, but hoped his honesty would translate into expedient action for God's ends. The many students whom he loved to teach are different because he was their teacher. They will recall how much Mark lived what he taught, pursuing what is noble and good, and how he achieved more than could be imagined in the all-too-short life span allotted him.

In the early part of his liturgical efforts in the United States, Mark had worked within the Center for Pastoral Liturgy at the University of Notre Dame precisely at a time when a flurry of international attention was being showered on the traditional liturgy of the Church he loved, with the aim that it speak its historic truths in twentieth-century accents of hope and promise. Mark's work was steeped in Vatican II theology and he used the full range of conciliar documents to promote the renewal of the liturgy. His insight and his depth provided wisdom during a unique world moment of elemental liturgical honesty. Later, with a faculty appointment in the Department of Theology, Mark moved fully, as it were, to the academic side of the equation, but he never forgot his earlier experience among God's people. Though many things academically, one could say he was always a "liturgist." As he put it, "Liturgy is always a moment of decision when the theorizing has to end and the ideal has to yield to the practical: something has to be said and something has to be done."[1] He saw liturgy as the theological focal point where theory and practice met.

His insistent questions arose from an equally insistent claim that liturgy should make a difference. In the pages that follow, for instance, he asks, "Why is the liturgy important to social justice?";[2] "Why not fully initiate infants and children into the sacramental life of the community?";[3] and "What difference should it make that a marriage is blessed by the Church, rather than allowed to occur, as it had for centuries, as a domestic issue only, between 'two families and . . . two households?'"[4] How, he wanted to know, can liturgy pass beyond naïveté to become "critical pedagogy?"[5] In the course of attending to these and similar questions, Mark began to see things differently than other people did. Or, perhaps more accurately, because he saw things differently than other people did, he found the right questions to ask: questions that were still open, Mark knew, even though others may have considered them already answered. He sought to go to the root of things with a version of Ricoeur's second naïveté—the state of mind from which a tenable new starting point can emerge, but only after painful confrontation or forthright suspicion destroys childlike initial innocence.[6] At such a moment, basic questions can be honestly posed all over again, in hope of a new set of answers that really do answer. Mark asked those questions. And when he was finished, he had begun crafting a new way of seeing old things.

It is not given to everyone to found a new discipline, but Mark did that. He was not altogether alone, it is true, for he had colleagues round about him, and was a faithful participant in a study group within the North American Academy of Liturgy (NAAL) that dedicated some twenty years to dreaming a new liturgical dawn. But Mark led the way. Though he did not live long enough to see it reach fruition, he at least predicted it in his call for a field of "Pastoral Liturgical Studies," precisely the intersection of theory and practice that Mark embodied.[7] He had arrived at this conclusion because of his conviction that liturgy could be approached as a "communications event."[8]

That insight was the academic catalyst that drew Mark and me together as coconspirators, if you will, intent on conceptualizing liturgy. His "liturgy as event," and my "liturgy beyond the text" seemed parallel forays in the same direction. By the time we first entered into conversation together, Mark had already given the matter enormous depth of thought. Synthetic to his core, Mark had been en route to a holistic conclusion from his earliest of days, when he had insisted on merging liturgical study with history on one hand and theology on the other. Theology was always his home base. "How can liturgy be anywhere else but in a theology department?" he asked me more than once, in that quiet certitude that marked his observations on just about everything he cared to comment on. But history was never absent, since theology, he believed, had to "reflect upon and complement the work of historical scholarship."[9]

It was in 1978, his second year at Notre Dame, when he was appointed associate director of the Center for Pastoral Liturgy, that the third and final plank of his emerging theory would fall into place: not just history and theology, but the actual liturgy as lived in the assembly of this American flesh-and-blood community he knew, theologically, to be the Body of Christ. This reality he had yet to comprehend in all its lived fullness, so his study thereafter would lead him to virtual immersion in psychological, philosophical, sociological, and anthropological evaluations of modernity, post-modernity, and Americanism. Even his historical reflections demonstrate his insistence on knowing what real people do—witness his reconstruction of marriage rites by depending on actual Church records ("the way Christian people throughout the ages actually contracted their marriages") as opposed to official "doctrinal, moral or canonical" texts, on one hand, and the romanticized tradition of courtly love on the other.[10] His 1983 vice-presidential address to the NAAL assimilated all this learning for the present, by laying the foundations for the study of liturgy in a new sort of way.

For Mark, liturgy could be approached—as we have seen—as a "communications event," by which he meant "liturgical actions, whether undertaken by the leadership or by the community as a whole," could be seen as "expressive actions" in which "even the silences are eloquent."[11] The structure of such events was intrinsically metaphorical. He noted that liturgical reforms toward greater and more immediate intelligibility had made a metaphorical approach to the liturgy more difficult. Mistaking the surface words and actions as the real thing compromised their ability to point beyond themselves and to capture the sense of the holy that eluded modernity. Modernity, in a philosophical sense, he said, was actually "corrosive of any sense of the holy."[12] Liturgy, properly done, would save us from it, even as we lived it.

This characterization of modernity stood at the center of Mark's life work. If he stood at the vortex of discrete and different disciplines, he also occupied the point of meeting between past and future, cheering for both. As a historian, he knew full well the contingency of human affairs. Not a single liturgical tradition had moved unscathed through time. The putatively ancient was often medieval, the universal often culturally specific. But even as he considered the rich histories of his subject matter—witness his treatments of infant baptism and marriage, included here—he avoided the historicist fallacy of imagining "early is better." He was willing to accord no single era the sole mantle of authenticity, and saw no reason, therefore, to return to any period of idealized perfection.

By the same token, however, our own era was hardly ideal either, though it was our own, and had to be lived through with integrity, by which Mark meant appropriate regard for the very past that the present anxiously discards. Modernity may stand out as the only era which sees no use in its own past. It was, for example, clearly "post-Christian,"[13] but not because its Christian past had nothing to say any more; only that it would have to say it differently. Liturgy was a form of "saying"—indeed, as a "communications event" rooted in metaphor, it had become the primary way of saying what other modes of expression could not articulate. But appreciating the role of Christian liturgy to Christians in a post-Christian world necessitated being fully of the world, a route to reality that Mark had chosen.

For people who read him right, he was the obverse of Nietzsche: he heralded a new age, as Nietzsche had, but from the inside of tradition, not outside it. He proclaimed the life, not the death, of God. Having to contend with forces enthralled by the first naïveté, Nietzsche had denounced the blind assumption that God was real, and announced the modernist project of thinking God dead. Mark implicitly pronounced this popular obituary of God a delusion. But without liturgical reform, mass culture would only underscore the Nietzschean message, since liturgy was the only mode of communication that could plumb the metaphoric depths of theology's heady claims and demonstrate God's indubitable reality in a post-Nietzschean and postmodern era.

Mark could reach these conclusions because he possessed a prophetic understanding of the culture wars through which he had personally lived. His early years in Trier, then Paris, gave him, as he put it, "an acute awareness of the human element in liturgy and the need to take contemporary conditions as well as historical tradition into account."[14] He was therefore uniquely able to balance the contemporary world with worlds long gone (or, at least, worlds in their passing), and to fuse them in a vision of a world yet to be. Tradition need not be its own worst enemy. It had the capacity to integrate serious cultural critique and be transformed without compromise. As much as tradition warranted cultural critique, tradition had also to critique culture. But would-be reformers would have to be up to the task of not simply burying necessary changes under the weight of theological debate; and, equally, not confusing surface issues with deep and serious transformation within.

Mark was convinced that people would believe serious liturgy if seriously done. He knew its power, which he had regularly experienced acutely. But that was because he knew better than to take it literally. The groups whom he sometimes took to task shared the fact that they were equally unimaginative, whereas "worship is, above all, an act of the imagination." Liturgical renewal, which Mark thought was "a function of ecclesial renewal" would have to bring about the "renewal of the Christian imagination."[15] The Church had attended to a change in liturgical imagery without attending to the deeper malaise of the failed imagination itself, which had become "sedimented," that is to say, "flat, substituting translation for contemplation."[16]

Also at issue was the deep, pervasive, and long-time brewing polarization of community and individual. Where once corporate identity merged the individual in a community of history, rampant individualism had flung the individual loose into ubiquitous religious privatism, causing atomic individuals to scurry about in search of any kind of get-together whatever. These could easily be mistaken for community, even if they were really still the opposite. "To the degree that we are there for our own private reasons, whether to express our faith or to enjoy singing and praying together, the liturgy is not yet that of community but merely an assembly of people all 'doing their own thing.'"[17] Liturgical reform had moved successfully from "private Mass" to shared celebration, but had yet to recover the meaning of public worship. That goal would require more than experimentation. It would demand a disciplined community of memory and of hope arising out of a sense of "baptismal vocation, personal and collective, to live as prophets, priests, and servants in the society where we have been placed."[18]

A community of memory was especially important, as it would have to remember "the things that our culture forgets."[19] Mark warned us in our time, as Jeremiah had in his, against crying, "Peace, peace, when there is no peace" (Jeremiah 6:14). Liturgy would have to learn to say not only "'Amen—so be it; that is as it should be,'" but also, "'This should not be; this must not be.'"[20] Members of such a community would do more than belong to churches "on their own terms." They would come because they were summoned "to historical tradition and religious discipline in response to God's call."[21] They would look to liturgy to do more than provide "feeling experiences." Rather, it would shape us, providing "quiet disciplining of Christian attitudes toward God, self and the world."[22]

As someone whose very being flowed from a decision to commit himself to such a historical tradition and religious discipline, the discrepancy between what liturgy could be and what liturgy was often troubled him. He was sometimes alone, for he spoke as a critic of archconservatives and liberals alike, representing no politically motivated group, but only himself and the fruits of his scholarship and reflection. He continued to speak from conviction, as a matter of principle, simply saying what he believed.

To the end of his life, Mark was on his journey of honest discovery, always at the cutting edge of things. Following Thomas Kuhn, it is customary now to differentiate paradigm makers, those who shift the horizons of a discipline, from "normal scientists," the mass of scholars who go about their business applying the popular paradigms indefinitely. The latter are not insignificant. They fill in the gaps, measure a paradigm's success, and build up mountains of data. Others with Mark's encyclopedic knowledge would have become such data accumulators. But Mark knew the limits of data, which he cited only to prove his point, no more. Scholarship had to be more than an exercise in the banking of knowledge that teachers "credited to a student's account and then drew upon in examinations."[23] Mark did not do this "normal science." He preferred to challenge paradigms. His call for a new discipline of pastoral liturgical studies was just the most evident claim in a life of scholarship that established paradigms beyond the horizons of what others were doing.

In the last years of his life, he became involved in yet another area of scholarship that had the potential to shift the paradigm he offered liturgical studies. His theory of liturgy as a communications event rooted in metaphor led him to wonder just what was being communicated by the various sign-systems in the liturgy and whether or not they reinforced or contradicted each other, a matter that standard ethnography seemed unable to demonstrate with any degree of certainty. That concern placed him in the very center of the evolving field of semiotics, "the study of how meaning is produced."[24] Mark devoured the writings of French critic, A. J. Greimas, and in 1988 he and his family set off for a year in Tilburg where he would study with Gerard Lukken and the Semanet Group, who were using Greimasian semiotics to explicate the liturgical event. That he would have to learn Dutch was, Mark told me, a minor matter. ("How hard could it be?" he asked rhetorically. He already knew English, French, German, Italian, Latin, and Greek.) While on sabbatical he completed the semiotic analysis of the interior of a church building, SS Peter and Paul in Tilburg, as a way of broadening his range of sign systems. He had already done and was continuing to do textual and gestural analyses on such liturgical events as the Anointing of the Sick, the Blessing of the Baptismal Water, Roman Eucharistic Prayer II, and the Blessing of Chrism. Had he lived longer, he would have amassed a body of work that accounted for more and more of the codes that interacted to produce meaning during the liturgical event.

But, of course, he did not live longer. During his last more or less healthy year, when I was commuting to Notre Dame from New York for a semester, Mark and I talked with some regularity. By then he was husbanding his inner resources, cared for by his life's partner, Barbara, and surrounded by their delightful children: Justin, Matthew, and Anna. One day I visited the home that he and Barbara had found in the country, a spectacular old building that had been renovated to blend the old with the new. The two of them had embarked on a macrobiotic diet, trying as best they could to fight off the cancer. My last extended memories of Mark are not scholarly at all. They are of Mark the husband and father, and that is as he would have wished things to be. He was devoted to his family, committed to sharing a lifetime with Barbara and raising their children with her. Mark loved life; lived it fully; thought about it always; and added to it with his endless wit, quiet grace, and intense commitment to the God who stood behind it. Sitting at table, I could not help but think, even then, that Mark and Barbara had found a home that epitomized all they believed. Living fully in the present, raising children for the future, they were a living response to that historical tradition to which they believed they were called.

Alas, Mark's lifetime lot was shortened. Why good people die young we will never know. But that their goodness remains behind in memory, who can doubt? This book is published precisely toward that end.

As Mark so deeply respected Jewish tradition, and as that is the historical tradition to which I am called, I end with what I believe Mark would have wanted me to: a lesson from the Jerusalem Talmud (ca. 400 C.E.). An earlier teaching from the Mishnah (ca. 200 C.E.) wonders what to do when a community raises more funds for charity than it actually needs. If, for example, a campaign for the poor and homeless nets more than we need this year, we may apply it to other poor and homeless at another time. If, however, the campaign was for a specific person, the extra money cannot be allotted to others, since people gave it with the understanding that it would be given to no one else. Whether needed or not, the person gets it all. By analogy, the rabbis wonder what to do if too much money is raised to bury a specific indigent man found dead in the streets. Presumably, people gave that too on condition it be applied to the person so designated; but the intended recipient is dead; once buried, what else can he possibly use? The rabbis conclude that the extra money can always be used to build a memorial over his grave.

But here is the interesting part. Though, in general, we build such a memorial, we are not obligated to do so for the righteous, because (the Talmud explains), "Their words are their memorial." The righteous, then, already have a memorial that they leave behind: it is what they teach us, how they touch us. A common response to a mourner, then, is to say *zecher tzaddik livrachah,* "The memory of the righteous is a blessing," by which we mean that their words live on to bless us.

Thus this volume: a memorial, and a fitting one for Mark Searle, a righteous man, who bequeathed his words of wisdom. We collect a sample of those words here, that they may conjure up his memory even in those who never knew him. Let all who read this see that Mark's memory remains a blessing.

Dr. Lawrence A. Hoffman is a rabbi, and the Barbara and Stephen Friedman Professor of Liturgy, Worship and Ritual at the Hebrew Union College—Jewish Institute of Religion in New York. He is also a cofounder of Synagogue 2000, an institute of transformation designed to help synagogues become moral and spiritual centers for the twenty-first century.

---

[1] "Marriage Rites as Documents of Faith: Notes for a Theology of Marriage" (1992).
[2] "Serving the Lord With Justice" (1980).
[3] "Infant Baptism Reconsidered" (1987).
[4] "Marriage Rites as Documents of Faith."
[5] "The Pedagogical Function of the Liturgy" (1981).
[6] Ibid.
[7] "New Tasks, New Methods: The Emergence of Pastoral Liturgical Studies" (1983).
[8] "Liturgy as Metaphor" (1981).
[9] "New Tasks, New Methods."
[10] "Marriage Rites as Documents of Faith."
[11] "Liturgy as Metaphor."
[12] Ibid.
[13] "Marriage Rites as Documents of Faith."
[14] Personal statement in preparation for Tenure Review, University of Notre Dame, 1986.
[15] "Images and Worship" (1984).
[16] Ibid.
[17] "Private Religion, Individualistic Society, and Common Worship" (1990).
[18] Ibid.
[19] Ibid.
[20] "Serving the Lord with Justice."
[21] "Private Religion."
[22] "Reflections on Liturgical Reform" (1982).
[23] "The Pedagogical Function of Liturgy."
[24] *Fons Vitae*: A Case Study in the Use of Liturgy as a Theological Source" (1991).

Lawrence J. Madden, s.j.

Introduction to "Serving the Lord with Justice"

In "Serving the Lord with Justice," Mark Searle demonstrated his profound insights into one of the most important dimensions of the celebration of the liturgy—the relationship between liturgy and social justice. This is an issue that only in recent years is receiving the serious attention it deserves from teachers, catechists, and pastors. Although the relationship between the liturgy and social responsibility was one of the unique features of the early American liturgical movement and was treated often in the writings of Virgil Michel, o.s.b., and a few of the early proponents of the movement, the connection was not easily grasped and was often missed by the rank and file. In fact, in the late 1960s and early 1970s, when the Liturgical Conference attempted to link the liturgy with social justice issues at their national conferences, many faithful followers complained in confusion that this effort was misplaced, that the struggle for civil rights and the critique of social structures had little to do with the liturgy. Of course, in this instance, the Americans were no different than most of the European scholars whose research and promotion of the liturgy contributed significantly to the writing and passage of the Constitution on the Sacred Liturgy of Vatican Council II. The constitution itself fails to make a clear connection between liturgy and social justice.

In his essay, Searle roots social justice in the justice of God. It is fundamentally God's self. We see the justice of God manifested in God's plan for the universe, and that plan is revealed and carried out in three relational areas: our relationship with God, with other human beings, and with the rest of the material universe. Searle then shows how the celebration of the liturgy can have a causal relationship with the development of a sense of social responsibility in the members of the assembly.

Two ideas are introduced in the article that reappear later in Mark Searle's writings on the nature of the liturgy. The first is the concept of the liturgy as an enacted parable. He employs this comparison to show the nature of the relationship between the celebration of the liturgy and concrete decision-making in the social or political arena. The liturgy cannot and does not give its participants answers to concrete political or social situations. It is like a parable that often turns our ideas upside down, forcing us to grasp the root values at stake that should form the inner context for concrete decisions.

The second idea is that of the liturgy as a rehearsal experience, a rehearsal for kingdom behavior. The Eucharist, for example, is a meal of the kingdom, a kingdom not fully achieved, but being rehearsed. Liturgical celebrations are not viewed, therefore, as isolated events, but as regular events in a lifelong process of gradual transformation.

Although this piece was written in 1979 it really needs no update. The reason for this, I believe, lies in the fact that Mark Searle was able to go to the heart of things and grasp the essentials with a mind that knew the tradition well and, just as importantly, understood it deeply. His ability to make the connections between liturgy and justice with such clarity and depth, therefore, renders his contribution timeless.

The article presents worshipers with some challenges. First, if we are to be molded by the liturgy, we must take its shape, its particularities seriously. We have to *attend*, that is, look, listen, and act contemplatively. If we serve the community in liturgical ministry, we must ensure that the celebrations of the sacraments are done with robust signs so that they can speak with their own power. If we preach regularly, we must ensure that the Word of God in the Scriptures is preached without distortion and with due attention to both its clarity and its complexity.

Second, we must continually be open to having our ideas of God, of our relationships with one another, and our relationship with the material universe changed and expanded by the Word of God heard in the assembly over the course of our lives and by participation in the ritual actions of the liturgies themselves. We must be ready to have our certainties questioned, our understanding of our role in God's plan amended, our field of concern broadened. We should not expect a quick transformation, but a gradual conversion of basic insights and attitudes.

We can help the Spirit in this process of personal transformation by performing some regular mystagogical reflection. For example, we might ask ourselves, "What did I see, hear, and feel at the liturgy?" "What was my experience?" "What does it mean to me?" And finally, "Do I need to make any decisions as a result of this experience?"

Mark Searle's article reminds us that the ultimate purpose of the Eucharist is the establishment of the kingdom of God, involving, indeed, our personal transformation through a deeper relationship with God, but also the transformation of the world in which we have a part to play.

Rev. Lawrence J. Madden, s.j., is founder and director of the Georgetown Center for Liturgy, Washington, D.C.

Serving the Lord with Justice[*]

In a thirteenth-century version of the legend of the Holy Grail, the story is told of how the poor knight Parsifal stumbles upon the castle where the Grail is kept. For miles around, the land lies desolate. Within the castle Parsifal finds a company burdened with sadness, surrounding a king suffering from a mysterious wound. Parsifal watches in amazement as first the bloody Lance and then the life-giving Grail are carried before him. He is disturbed by the strange suffering of the people, but he asks no questions. The next morning he awakes to find the castle deserted; the wounded king and all his sorrowful court have disappeared, and with them the Holy Grail.

A long time later, after years of fruitless adventuring and after forty days of penance, Parsifal is given a second chance. He returns to the castle a changed and chastened man. Now, humbly, he is moved to ask two questions: "What is your sorrow?" and "Whom does one serve in serving the Grail?" He is given no answer to his questions—it is enough that he asks them. The afflicted king is immediately healed, the people sense the lifting of a great burden of misery, and the land itself bursts into life.

The quest for the Grail is a famous and powerful symbol of the quest for the source of life itself, of the search for wholeness and healing, of the quest for God. The release of its power affects not simply the wounds of the stricken king but the vitality of the land and the well-being of the people as a whole.

There has always been a certain tension between the inner life and social reform. On occasion the dichotomy has been transcended by mystics who were also social reformers, but the history of Christianity is for the most part a history of vacillation between contemplation and

* This essay first appeared in *Liturgy and Social Justice,* ed. Mark Searle (Collegeville: The Liturgical Press, 1980) 13–35.

action, as first one and then the other has enjoyed higher esteem. At times, matters of charity and social justice have appeared to be at best appendages to the really important business of saving one's soul or even as means to that higher end. At other times, including perhaps our own, recognition of the practical and social implications of Christian commitment has rendered the cultivation of the spiritual life suspect as a kind of self-indulgent luxury.

The story of Parsifal offers us a symbolic image in which pursuit of the Grail and concern for the suffering neighbor are intrinsically and inseparably connected, without either being reduced to the other. We have to ask of the needy, "What is your sorrow?" Yet, at the same time we must also raise the question, "Whom does one serve in serving the Grail?"[1] It is not so much a matter of the first question relating to the active dimension of Christian life and the second to its contemplative dimension, for the Grail is a symbol of total healing—personal, social, spiritual, and communal. Somehow the questions are more closely linked than that. Each is a dimension of the other, and we want to explore how that might be the case, and particularly why the liturgy is important for Christians committed to social justice.

I. Justice in Liturgy and in Christian Life

Let us begin with a clarification of terms. In the first place, "liturgy" means much more than texts or rubrics; it comprises the whole event of a Christian community gathering to celebrate the rituals of the Church. The term is used here as referring to the actions of a gathered community in hearing the Word of God, breaking bread, initiating new members, anointing the sick, celebrating conversion and renewal, marrying and giving in marriage, ordaining its leaders, or joining together in the praise and acknowledgement of God.

The question we want to ask is this: What has all this liturgical activity to do with the cause of justice? For some people, the answer would be "Nothing." Others would see an indirect link insofar as they believe that churchgoing is a stabilizing influence in society and that religion helps people to keep the law and to live as conscientious citizens. Others again would like to see religion more explicitly endorse specific political options, and the ritual of the Church take on the role of deliberate social consciousness-raising.

Part of what is at stake here, of course, is the question of the larger relationship between personal beliefs and social engagement, but there are also different concepts of justice involved. Whatever people's social philosophy might be, justice very often comes down to what the law defines as just or unjust; or, where the law itself is deemed inadequate or unjust, it comes to what the Constitution can be argued to provide. In short, in a pluralistic society such as ours, where agreement upon any kind of absolute principles is virtually impossible to achieve, justice in fact means legal justice, and the struggle for justice means seeking legal redress or Constitutional amendment for situations felt to be unjust.[2] Even basic human rights have to be argued as a matter of positive law when arguments over them take the form of an appeal to the law or to the Constitution or to international agreements.

But it would be confusing to look to the liturgy for support or insight in the pursuit of legal arguments, for the justice that it celebrates, while not unrelated, is fundamentally of a very different kind. The liturgy celebrates the justice of God himself, as revealed by him in history, recorded in the Scriptures, and proclaimed in the assembly of the faithful. This is not the kind of justice that consists in arbitrating between conflicting claims or enforcing observance of legal codes. Not that such things are any the less important for that, for, as Robert Bolt's Thomas More knew full well, we must often seek refuge from tyranny in the thickets of the law.[3] What this does suggest, however, is that the justice of the law or of the Constitution or of the Geneva Convention cannot simply be identified with the justice of God; and it is with his justice that the liturgy is concerned.

For its own part, the justice of God is not to be understood, as it often is in the popular imagination at least, as a matter of legal enactment or as the expression of a certain divine wisdom in tailoring exquisitely fitting punishment to the crimes of the inescapably guilty. The justice of God is ultimately God himself, just as he is. It is a justice that is revealed in all that God does to reveal himself. In creation it is revealed by things being the way he made them and serving the purpose for which they were made. In history God's justice is manifest in the people and events that embody and fulfill his will. In short, the justice of God is satisfied when things conform to the purpose for which he made them. (And this would suggest, incidentally, that questions of beauty and authenticity are, for the Judeo-Christian tradition, not simply matters of personal taste but of God's justice.)

Human justice, it might be said, is at best a bridle on evil; God's justice is the flowering of the good. That is why God's justice must transcend legal justice: "I tell you, if your justice goes no deeper than that of the scribes and the Pharisees, you will never get into the kingdom of heaven" (Matt 5:20). God's justice is done when arbitration is transformed by reconciliation; when people become more than objects of desire, manipulation, and profit; when poverty is confronted by asking, not how much the poor require, but how much the rich need; when the goods of the earth are looked upon, not as sources of private profit, but as sacraments of divine and human intercommunication. As and when such things occur, however rarely or fleetingly, then God's justice is done, and there the rule or kingdom of God becomes manifest. For the justice of God that the liturgy proclaims *is* the kingdom of God.

It is true that the reign of justice in this sense is at best intermittently realized in human history and that its full and definitive realization awaits the parousia, but it is a matter of hope, not just of vague optimism. It is a matter of hope because it has already happened. The justice of God has been revealed among us in many and various ways throughout the course of human history, but above all it has been seen in all its dimensions in the person of Jesus. He was the Just One. He not only spoke about the coming kingdom, speculatively as it were, but he embodied it in his own person. In his life and activity he modeled the radically different justice which is that of the kingdom of God. By living and dying in total accord with his Father's will and by doing all he did in fulfillment of the Father's intentions for the world, Jesus lived the justice of God. He was a just man, not because he kept the law, but because he lived according to the order and vocation of the One who predetermines all things. Not surprisingly, this brought him into conflict with contemporary systems of justice in his own society. But the fact that such divine justice has been realized in human form upon this earth means that it is no escapist utopia but a real possibility and the object of a well-founded hope. And the fact that the same Spirit that animated him has been poured out upon the rest of humanity means that the realization of such justice may henceforth always be looked for and worked for.

In every generation some people are called by name consciously to serve this kingdom and its justice as revealed in Jesus. They are called Christians, and together, as a new humanity, they have the unenviable responsibility of representing the hope of a higher justice and working for its realization. It is not that the kingdom and justice of God are to be found only among them, but they are called and commissioned in its service. The form in which they receive that commission is the ritual known as baptism, in which they are called to surrender themselves to the God who revealed himself in Jesus and whom they acknowledge as the Creator of the world and the Lord of history. These disciples of Jesus, who die to the man-made and demonically disjointed world of their times, begin to live according to a new order and according to a new principle: the Spirit of God who enables them to do the works of God.

The position of these disciples is well summarized in the words of an anonymous early apologist:

> Christians are not distinguished from the rest of mankind by either country, speech, or customs; the fact is, they nowhere settle in cities of their own; they use no peculiar language; they cultivate no eccentric mode of life. . . . Yet, while they settle in both Greek and non-Greek cities, as each one's lot is cast, and conform to the customs of the country in dress, diet, and mode of life in general, the whole tenor of their way of living stamps it as worthy of admiration and contrary to expectation. . . . They spend their days on earth, but hold citizenship in heaven. They obey the established laws, but in their private lives go beyond the law. They love all and are persecuted by all. . . . They are poor and enrich many. . . .

This same writer goes on to summarize the position of the Christians by saying: [W]hat the soul is in the body, that the Christians are in the world. . . . Such is the important post to which God has assigned them, and it is not lawful for them to desert it.[4]

Politics has been defined as the art of the possible, but the post to which God has assigned Christians goes far beyond this. What is possible or realistic or prudent for the unconverted is, as we are too well aware, not very much. In this new order, however, we are called to live beyond our own very real limitations. By virtue of the Spirit of God, it is possible to offer hospitality to strangers, to do good without charge, to share one's bread, to care for the afflicted without seeking to profit from another's misfortune, to exercise authority in a way that invites free assent instead of compelling grudging conformity. These may not appear to be great matters, but they illustrate in a simple and traditional way the sort of thing that the justice of the world cannot demand but the justice of God requires.

Perhaps this was why, in the third century,[5] the criteria for deciding whether apparent converts were really being called by God to this community of witness were simply: Have they, after being in contact with the Church, learned to live an honest life? Have they honored the widows? Have they cared for the sick? Have they shown themselves assiduous in doing good? In translation that might read: Have they come to appreciate the new justice? Have they learned to share their surplus? Have they had their eyes opened to the egotism of a consumer society? Have they learned to overcome the cannibalistic individualism of the age and put themselves at the service of the needy and oppressed?

Yet it is important to understand the motivation of this new order. These were not "do-gooders," working out their own problems under the guise of helping others. They were more like reformed alcoholics: people whose conversion to justice had inevitably confronted them with their own injustice and poverty. Once they had been caught up, as victims and perpetrators, in the injustice of the world, but then they had experienced the liberating power of God's justice. That liberating justice of God continued to operate in history in the daily life and work of Christian people. The power of God's justice, which lifts up the lowly and undermines the pretensions of the powerful, was recognized both in the shape of the community's worship and in the shape of its common life. The two were not separable: both liturgy and the events of daily life were equally occasions for bearing generous and faithful testimony to the fact that God's merciful justice finds its scope in human history.

The close continuity between liturgical celebration and social action is evident in the early history of the liturgy. It was the role of the bishop not only to preside at the liturgy and to preach but also to oversee the general welfare of his people and to involve himself directly in settling disputes, feeding the poor, caring for the sick, providing for orphans and widows. In this he was helped by deacons and deaconesses, whose social role was likewise carried over into the community celebration. One might also mention the merging of liturgy and life in such matters as the holding of agapes, the importance attached to the collection, the care and anointing of the sick, the formation of catechumens, and the institution of public penance and public reconciliation for grave sins.

Moreover, given that the concept of *anamnesis* meant more than simply remembering the past and implied a real participation in the events remembered, the eucharistic prayers, too, may be read as testimony to the continuing experience of God's saving justice. A common appellation of God in the eucharistic prayers of the East is "lover of the human race." Thus the account of the *mirabilia Dei*, especially as it focuses on the life of Christ, constitutes not only an account of the past works of God's justice but an implicit program for the ongoing life of the Christian community.

One Egyptian anaphora, the Alexandrian anaphora of Gregory Nazianzen,[6] speaks of the *mirabilia Dei* as having been wrought among, and on behalf of, the worshiping community; this sense of intimacy and immediacy is emphasized by the prayer being offered largely in the first person singular and punctuated throughout by the congregation's cries of *Kyrie eleison*. The proclamation of God's mighty works is brought to a conclusion and tied into the institution narrative with the words, "I offer you the symbols of this my liberty. . . ." This liberation, which is the freedom enjoyed by the praying community, is attributed to him who has been acclaimed as the "lover of the human race." It is a liberty wrought both in the saving acts of God in the past and realized in the ongoing life of Christian people, for the justice of God continues to bless and redeem the earth through the lives of those who love him and acknowledge him.

II. Justice as Revealed in the Liturgy

We have seen that the liturgy celebrates the justice of God as revealed above all in Jesus, and we have further suggested that such justice prevails when the will of God is done: when the relationships that God intends to exist within his creation, and between his creation and himself, do in fact exist. This is not a justice, then, that begins with human rights abstractly conceived, but with a divine economy in process of realization. It starts with a God-given order in which everything is assigned its rightful place or, better, with a divine teleology in which all created things are called to fulfill their rightful purpose and destiny under God.

It is probably true to say that, given the unfolding and always incomplete understanding of our purpose and destiny, it is easier to recognize injustice than it is to say precisely and specifically what the kingdom of God demands under all circumstances. Nevertheless, the liturgy does reveal, at least in outline, the positive dimensions of the kingdom and indicates the kind of God-given relationships that constitute the justice of the kingdom. These relationships are of three kinds: our relationship with God, our relationship with one another, and our relationship with material creation.

1. Our Relationship with God

Every eucharistic liturgy contains at least one clear and apodictic statement about justice; it occurs at the beginning of the eucharistic prayer:

> Let us give thanks to the Lord our God.
> It is right to give him thanks and praise.

Vere dignum et iustum est . . . tibi gratias agere: it really is right, it is a matter of justice, that we should always and everywhere give you thanks. In view of this sentiment, which belongs to the original and indispensable core of the eucharistic liturgy, it is hardly surprising that St. Thomas Aquinas should have seen the virtue of religion as part of the moral virtue of justice. "He is our unfailing source and to him more than to any other we must be bound; he is our last end and to him our choice must be constantly directed; it is God whom we spurn and lose when we sin; it is God whom we must regain once more by believing in him and pledging our loyalty to him."[7] Significantly enough, Pius XII took this quotation from St. Thomas as the starting point for his encyclical on the liturgy, *Mediator Dei* (1947).

The Christian liturgy, true to its ancestry in the Jewish *berakoth*, acknowledges the God who created and sustains the universe and who has intervened as Savior in the course of human history to shape it to its proper end. Thus the liturgy proclaims God as the source of all justice in his own being, a justice that has been revealed both in creation and in history and that has gained for him the accolade "lover of the human race." So it is that the official prayer of the Christian community begins each new day with the invitation:

> Come, then, let us bow down and worship,
>> bending the knee before the Lord, our maker,
> For he is our God and we are his people,
>> the flock he shepherds.[8]

Such acknowledgment of God is basic to the Judeo-Christian prayer tradition, finding expression in the Jewish *berakoth*, or blessings, and in the major prayers of all the Christian sacraments. But it is also essential to the cause of justice, and this for two reasons.

First, the acknowledgment of the absolute claim of God and of his justice as something that transcends any historical attempt to be faithful to such a claim relativizes all social programs, all political systems, and all just causes. The kingdom of God is certainly present among us, but it is not to be identified with any particular form of the social order or with any given political system. For this reason no form of government, no program of reform, can ever claim absolute rights over individuals or communities, no matter how good and beneficial it might appear to be; and no institution or cause can claim the total and unquestioning loyalty of any person. When they do make such claims, they become demonic, arrogating to themselves what belongs properly to God alone. We must join institutions and movements, but we may not sell out to them. Thus, acknowledgment of the absolute claim of God's justice becomes a source of critical consciousness vis-à-vis all political and social programs.

Second, the acknowledgment that the work of justice—the work of liberation, development, and reconciliation—is the work of God must save us from any messiah complex. The Christian must necessarily engage in such work, but the cause is God's, as are the power and the glory. Without this sort of conscious awareness and the humility it entails, there is always the grave danger of people imposing their own ideas and ambitions upon the less fortunate, further compromising their freedom and condemning both the would-be helper and the client to eventual disillusionment and perhaps despair. Thus, acknowledgment of the transcendent source and goal of all justice becomes a source of critical self-awareness for all who would commit themselves to the service of others.[9]

2. Relationships in the Human Community

We have seen that relationships within the human community are themselves affected by the existential awareness (or lack of awareness) of who it is we serve. For the Christian—so the prayer of the liturgy would suggest—the motivation for philanthropic work is one's own profound awareness of the divine philanthropy. We stand to one another not as the rich to the poor, the wise to the ignorant, the strong to the needy, the clever to the simple; we stand rather as the poor to the poor, the weak to the weak, the loved to the loved. The history of charitable, political, and social enterprises is full of instances of paternalism, manipulation, and exploitation inflicted upon the unfortunate in the name of good. Power corrupts and knowledge inflates, unless the power and the knowledge are recognized as gifts over which we have only stewardship, not ownership. We are not the leaders; we all belong to the flock that is led by God's hand.

Moreover, for the members of the worshiping community, relationships with one's fellow human beings are based not simply upon their common humanity but upon their common humanity as assumed and redeemed by the love and obedience of Jesus, and raised to a new level by the Spirit of Jesus at work in the world. This realization makes the believers' love for one another not just a vague ethical imperative, but an expression of the new life to which they have, by no merits of their own, been reborn and which is essentially communal. It is in the actual historical community into which they have been incorporated by baptism that the new life is to be worked out and brought to full realization in the perfected personhood of each of the children of God. This happens, as does all personal development, through interaction in which each person's unique combination of gifts is called forth in response to others. The liturgical assembly, at least in its ideal form, offers a model of such interaction. It is not a community of equals but a community of God-given and complementary charisms, gifts that cannot be identified a priori by the categories of the secular community—age, sex, race—but are distributed by God indiscriminately among all for the sole purpose of building up the community in perfect justice.

Furthermore, the work of the Spirit to renew the face of the earth is different from his creation of the material world in that it calls for the free response of every person, inviting each to surrender to the liberating will of God in the community of the human family. The work of the Spirit is intensely personal and thoroughly liberating. As such, it saves us from the chilling anonymity of clienthood and the faceless inhumanity of being reduced to a statistic—people are not just cases to be counted, documented, and processed. The experience of God's justice as grace and gift might also save us from compelling people to accept help they do not want, or to submit to programs designed without their consultation, or to accept new forms of dependency upon those who claim to be liberating them. (It is perhaps because the Church has not always recognized the existential freedom which grace brings that she has submitted people to moral, economic, and even physical compulsion in the name of the Gospel, while theologians sipped tea and debated the niceties of prevenient grace and free will.)

To put the matter more positively, the liturgy presupposes a group of people who can reach across the social, political, and economic barriers that structure our world to say "Our Father" and to speak of themselves as "we." Such a community, even in its liturgical manifestations, is unable to realize perfectly all the demands of justice. For that to happen, it would have to be truly universal and truly particular, intimate enough for all to know one another and to accept one another profoundly, and at the same time open to all and sundry without exception. In fact, as we know only too well, the liturgical assembly reflects, not the justice of the kingdom, but the divisions of social groupings. That is the torment and the tension of being confronted with the kingdom in the assembly of the faithful, but the tension has to be retained. Justice is properly a mark of the Church, like her being one, holy, catholic, and apostolic. Like these other qualities, it constitutes a tension rather than an achievement; something given, yet always to be realized. If that tension is relaxed, however, the Christian community falls from the justice of God and relapses into the thoughtless acceptance of an unjust world, taking as normal and unexceptionable the ambitions of power, the maldistribution of wealth, and the social and racial divisions that characterize our world.

3. Relationship to Material Creation

The justice of God, as it finds expression in the quality of human relationships, has everything to do with his justice as it affects the goods of the earth. Material goods are not just neutral objects, but, as our economic system makes us aware, they are the mediators of human relationships. As valuables, items of necessity, usefulness, or luxury; as fruits of labor, marketable commodities, cherished possessions, or desirable acquisitions, they represent not themselves alone, but the values and aspirations and experiences of the human community of users. It was as such that they were intended from the beginning. The goods of the earth were set at our disposal to be transformed, through manufacture and use, into vehicles of human communication and carriers of human meaning. Perhaps we see this most clearly with gifts. A gift is not just an object, a thing; it bespeaks the giver and conveys to the recipient, not just the transfer of ownership and use, but the bond of a relationship.

When God, according to Genesis, created the world, saw that it was good, and then entrusted it to the human race, it was to serve the ongoing development of that race into a community of mutual exchange and growing complicity. Yet all material goods put into human hands immediately acquire a certain ambivalence. They can be used to build up relationships as God intended, or they can be turned into instruments of division and violence. Everything, from a piece of rock to nuclear energy, has the capacity to be used constructively or destructively. Unless material creation is recognized as belonging to its Creator, with a meaning and destiny that derive from the place assigned to it in his historical economy, it becomes the mute victim of our lust for possession and of our egotistical will to power. What was meant to speak to us of God and to further our ties with one another now becomes a matter of personal possession, arbitrary exploitation, and alienated self-sufficiency.

But when Jesus took bread and wine or a few fish and blessed God for them and shared them with his disciples, creation found its purpose once again.[10] When the wood of the cross, itself the innocent victim and unchoosing collaborator in man's inhumanity to man, became the means of expressing a hitherto undreamed of relationship between God and his people, the wood itself was redeemed. In each instance the true order of things was restored and justice reigned insofar as created things could now once again speak of God, the "lover of the human race." At the same time, and inseparably, they spoke of the right relationship that should exist between human beings. When Jesus took the bread, said the blessing, broke the bread and shared it, he demonstrated, unforgettably, the proper use of all material things. The early Christians realized this: they "eucharistized" their lives by blessing God in all things and by making their possessions available to one another. And when Jesus took the cup and gave thanks to God and passed it among his disciples, he rediscovered for the human race the joy of not claiming anything for one's own—not even life itself.

It used to be thought that the "matter" of the sacraments was bread, wine, oil, water, and so forth. More recently there has been a healthy tendency to suggest that it is not bread that constitutes the sacramental sign of the Eucharist, nor oil that is the sacramental sign of confirmation or anointing the sick, but bread that is broken and shared, the cup of wine passed around for all to drink, the oil applied by one person to another. The sacraments are actions of the body, through which we become present to one another and touch one another's lives. Thus, created realities, including in the first place the human body, find their fulfillment in being used to build up the human community in accordance with the designs of God.

Creation, groaning to be redeemed from the homicidal perversions to which our sinful use has subjected it, finds it liberation when it is used as it is used in the liturgy: to acknowledge and express the justice of God in the midst of his people, who are being bonded into a community by their common and respectful use of material things. Over against that stand all forms of selfish appropriation and misuse of created realities, an appropriation and abuse that seem inseparable from unjust relationships between people. It is a long way from Cain's murder of Abel to the stockpiling of nuclear armaments or the mutual exploitation of Western capitalism, but the simplest celebration of the Eucharist, the breaking of bread, cries out against the normalization and rationalization of injustice in the use of material goods, and against the way we turn the creation committed to our care into weapons of power and destruction.

III. Liturgy as Social Criticism

It has been argued here that the justice proclaimed in the liturgy is the justice of God and of his kingdom. Further, such justice involves right relationships between human beings and God, between human beings themselves as individuals and as communities, and between human beings and material creation. Such relationships are right insofar as they allow each party to be what it is: allowing God to be God, human beings to be human, and creation, whether animate or inanimate, to be treated gratefully and respectfully. Moreover, the justice of God and the integrity of the human person are such that failure in one set of relationships constitutes a failure in all—justice is indivisible.

All this may sound idealistic and remote, indeed so remote as to be useless as a guide to action. On the other hand, the justice of God presented in the liturgy is anything but an abstraction, for the liturgy of the Church sacramentalizes the presence of Christ, the Just One. For that reason, and for that reason alone, we can say that the liturgy not only proclaims the justice of the kingdom of God as something to be done but actually renders it present, not as an achievement of ours but as a gift of God. In its presence we are confronted with that which we are called to be, with that which God would make us be, if we permit it. Thus the liturgy not only provides us with a moral ideal but confronts us with an ontological reality in the light of which the ambivalence of our own lives is revealed for what it is.

Like the Word of God in history, the liturgy is the revelation of God's justice in both event and word, cutting into human life both as good news and as denunciation. It proclaims and realizes the saving presence of the Spirit in the world, brings the presence of the kingdom, and enables us to realize where this is happening even outside the liturgy.

Celebrating the liturgy should train us to recognize justice and injustice when we see it. It serves as a basis for social criticism by giving us a criterion by which to evaluate the events and structures of the world. But it is not just the world "out there" that stands under the judgment of God's justice, sacramentally realized in the liturgy. The first accused is the Church itself, which, to the degree that it fails to recognize what it is about, eats and drinks condemnation to itself (1 Cor 11:29).

In saying "Amen" to the justice of God proclaimed in the liturgy, we are implicitly saying "Anathema" to all that fails to measure up to that justice. Perhaps we need on occasion to make that explicit. Perhaps we need in the liturgy not only ways of saying "Amen—so be it; that is as it should be," but also ways of saying "This should not be, this must not be!" Maybe we need to borrow, as the old *Book of Common Prayer* did, the liturgical comminations or curses of Deuteronomy:

> A curse on him who treats his father or mother
>   dishonorably. . . .
> A curse on him who displaces his neighbor's boundary
>   mark. . . .
> A curse on him who leads a blind man astray on the road. . . .
> A curse on him who tampers with the rights of the stranger,
>   the orphan and the widow. . . . (Deut 27:16-19).

But while the liturgy does provide us with a basis for social criticism, it neither dispenses with the need for policy planning and programs of social action nor provides us with any specific guidelines for setting about such undertakings. Consequently, Christians as such can claim no special gifts of practical wisdom or infused knowledge in the political arena. On the other hand, they are equipped by the Gospel and the liturgy with a sense of the overall meaning and direction of the struggle for justice and with an ideal (the kingdom) which, while its positive dimensions may be difficult to spell out in specific terms, at least enables us to evaluate critically the direction and value of our work and the attitudes out of which we operate. The liturgy provides a model or ideal in the light of which all human justice is judged and all mere lip service to God is itself denounced as injustice.

It would be misleading to look to the liturgy, as it would be to look to the Scriptures, for detailed prescriptions for dealing with contemporary problems.[11] On the other hand, while the liturgy does serve as a negative criterion for recognizing injustice in all its forms, it also has a more positive function. It functions, I would suggest, as an enacted parable.

The point about a parable is that when its character as parable is recognized, it is characteristically nondirective. Thus, the story that Jesus tells in response to a question or to a particular situation is one whose unexpected contrasts enable the listeners to come to an entirely different perspective concerning the matter at hand.[12] Having come to that new point of view, they are then left free to decide how to react. It is typical of Jesus—and therefore of God's justice—that he does not attempt to force people in a particular direction but invites them to discover the true dimensions of the kingdom and to act accordingly. By opening up new horizons, Jesus allows his hearers to exercise their freedom in a more complete way. (One might add that the meals of Jesus recorded in the Scriptures have this same characteristic and may be understood as enacted parables of the kingdom.) The liturgy, then, is intended, like the parables of Jesus, to generate insight and to offer a call rather than to impose moral imperatives; or rather, the moral imperative arises from within the person as a free and personal response to the insight that Jesus gives.

What is true of the parables and parabolic situations of Jesus in the Gospels is true for the liturgy also, though the liturgy has generally suffered the same fate as the parables in the hands of preachers and teachers, in being moralized and used to prove an ethical point. Yet the liturgy retains its parabolic potential to subvert all human perspectives and to offer us a way of seeing the world from the vantage point of God's justice revealed in word and sacrament. We are left to draw our own conclusions, or rather, we are left as a community to decide what appropriate forms of action might be called for in view of the newly recognized disparity between the order ordained by God and the order that actually prevails. The parable of the mustard seed, for example, retold in a large, anonymous congregation, might generate one set of insights; in a small, impoverished, and perhaps persecuted community it would generate others. The exercise of assembling for Eucharist, or the gesture of breaking the bread, will likewise generate insights of different kinds in different situations. The insight is generated by the contrast between what is and what might be, between the story of the participants and the story implied in the rite.

Another important parallel between the liturgy and the parables of Jesus is to be found in the fact that Jesus not only told parables but also engaged in parabolic actions, for example, eating and drinking with sinners. This makes it easier to recognize the parabolic character of the liturgy, insofar as liturgy is not a text but an event; not an object but a participatory activity; not a story told but a drama enacted. Thus it shares the same function as the actions of Christ, namely, that of being not just a description of what the kingdom of God is like, but the very presence of that kingdom and its justice in the person and action of Christ, now present sacramentally in the assembly of the faithful. "Do this. . . . ," Jesus said, referring to the parable we call Eucharist. In doing it, justice is done and the kingdom is present sacramentally, for all sacramental acts are the actions of Christ, the Just One. Their effectiveness depends upon the eruption into time of the eschatological reign of God's justice as a real and present gift; and it depends upon the community's appropriation of that gift, that is, making that justice its own.

The liturgical assembly, then, is the place where justice is proclaimed, but it is neither a classroom nor a political rally nor a hearing. It is more like a rehearsal room where actions must be repeated over and over until they are thoroughly assimilated and perfected—until, that is, the actors have totally identified with the part assigned to them. The liturgical action is a rehearsal of the utopian kingdom first enacted upon the human stage in the meals that Jesus shared with outcasts and sinners. In it we learn to understand the drama of God's justice as it unfolds in our world and to identify with the role assigned to us so that we may play it effectively in our lives and eventually before the throne of God for all eternity, when his justice will be established beyond all compromise.

This, of course, it not to say that every liturgical celebration is a triumph of divine justice—we are obviously far from it. But the nature of the sacraments is such that, where the Church celebrates them as Christ intends, the justice of the kingdom is more or less apparent for those who have eyes to see and ears to hear and allow themselves to be drawn into it. On the other hand, when the community fails to practice justice, it fails to celebrate as Christ intended. Then we have the laconic and chilling verdict of Paul: "It is not the Lord's Supper that you are eating" (1 Cor 11:20).

Conclusion: The Exaltation of Justice

At the beginning of this essay, the question was posed as to why the liturgy might be important to Christians committed to social justice. Perhaps the foregoing reflections can offer some hints as to an answer. It should be clear, however, that while not every Christian is necessarily called to become a social activist in the usual sense of that term, no one can safely celebrate the liturgy who is indifferent to the claims of God's justice upon the world or who is not willing, in Paul's terms, to offer his or her living body as a sacrifice by breaking with the injustice of the world (Rom 12:1ff.). For it is in the nature of the liturgy that it presents us with the kingdom of God and draws us into its justice.

In other words, liturgy and justice go together because they are both going in the same direction: Godward. The Christian vision does not allow for pulling in two directions, one vertical and the other horizontal. In Christ these opposites are reconciled. Henceforth there is movement only in one direction: toward God our future. The word of justice has issued from his mouth and is now returning to him enfleshed in humanity. For this reason we can agree with Alexander Schmemann when he writes:

> Christianity falls down as soon as the idea of our going up in Christ's ascension—the movement of sacrifice—begins to be replaced with his going down. And that is exactly where we are today: it is always a bringing him down into ordinary life, and this we say will solve our social problems. The Church must go down to the ghetto, into the world in all its reality. But to save the world from social injustices, the need first of all is not to go down to its miseries, as to have a few witnesses in this world to its possible ascension.[13]

The Christian attitude toward the world, then, is not one of condescension, but one of witnessing to the hope of exaltation. This hope is realistic only insofar as it is experienced, but it is experienced only by those who have learned to recognize the disparity between the values of the kingdom and the values by which our world is organized, and who have learned to surrender to the former and break with the latter.

Dostoyevsky expressed a similar point of view in his novel *The Brothers Karamazov*.[14] Satan admits to Ivan Karamazov that if he, Satan, had only been able to bring himself to shout "Hosanna!" when the Son of Man was ascending into heaven, history would have come to an end. What did Dostoyevsky mean by this? Presumably that if injustice, which he personifies in the best liturgical tradition as Satan, had acknowledged the sovereignty of God, the kingdom would no longer have been contested, opposition to it would have ceased, and the world as we know it would have passed. It is an idea not far removed from the belief that if every Jew observed the Torah for one day, the Messiah would come; for if every Jew submitted to the justice of God, the messianic era of justice and peace would have arrived.

Christians, however, believe that God has not waited for the full observance of the Torah before sending the Messiah. In fact, Christ has appeared to deliver us from the impossible task of trying to fulfill the demands of God's justice unaided. Instead, in the person of Christ, justice has at last been done, and has been seen to be done. In him the earth has witnessed a human being who perfectly embodied the justice of God, so that in his life others became the fortunate beneficiaries of God's justice, while God himself was given what was in justice his: the surrender of a free heart to his will for the world. The two—justice toward God and justice toward one's fellows—are inseparable, and both reached their consummation in the death and resurrection of Jesus.

The ascension of Jesus is perfect justice, for it means the drawing of humanity into the reign of God. It is the vindication of God's justice in the face of human injustice. It makes it possible for the whole human race in principle to find that justice which was realized in Christ. That is where Christians find themselves today: exploring the possibility of justice through surrender to God. The world cannot find justice until it is surrendered to God in Christ. When that happens, Christ will "hand over the kingdom to God the Father, having done away with every sovereignty, authority and power. . . . And when everything is subjected to him, then the Son himself will be subject to his turn to the One who subjected all things to him, so that God may be all in all" (1 Cor 15:24, 28).

In the meantime we sing the song of the Lord in an alien land. It sometimes seems naïve, if not entirely inappropriate, to break bread and dream of the justice of the kingdom in a world that takes the insanities of war, violence, and exploitation for normal. Yet, as the anonymous Christian of the second century reminds us, this is the post to which God has assigned us, and we may not lawfully desert it. In trying to remain faithful to the breaking of bread and to all that it implies, and in continuing to work, look, and pray for the coming kingdom, Christians might take heart from the words of the Second Vatican Council:

> We can justly consider that the future of humanity
> lies in the hands of those who are strong enough
> to provide coming generations
> with reasons for living and hoping (GS 31).

---

[1] "The Fisher King," a retelling by Ann Himmler based on Wolfram von Eschenbach's *Parzival*, in *Parabola* 3, no. 2 (1978) 16–22.

[2] On the need to return to the classical treatment of justice in terms of order, see D. Burrell, "Justice . . . What Is It All About?" *Occasional Papers on Catholic Higher Education* 4, no. 2 (Winter 1978) 12–7.

[3] For an illuminating discussion of More and the law, see S. Hauerwas and T. L. Shaffer, "Hope Faces Power: Thomas More and the King of England," *Soundings* 61, no. 4 (Winter 1978) 456–79.

[4] *Epistle to Diognetus*, trans. H. G. Meecham (Manchester University Press, 1949) 78–80.

[5] *La tradition apostolique* 20, ed. Bernard Botte (Paris: Editions du Cerf, 1968) 78.

[6] *Prex Eucharistica*, ed. A. Hänggi and I. Pahl (Fribourg: Editions Universitaires, 1968) 363.

[7] *Summa Theologiae* II–II, q. 81 art. 1. See also art. 4.

[8] Psalm 95, the invitatory psalm of the Liturgy of the Hours.

[9] For a psychological study of this question from a Jungian perspective, see A. Guggenbuhl-Craig, *Power in the Helping Professions* (New York: Spring Publications, 1971).

[10] John Mosier, "A Promise of Plenty: The Eucharist as Social Critique," *Downside Review* 91, no. 305 (October 1973) 298–305.

[11] For a summary of views on this matter, see David Hollenbach's excellent article "A Prophetic Church and the Catholic Sacramental Imagination," *The Faith That Does Justice*, ed. John C. Haughey (New York: Paulist Press, 1977) 234–63.

[12] On the subversive character of parable, see John D. Crossan, *The Dark Interval* (Niles, Ill.: Argus Communications, 1975).

[13] Alexander Schmemann, "Sacrifice and Worship," *Parabola* 3, no. 2 (Winter 1978) 65.

[14] Fyodor Dostoyevsky, *The Brothers Karamazov*, trans. D. Magarshack (Harmondsworth: Penguin Books) 2:761–2.

Theresa F. Koernke, I.H.M.

Introduction to "Liturgy as Metaphor"

Is it possible to articulate the faith of the Church and move Christian hearts regarding the liturgies of the sacraments in other than the Scholastic categories such as cause and effect, matter and form, substance and accidents, created grace and uncreated grace? The New Testament scriptures have no difficulty in doing so. Yet, with the absorption of the Neoplatonic-Aristotelian philosophical language and the social and cosmological structures that ground it, the imagination of the teaching authority of the Church has been kidnapped and held hostage by it. This is so profoundly the case that, in many instances, such as the refusal to use inclusive language or in further clericalizing liturgical behavior, the magisterium presumes that its directives are a matter of faith, rather than seeing that they are grounded in the presumptions of Platonic and Aristotelian cosmology and social order. Inherent in that system of thought are notions that evacuate the meaning of symbol and lead to the thought that the really real is somehow in a spiritual realm and that the physical world is but a shadow of it. As well, it has led to the thought that these categories can actually explain divine-human communication.

I write this reflection on "Liturgy as Metaphor" in the midst of negotiating several matters of liturgical import: (1) the statement by young adults that the celebration of the Eucharist does not capture their imaginations, that the preaching does not enable them to engage the serious concerns of their lives, and that the experience is almost always devoid of any sense of the Holy; (2) the statement that parishes should provide for the perpetual exposition of the Blessed Sacrament because the seeing of the "real body" of the Lord will keep people from having abortions; and (3) the encouragement on the part of presiders of the Eucharist to "hold hands, to express our unity with each other."

Given these and similar experiences in 2002, "Liturgy as Metaphor" is as significant to today's liturgical concerns as it was over twenty years ago. By exploring the meaning of metaphor, symbol, and speech acts, Mark Searle provides a fresh view of the significance of the public worship of the Church as divine-human engagement, names the source of flatminded literalness regarding the sacraments, provides insight into the skewed notion of what "communion" means, as well as the bases for the practice of preaching mystagogical homilies rather than informational sermons.

In retrospect, the years immediately before and after Vatican Council II witnessed the presumption that the very reforms of the liturgies of the sacraments would, ipso facto, precipitate or facilitate the following realizations: that we are baptized into a set of relationships, with Christ and each other, precisely in his saving act on the cross; that our entire lives, therefore, participate in the justice of God, that is, that we participate in the sacrifice/self-offering of the Father in Christ, through the Spirit to the world, *and* that those who are baptized participate in Christ's self-offering/sacrifice to the Father, intimately united with Christ and each other, through the working of the Spirit; that there is only one Liturgy, that of Jesus Christ, and that we celebrate it, or as Searle would say, that "we rehearse the reign of God until we get it right." Yet, forty years since the promulgation of the Constitution on the Sacred Liturgy, the cautions of Romano Guardini's oft-cited letter to the 1964 German Liturgical Congress are as unnerving as ever. Moving furniture, removing anomalies, use of the vernacular, and so on, have not changed the deep down shaped-by-Scholasticism *subjective expectations* of our people as pervasively as we had naïvely hoped. As Mark Searle once wrote, referring to Einstein's reflection on the New Science, "everything has changed except the way we think," that is, even though the fruits of the biblical and liturgical movements led to the liturgical reforms published in the Constitution on the Sacred Liturgy, there has not been the sort of conceptual and spiritual-dispositional conversion away from the rigidity and clericalism of Scholasticism presupposed in that document.

Mark Searle points to the inadequate understanding of the meaning of participation in the public worship of the Church (doing something like a ministry) and, as I read it, clearly names the corruption of the Catholic imagination by Western metaphysics. While not the first liturgical theologian to make these observations—in the early twentieth century Dom Odo Casel, O.S.B., regularly referred to the categories of

Scholastic metaphysics as positive obstacles to the articulation of the faith—Mark Searle was among the post-Vatican II theologians consciously to offer another set of categories, another "language," based on categories from the humanities and the human sciences, especially "metaphor" and "speech acts," by which we might grasp and catechize the meaning of the public worship of the Church.

My own studies have carried me to the history of Western thought, especially as it is manifest in Neoplatonic-Aristotelian metaphysics in any of its variations. I have found that, even though Copernicus and Galileo heralded the demise of Neoplatonic-Aristotelian philosophy, the magisterium has, until and in spite of the issuance of *Fides et Ratio* (1995), continued to cling to the Scholastic worldview. In other words, even though Pope John Paul II says that the Church as a whole does not adhere to one philosophical system, thereby opening the door to healthy theological pluralism, the actions of the Congregation for Worship are clearly rooted in the assumptions of Scholasticism.

By distinction, Mark Searle's contribution to theology of the liturgy is part of the vast intellectual movement called "Postmodern." With others like Edward Schillebeeckx, Karl Rahner, Edward Kilmartin, Louis-Marie Chauvet, and David Power, theologians have challenged both the debilitating effects of Scholasticism on the articulation and practice of the public worship of the Church, as well as the "Modern" presumption that we can intellectually "figure everything out." Indeed, what we had for centuries presumed to be the universally common sense Catholic way of thinking and doing has been shown to be a culturally conditioned Hellenistic construction. Given this insight, Searle recognized the death of the presumptions of Scholasticism and Modernity and called for new ways of viewing the reality of faith that profoundly regard the fact of persons-in-relationship-in-the-world. If that Scholastic metanarrative (explanation of reality) has exercised such a crippling effect on the Catholic imagination, then it needed to be deconstructed or demystified.

Mark Searle took the Constitution on the Sacred Liturgy, especially paragraph seven, seriously: "In the liturgy the sanctification of persons is manifested by signs perceptible to the senses, and is effected in a way which is proper to each of these signs; in the liturgy full public worship is performed by the Mystical Body of Jesus Christ, that is, by the Head and its Members." If everything means or signifies something, then Mark Searle is among the persistent heralds of attention to language and space and behavior in the public worship of the Church.

The celebration of any of the liturgies of the sacraments is a speech act on the part of God and on the part of the assembly. Every celebration of any of the liturgies is an extended metaphor for the initiative of God in Christ through the Spirit and of the response of Christians in Christ through the Spirit to the glory of God.

Mark Searle is among those who have disturbed the apparent certitudes of Scholasticism and replaced them with images rooted in the human experience sanctified by the Word who took on our flesh.

Theresa F. Koernke, I.H.M., is assistant professor in the Department of Word and Worship at Washington Theological Union, Washington, D.C.

Liturgy as Metaphor*

There can be no doubt that the bringing together of the two fields of religion and literature is an extremely fascinating and fruitful enterprise. The study of the religious themes, preoccupations, images and sensibilities which recur in the literary productions of different ages and of individual writers is making an important contribution to the study of the religious dimension of human life. In this paper, however, I want to take a different approach and to indicate what I perceive to be one basic area in which the literary enterprise—and the speech event which literary productions both serve and preserve—can shed light upon the phenomenon of Christian worship.

The study of metaphor has long since been recognized as significant for fields other than those of the grammarian and the literary critic. It has come to play a significant role in epistemology, in the philosophy of science, in philosophical theology, all of which in turn draw upon the work being done on metaphor in the philosophy of language. This paper does not pretend to offer any new contribution to the study of metaphor as such, but hopes simply to suggest ways in which such study might have implications for the study and practice of Christian worship.

The Problem

The ground and justification for any such attempt, of course, is the conviction that the liturgical event is best understood as a communications event. It rests upon the conviction that a liturgical service as a whole, together with all its constitutive elements, says something. It supposes that liturgical actions, whether undertaken by the leadership

* This essay first appeared in *Worship* 55:2 (1981) 98–120. It was reprinted in *Notre Dame English Journal* 13:4 (1981) 185–206.

or by the community as a whole, are expressive actions, and that even the silences are eloquent. Thus, when I speak of the metaphorical character of liturgical language, I do not thereby intend to restrict my meaning to the verbal elements of praying and preaching and reading and singing, but to include all the nonverbal elements and the totality of the service as a whole. My aim is not so much to explore the use of metaphor in the liturgy as to look at the liturgical event in its entirety as having a structure which is intrinsically metaphorical.

The history of Christian worship reveals that, while such an approach to liturgy has an impressive precedent in the sacramental sermons of the Fathers, it has not effectively influenced either sacramental theology or popular catechesis during the medieval or modern periods. The rediscovery of liturgy as communication is one of the achievements of the liturgical movement and one of the underlying principles of the liturgical reform emanating from the Second Vatican Council. Yet it may be seriously questioned whether the understanding of human communication which prompted the reintroduction of the vernacular and encouraged the active participation of all believers in the liturgical rites was really adequate to these rites. Like the sixteenth century liturgical reforms, the reform program of Vatican II seems largely to have been motivated by the desire to render the rites more easily intelligible, so that participation in the rites might serve profitably as an occasion for instruction and edification.

In fact, however, the reforms have not been an unmitigated success. Far from curing the communications problem, they have rather served to reveal its real dimensions, forcing us to recognize that the difficulties we have with the liturgy lay not only in the rites, but in ourselves.

One person who recognized this very early on was the German writer, theologian, and liturgist, Romano Guardini. In an open letter to the German Liturgical Congress meeting at Mainz early in 1964, he warned of the danger of allowing the necessary process of revising the texts and rites to obscure the deeper issue which he identified as "the problem of the cult act or, to be more precise, of the liturgical act." "The question is whether the wonderful opportunities now open to the liturgy will achieve their full realization; whether we shall be satisfied with just removing anomalies, taking new situations into account, giving better instruction on the meaning of ceremonies and liturgical vessels, or *whether we shall re-learn a forgotten way of doing things and recapture lost attitudes*."[1]

This is really the heart of the matter. Our experience over the last few years has forced us to acknowledge that our alienation from the liturgy cannot be overcome simply by further reforms, nor by further experimentation, but only by relearning, from the tradition what we have received, "a forgotten way of doing things." On the other hand, it is not a problem which can be solved by new and better theologies, either, though these are needed, too. Theology is necessarily a conceptual exercise, whereas it was precisely a too conceptualized understanding of the liturgy which led many to place unrealistic expectations upon the simplification and clarification of the rites. As Guardini puts it, "Our problem is to rise above reading and writing and learn really to look with understanding."[2]

What Guardini seems to be suggesting here is that the problem of liturgical worship for contemporary people is not simply a problem of faith but a problem of culture. The question is whether the common mindset which characterizes our Western culture is capable of understanding the kind of thing the liturgical act is, and so of entering into it. Could it be that, while we try to worship with all the faith and devotion we can muster, we are alienated by our own culture from the very tradition to which, as believers, we continue to cling? Writing nearly ten years after Guardini, Langdon Gilkey described the contemporary crisis of faith. To him the most fundamental manifestation of that crisis seemed to be "the elusiveness for all of us in our time of the holy, the absence for countless persons of a vivid sense of the presence of the divine—an absence felt not only in our daily life in the world but (even more devastatingly) an absence brought from the world into our holy places and experienced when Christians gather in worship."[3] Gilkey sums up this cultural problem under the term "modernity," "a secular consciousness that has tended to dissolve the sense of the holy wherever that consciousness has become dominant."

This "modernity," then, the argument would run, consists of a form of consciousness, a whole frame of reference within which we experience and interpret reality and which is corrosive of any sense of the holy. It would manifest itself as a prejudice in favor of rationalism and a corresponding distrust of the imagination. Its symptoms would include the conviction that knowledge is a tool for mastering reality, that every mystery ultimately has an explanation, that the use of time is justified only in terms of the benefits it produces and that the quality of life is to be measured in terms of the amount of goods available for consumption.[4]

But perhaps the most insidious and basic problem posed by the spirit of the age is what John Shea has called its "flatminded literalism." He writes, "The scientific mode of knowledge is popularly considered the only way to the real. This cultural mood induces a flatminded literalism, where religious symbols are not allowed to flourish symbolically, but are frozen into statements about some ontological deity. They do not configure and mobilize human experience, but are considered solely as independent entities susceptible to a detached scrutiny. In this way religious symbols are victimized into literal language designating invisible objects. For most people religious language is a form of supernatural positivism. The first step to a second naiveté is away from a literal understanding of religious language and towards an awareness of the relationship between symbol and experience."[5]

Posing the problem in this way makes it immediately clear why the study of metaphor as a phenomenon of human speech would be of interest to liturgists, for the continued and indeed inescapable use of metaphor provides evidence of the need of the human spirit to break out of the straitjacket of literal language, and thus points to the possibility, even today, of people being able to understand religious language in general and liturgical language in particular as it is meant to be understood, on its own terms.

The thesis of this paper, then, is that the celebration of the liturgy is a communications event, but that it is faced with the problem of the communication process being understood in our culture almost exclusively as a process of conveying information. The study of metaphor, however, reveals the inadequacy of such an understanding and can help us "relearn a forgotten way of doing things and recapture lost attitudes." If that happens, the reform of the rites will then appear simply as a necessary prelude to the more significant phase of liturgical renewal, that of a renewed understanding of the language of the rite and a recovery of its communicative potential. In short, we are starting from the supposition that the role of liturgical language is not simply to convey supernatural "facts," but to engage us in relationship; and that the actions of the liturgy are not undertaken for the purpose of getting a job done, so much as to constitute and express attitudes. The problem would be that most people "read" the liturgy in terms of something educational and purposeful, whereas the task of the liturgist is to help them enter into it in such a way that they discover it as an encounter with mystery, generating both insight and commitment.

The Classical Theory of Metaphor

In the classical study of language, metaphor was treated almost entirely in terms of its being a rhetorical conceit, as a means to engaging and persuading an audience. As such, it was not considered to convey any additional information, but rather to constitute an appeal to the imagination and emotions. Since it was considered an embroidering of the truth, a distraction or ornamentation to be employed when the truth was not persuasive enough to speak for itself, it was inevitably to be treated with some suspicion. At the very least, it was something superfluous, which could be left aside without loss of cognitive content. Even if it meant a sacrifice of some wit and grace, the same truth could be expressed in other, more direct ways.

While there are trivial uses of metaphor which might fit this definition, it has long since been abandoned as an adequate account of what metaphor is and how it functions. It is worth remarking, however, that this "substitution theory" of metaphor had its theological counterpart in the theology of sacraments which formed the religious consciousness of most modern Catholics. It is a matter of more than passing interest that the theology of seminary manuals and popular catechisms explained the meaning of the sacramental rites with minimal reference to their liturgical celebration. Baptism would be discussed in terms of the pouring of water to the accompaniment of a brief verbal formula, and the whole solemn ritual of prayers, signings, exorcisms, renunciation of Satan, profession of faith, giving of salt, use of two different kinds of oil, lighted candles, baptismal robes, and the rest were totally ignored. The theology of the Mass went into elaborate explanations of the real presence and the expiatory sacrifice without so much as a nod to any actual element of the Mass ritual beyond perhaps the words of consecration. The preoccupation with causality, rather than signification—the shift from seeing the sacraments as communications events to seeing them as causal operations—meant that the actual liturgical performance was not taken seriously as a source of understanding. Instead, the Thomistic axiom, *significando causant*, was effectively cut in two and the first half promptly forgotten as causality was discussed without reference to the meaning inherent in the liturgical structure as a whole. The development of ceremonies was considered a useful but ultimately arbitrary phenomenon, while the study of matter and form, usually in terms of justifying them historically and defining them juridically, recognized them at best as appropriate to the grace offered but hardly as the very form of the grace itself. So, for example, after establishing the divine institution of the sacraments as to their matter and form, the Catechism of the Council of Trent goes on to treat of "ceremonies" in a way that must strike us now as extraordinarily offhand: "To these [the matter and form] are added ceremonies, which, although they cannot, unless necessity compel a different course, be omitted without sin, yet, if at any time they be omitted, not being essential, are not to be considered at all to affect the validity of the sacrament."[6]

In short, the sacraments were identified as causal acts, consisting of a minimum of one sign and a form of words, to which a number of ceremonies had in the course of time been advantageously added for the instruction and edification of the faithful. This edification and instruction, however, could equally well be achieved by catechesis, spiritual reading and private devotions. In other words, the metaphor could be translated and, as the theologians showed in their commentaries, effectively dispensed with in favor of more conceptual statements. The elaboration of allegorical and moralistic commentaries on the Mass, which sought to entertain and edify the faithful with explanations of the rites that had nothing to do with the original and intrinsic meaning of the parts of the Mass, is proof of this same approach. The same fate overtook the Scriptures which became but a source of proof texts to bolster an interpretation of revelation that saw it in terms of the promulgation of a series of divine decrees and the unveiling of a number of truth statements. The net result was the constant effort to define faith in conceptual terms and to define sacramental liturgy in terms of cause and effect. It is in this tradition that our contemporary congregations have largely been formed.

All that is now changing. The profound changes that have overcome theology in the twentieth century are merely symptomatic of a broader shift of consciousness which has been occurring in the Western mind in our times.

This may be due in part to the encounter with Oriental languages and with non-Western ways of thinking[7] and in part to the bankruptcy of that line of philosophical inquiry which culminated in Anglo-Saxon logical positivism. Whatever its causes, and whatever later historians will make of its complex developments, it is undeniable that at the heart of this shift of thinking lies the abandonment of that radical distinction between objectivity and subjectivity which has been so basic a dialectic of modern thought. This implies a radical reevaluation of the act of knowing itself. Susanne Langer characterizes this reevaluation or shift of perception as a dawning realization that all facts carry symbolic meaning, so that "the edifice of human knowledge stands before us, not as a vast collection of sense reports, but as a structure of *facts that are symbols* and *laws that are their meanings*."[8]

Thus symbolization has come to be seen as the most fundamental characteristic of the human enterprise and its study has come to occupy a central place in every discipline which touches upon the complexities of human life. Despite wide areas of disagreement in defining a term like "symbol," the importance of symbolization is nevertheless universally recognized, and this in turn is altering our ideas about how we relate to reality and how truth is mediated.

The study of metaphor as a way of relating to reality has been very significant in this regard. From being a frill on the texture of language, it has come to be seen as a semantic necessity. Too important to be left to the grammarians, it has become a major preoccupation of philosophers concerned with the relationship between knowing and telling.

The rehabilitation of metaphor has come about through the development of a distinction between what Philip Wheelwright calls "steno-language" and "tensive language."[9] These are not so much clear categories as two different directions in which language may attempt to move. By "steno-language" he means words and symbols which have a more or less clearly defined reference, shared by all who speak the same language. Such words and symbols would then be capable of ostensive definition and would point to their reference with a minimum of ambiguity. If I speak of a house or a tree or a square, people who speak English would immediately recognize the kind of thing that was being referred to. Such language can be made even less ambiguous, in scientific or technological discourse, for example, by careful qualification and definition, and this is its strength: it aims at a maximum of precision and a minimum of irrelevant associations.

In contrast to "steno-language," tensive language is open, undefined, ambivalent and consequently rich in associations. It refers not so much to a single and definite item of reality as to a pattern of related kinds of experience. It thus conjoins, rather than distinguishes, realms of experience and in doing so gives expression to the continuities and ambiguities of human experience. The flatminded literalism to which we referred consists of the prejudice in favor of steno-language, the supposition that truth is best served by minimizing ambiguity, so that each word refers to one thing and one thing only. The shift in the Western intellectual tradition to which we referred consists in the rejection of such a bias and a recognition that whole areas of human experience can only be acknowledged through the legitimate use of tensive language, which expresses the constant outreach of the human mind and spirit beyond that which is already known and that which can be put into words already defined. The axiom of logical positivism, that statements incapable of empirical verification are a non-sense, has been replaced by the axiom that we know more than we can tell.

But tensive language is not a new invention. It simply represents the philosophical recognition of patterns of thought and expression which have always characterized human speech, but which have not hitherto been taken seriously. This is important, for it means that the starting point is ordinary, everyday language. The man in the street may be surprised to know that he speaks and writes prose, but the thrust of contemporary philosophy of language is towards the recognition that the man in the street also speaks poetry! The significance of this development, for the liturgist as for the English teacher, is that it enables us to find in the speech of the people we work with evidence of their own unreflective acknowledgment of the mystery of existence. This, in turn, presents a powerful pedagogical tool for helping them to come to a more reflective understanding of the ultimately mysterious character of the real world.

The key to such a process would be a study of metaphor which fully recognizes its irreducibility to any other, more prosaic formulation. In place of the old "substitution theory" of metaphor we now have what Max Black calls the "interaction theory,"[10] a term which can serve us as well as any other for our purposes here, as we look more closely at how metaphor operates.

Metaphor as Interaction

Strictly speaking, metaphor involves not so much the nonliteral use of a word, as if a word could ever stand alone, but rather the use of language proper to one area of human experience to refer to a different realm of experience. But what precisely is the relationship between these two domains? According to Max Black, "A memorable metaphor has the power to bring two separate domains into cognitive and emotional relation by using language directly appropriate to the one as a lens for seeing the other; the implications, suggestions and supporting values entwined with the literal use of the metaphorical expression enable us to see a new subject matter in a new way."[11]

Thus, when we speak of old age as "the autumn of life," our memories, experiences and associations of that season of the year become a way both of looking at and of speaking about a particular stage in human life. The metaphor thus does two things: it offers insight and it lends a vocabulary in which to play out the insight. It is not just a matter of lending a vocabulary, for the use of the vocabulary will be guided and restricted by the insight itself and some extensions of the metaphor will be excluded as inappropriate: talk of "mellow fruitfulness" may well be appropriate, whereas talk of bonfires may not. Moreover this reflection on the way metaphors allow themselves to be played out into a whole series of metaphors may also serve to remind us that it is properly the sentence rather than the word which is the true bearer of metaphorical meaning and that more often than not it is a whole opus, whether it be a poem or a novel or, indeed, a liturgy, which carries the overarching metaphor within which a whole series of otherwise literal references will be enabled to function metaphorically in their turn.

Philip Wheelwright adds a useful refinement to Black's analysis of metaphor as the interaction between the two domains when he distinguishes between two moves which the use of metaphor may involve.[12] The first, which he calls the "epiphoric," is virtually identical with what Black calls a metaphor *tout court*, namely, the move from the literal meaning of an utterance to its application to something else on the grounds of a perceived isomorphism: a sort of shift from the lesser to the better known. What is essential here is that the literal meaning be grasped and appreciated, or else the metaphor falls flat. The tension is maintained, therefore, by the simultaneous assertion and denial of the literal meaning, or by the cracking of the literal meaning, under the weight of its own impossible literalism, to reveal some nonliteral reference. The second kind of move is really a different kind of metaphor: what Wheelwright calls "diaphor" or diaphoric movement. In this case, two literal meanings are put side by side, producing a conflict of interpretations which pushes the mind beyond either in its quest for intelligibility.

One could cite literary examples in illustration of these two moves, but since our purpose is to relate liturgy and metaphor, perhaps some liturgical examples would be in order.

One cannot but be struck by the close parallelism between this approach to metaphor as the intersection of domains and the classic Augustinian definition of sacrament in terms of the *sacramentum* and the *res sacramenti*.[13] Sacraments, like metaphors, are successful to the degree that they succeed in pointing beyond their literal meaning, yet also like metaphor they cannot dispense with that literal meaning. Bread has to be bread in the usually accepted sense of the term (*in communi aestimatione hominum*) for it to be an adequate sacramental sign. Similarly, the use of an absolute minimum of water in Christian baptism serves at best to domesticate the metaphor and at worst manages to sever any connection between the meaning of the rite and human associations of water as both sustainer of life and agent of destruction. This attenuation of sacramental signs is sometimes defended on the grounds that the use of real bread or the practice of baptizing by immersion might be irreverent, which is another way of saying that they would lose their metaphorical potential to point beyond themselves. Yet the experience of metaphor in language goes to show that metaphors fail when their literal meaning is no longer recognized and that it is the context, not the symbol itself, which makes it impossible to stick to the literal reference.

Conversely, the epiphoric move in metaphor occurs when it is not simply the context, but the juxtaposition of a second irreconcilable literal meaning, which creates the explosion of insight. When Christ took bread and said "This is my body," two significant units, one an object and the other a verbal phrase, were set in uncomfortable juxtaposition, forcing the disciples to move beyond the literal meanings to a new kind of seeing. Further examples of similar clashes of meaning are to be found throughout the words and actions of the liturgy. To address God as "Lord" and "Rock" in the same breath is to conjoin irreconcilable literal references in such a way as to force the mind beyond them to a transcendent reconciliation of opposites, to the disclosure of something which has features in common both with lordship and rockfastness, but which cannot be identified with any lord or any rock that we would recognize.

Metaphor as Disclosure

The question of what it is that is actually known in the insight that metaphor offers is one that has been addressed by the late Ian Ramsey. It was his persuasion that what is disclosed in a successful metaphor is an insight into reality as such. Whether the metaphor offers a sudden flash of recognition or a slowly dawning realization, there is something objective which the metaphor reveals—and which only metaphor can reveal—a recognition of the way the universe is, a glimpse of how things are. Hence Ramsey talks about "cosmic disclosure,"[14] for, he argues, a good metaphor yields a kind of undifferentiated knowing which transcends the particular categories within which we may thereafter speak of it. And what is known is undifferentiated reality, reality in its wholeness, the really real, the unfathomable, unspeakable mystery of things—or, to use Tillich's term, the ground of our being.

At the risk of simplifying Ramsey's thought, we can perhaps distinguish three elements in the birth of a metaphor and three elements in its operativity. First, there is a hunch or intuition: a person watching a mother with her child, or someone fascinated with the way the waves swirl and crash upon a cliff, or someone seeing an empty shoe lying discarded in the street is struck by the intuition that there is something about reality itself, about life and existence, about the universe, which transcends this particular woman or rock or worn-out shoe. That is the hunch, the insight, the encounter with reality itself. Secondly, the image of the woman or the rock or the shoe remains as an image to be lived with, savored, mulled over. Thirdly, the image gives rise to discourse, to speaking and thinking about reality in terms of the mother's care of the child, the steadfastness of the rock, of the untold yet piteous story of the shoe. Thus the birth of a metaphor moves from the intimation through the image to the discourse, and the discourse tries to do justice to the image while the image calls up other images to help it hold and reveal the insight. Thus in its operativity the metaphor moves from discourse to image to insight. When we hear someone else's metaphor, we move from the discourse (speech or text) to the literal meaning which constitutes the image, in the hope of glimpsing the original insight and experiencing the encounter with reality which gave rise to it.

Ramsey insists very strongly on the objective reference of metaphor, on the transcendence of what is revealed over the image which reveals it. "The very aptness of the word I use—disclosure—is that the objective reference is safeguarded, for the object declares its objectivity by actively confronting us."[15] It is the word "actively" in this quotation which is important, for it is meant to point to that aspect of insight which is its gift character. Knowledge can be acquired and mastered: insight is something that dawns on us and masters us as objective reality discloses something of itself to us. It is this characteristic of reality—its autonomy and transcendence and yet its ability to impose itself upon our awareness—that to Ramsey's mind justifies talk about that reality in personalist terms. "God," he points out, is not strictly a proper name. Of itself, it has no more meaning than x, standing for the unknown, always elusive, ultimate mysteriousness of things. If we then speak of this reality, of God, in personal terms, even to the point of presuming to address it in the way we might address another person, it is precisely because the experience of other persons as autonomous centers of activity suggests an isomorphism with this experience of reality as autonomous mystery.[16] Yet the metaphoric quality of such language would be lost if we were thereby led to think and speak about God as a kind of invisible person. That would be flat-minded literalism.

It is, of course, the fate of most metaphors either not to catch on or else to degenerate quickly into clichés whose metaphorical potential is no longer realized. Once recognized and appreciate, this tendency to degeneration can shed valuable light on the problems of liturgy, but before we go on to that, a couple of brief remarks on some further ramifications of Ramsey's view of metaphoric disclosure might be in order. These have to do with the way metaphor demands the involvement of those who use it.

The most powerful metaphors in human language are those that touch on areas of experience which clearly engage our own mystery, opening up for us the wonder and ambiguity of human existence, yet there are two particular ways in which all metaphor lays claim on us. In the first place, metaphor requires the *engagement* of those who would understand it. Black speaks of the metaphorical image as a lens through which something else is viewed. It thus constitutes an invitation to look at reality in a particular way. It requires an act of contemplation, rather than analysis which takes it apart and destroys it, dissipating its power. Contemplation, on the contrary, suggests an entering into that which is contemplated, a kind of in-dwelling. In this sense, metaphor calls for the hearer or reader to yield his ground, to part with his usual descriptions of variety, to move over onto the ground of the image, to live inside it, to look around and get the feel of it. It calls for a suspension of disbelief, a closure of critical distance, a commitment of trust to this way of seeing.

Once inside, when a metaphor yields up its secret, it demands a second kind of commitment: that of *loyalty* to the insight offered. Ramsey compares this with the kind of loyalty required of the mathematician who discovers the meaning of a formula or with the loyalty required of us when we have gained an insight into another person: once we know, we cannot go back and pretend we never knew.[17] In short, a good metaphor not only carries cognitive content but it also has attitudinal import. To speak of old age in terms of autumn prompts quite a different attitude than would be the case if the metaphor used were that of the hourglass running out, leaving nothing but emptiness. Thus a good metaphor not only offers a powerful insight, but actually enables us to relate beneficially to the reality of which we speak. In that sense, metaphors, like models in science, permit of verification. They are verified by their fruitfulness not only for understanding life, but for living it.

This view of metaphor, then, sees it as mediating an encounter with objective reality. It demands a kind of faith as its precondition and a loyal obedience as its consequence. Yet what that reality is that we have glimpsed is always more than we can say. We know we have been confronted with something real, but what we try to say about that reality is always open to correction by the experience itself as well as by other experiences.[18]

This understanding of how metaphor works and what it yields is of greatest interest for Christian liturgy. All Christian liturgy plays out a single root metaphor, that of the death and resurrection of Jesus as the disclosure, for those who will enter into it, of ultimate reality. For the Christian, Jesus is the metaphor of God and all other experiences and the metaphors to which they give rise are shaped and qualified and reinterpreted in the light of this one.

Yet, as Ramsey again reminds us, it is not so much through a single metaphor that our sense of the cosmos is created as through a certain convergence and even conflict of many metaphors. Consequently, while the believer speaks of Christ as the self-disclosure of God, Christ himself becomes the medium of such disclosure only through a whole series of presentations in different contexts. Thus we have not one but four Gospels. In the Gospels he is presented in a whole series of stories and sayings, as well as under a series of explicit metaphors such as the way, the truth, the life, the gate, the sheepfold, the shepherd, the vine, the suffering servant, the new Moses, the Christ, the Logos of God and so on.

Similarly, the liturgy may be said always to be an enactment of the root metaphor of the paschal mystery of the death and resurrection of Jesus as the disclosure of God, yet it celebrates that mystery in a whole series of rites and ceremonies, in successive seasons of feast and fast, in a variety of liturgical traditions, Eastern and Western. All these serve to disclose, under the circumstances of particular times and places and occasions, the single indivisible mystery, disclosed in the person of Jesus, which we intuitively know and encounter without either being able to understand it exhaustively or to articulate at all except in the metaphorical language of disclosure. The one unnameable mystery of reality is refracted through the variegated lenses of historical tradition and contemporary liturgical practices.

To say this is simply to make the same claim for the liturgy as Ramsey makes for metaphor when he argues that, because what every metaphor offers is a cosmic disclosure, that is, an undefined and undifferentiated grasp of reality, they all give access to the same reality,[19] the unknown and indefinable that we refer to when we use the word "God." The disclosure which gives rise to metaphor and which metaphor seeks thereafter to convey, provides us with a model for thinking about—and relating loyally to—the single, undifferentiated reality which is thereby disclosed. Whether in liturgy or in literature, metaphor represents the "interaction of the timeless with time," a moment in which we become intuitively aware of what it is, behind the immediacy of the shortsighted here and now, that we are related to. These are moments when the randomness and disconnectedness of mundane living are fleetingly dispelled by an intimation of the order and harmony that underlies all things and contains them.

In principle, of course, any occasion could serve for such an insight—watching a potter at his wheel, a mother with her child, or the seawaves pounding on a rock—but the language of model and metaphor which has arisen out of such disclosures in the past prepare us again to recognize such experiences as disclosure situations. In works of literature, it is the continued ability of certain works to offer compelling disclosure of reality which gives them the status of classics.[20] In much the same way, Christian liturgy is essentially traditional in character: the constant reading of the Scriptures and the tireless repetition of ancient rituals present us with a rich system of related metaphors, both verbal and enacted, which were not only born in encounter with objective reality (hence the claim of divine inspiration and institution), but have continued to disclose that cosmic reality that we call the God and Father of Jesus Christ to successive generations of believers. For believers, these metaphors, all playing out and playing off the root metaphor of Jesus, "the image of the unseen God" (Col 1:15), are the normative, but not the exclusive media of "cosmic disclosure." Rather, they prepare us to recognize the metaphorical or sacramental character of all tangible realities, as long as they are not themselves perceived simply as steno-symbols for nontangible realities, devoid of metaphoric tension.

The Fading of Metaphor

The vocabulary of our language continues to develop and grow through the invention of new metaphors and their eventual decline into steno-language. As Philip Wheelwright remarks: "They grow old and moribund, losing the vital tension of opposed meanings, dramatic antithesis, paradox, which was theirs at their inception. They become fossilized and enter into everyday life as steno-symbols which have lost their one-time allusiveness and power to stir . . . consequently they are no longer living metaphors, but merely ex-metaphoric corpses, steno-terms, units of literal language."[21]

Religious language is not invulnerable to such a fate, particularly in a culture that tends to regard truthfulness as being the prerogative of literally descriptive statements. Religious statements are commonly believed to be true in the sense that they were once verifiable or will be after death. Many Christians believe that, had you been there, you might have seen Christ ascending into the clouds to sit at God's right hand and that, should you happen to be alive at the time, you might one day see him coming back riding on the clouds. In other words, religious metaphors commonly lose their tensiveness and become fossilized steno-symbols, so that those who believe and those who have given up believing are united at least in the conviction that such language is either literally true or it is not true at all. Or, to put it another way, the effect of literal interpretation is largely to relegate Christianity to a message about a distant past and to a future outside time, leaving the present void of the presence of God.

In the area of liturgy, the problem manifests itself as a problem of participation. In remarking on the parallel between the emphasis on the objectivity of truth statements and language and the stress on the objectivity of sacramental causality in liturgy, we noted that this created problems for participation which revision of the rites has not of itself been able to resolve. It may be, then, that reflection on the kind of participation metaphor requires can offer some guidance in deepening our understanding of what liturgical participation demands.

Entering Into Metaphor

Metaphor, in the first place, calls for a certain amount of trusting imagination, the willing suspension of disbelief. The reader or hearer has to overcome critical distance and let the metaphor teach him to see. We have to enter into the metaphor with a certain measure of sympathetic expectation and to linger with it until it yields up its secret. The dawning of insight, the gradual realization of disclosure, comes slowly and unpredictably to one who becomes immersed in the metaphor, plays with it, savors it imaginatively.

This the language of the liturgy gives us the opportunity to do in the poetry and song of psalms, hymns, and canticles; in the provision for silence; in its provision for communal prayer; in its provision for imaginative—or contemplative—looking; and not least in the gestures and actions of the community, if only we knew how to enter into all this

> . . . kneeling, this singing, this reading from ancient books,
> This acknowledgement that the burden is intolerable, this
>   promise of amendment,
> This humble access, this putting out of the hands
> This taking of bread and wine, this return to your place not
>   looking about you. . .[22]

The language of the rite, as we have reminded ourselves already, is not only the language of spoken words but also the language of actions undertaken, where the performative word is accompanied by the significant gesture, each a commentary upon the other, each sustaining the other. To us who have become distrustful of the word, the liturgy offers the opportunity to rediscover its power by submitting to the gesture as well. We kneel to confess, stand to salute and to praise; we bow, we beat the breast, we raise our hands, we genuflect, we make the sign of the cross—and in all this we discover the meaning of the rite by putting ourselves as best we can into what we are doing. In all these ways and more, the liturgy encourages us to try on the metaphor; not just to stand there, but to body it forth.

But the attitude of mind is all-important here. Once again, Guardini makes the point very well when he asks whether the liturgical act means the same to us as to "the priest of the late nineteenth century who said: 'We must organize the procession better; we must see to it that the singing and praying are done better.' He did not realize that he should have asked himself quite a different question: how can the act of walking become a religious act, a retinue for the Lord progressing through his land, so that an epiphany may take place."[23] He might also have asked: how can we process up to receive Communion in such a way that it is experienced as something different from standing in line at a supermarket checkout? Fortunately, the liturgy already has the resources to fire our feeble imaginations. The Communion chant is intended to accompany the procession to Communion both to indicate that this is not a supermarket and also to provide us with another set of lyrical metaphors by which to walk. Then there is the very invitation to Communion, "Happy are those who are called to his supper," with all its associations of the huge and joyful throng described in the book of Revelation as celebrating the marriage feast of the Lamb.

Thus the liturgy contains a whole plethora of images, playing off one another, all pointing beyond their literal meaning to something else. To quote Ramsey again: "God is revealed in the cosmic disclosure which may occur at some stage as the pattern of models is developed without end, just as there may dawn on us that to which an infinite convergent series points as its terms are endlessly developed."[24] The temptation to explain these images—whether they be scriptural images or liturgical gestures—is something that has to be resisted: it is not explanation we need, but contemplation; not ideas but disclosures. For the language of the rite is never a statement about what it contains, so much as the coming to light of the mystery itself. What this mystery is in its fullness can only be explored by playing with the images until it is glimpsed, acknowledged, and surrendered to. Carl Gustav Jung spoke of "the great spirit adventure of our time" as being "the exposure of human consciousness to the undefined and the undefinable."[25] That, I would suggest, is what the liturgy has always been about.

From this it should be clear that the encounter with God the liturgy promises is not something that will usually be attended by the overwhelming and ineluctable quality often associated with theophanies. The liturgy does not pretend to offer instant gratification of the contemporary craving for experience. It is neither instant gratification nor emotional catharsis. Instead, the awareness of God-in-Christ which it holds out, and the encounter with him that it promises, come slowly to those who persevere and who give their eyes time to adjust to the light. What Bernard Lonergan says of religious conversion is quite applicable here: "it is revealed in retrospect as an undertow of existential consciousness, as a fated acceptance of a vocation to holiness, as perhaps an increasing simplicity and passivity in prayer."[26] That, I think, is what the liturgy can engender in those who frequent it and give themselves to its discipline. In brief, just as metaphor can only operate as metaphor for those who recognize its metaphorical character, so liturgy can only act as a disclosure of God to those who surrender their claim to know beforehand what it means and who will allow its literal meaning to serve each time afresh as the starting point for the discovery of further meaning. This, in turn, leads us to ask what it is that a fresh metaphor has that a faded metaphor has lost.

Grounding of Metaphor

If we take a very common term, "broadcasting," and look at its history, it is easy to recognize that it came to acquire its present meaning because, when the wonder of wireless radio was still new, a certain isomorphism was glimpsed between the operations of the radio broadcaster and the operation of the farmer broadcasting his grain at sowing time. Perhaps the far older metaphor of the word as seed played a part in this, but in any case the term "broadcasting" has lost its metaphorical tension because the experience of sowing seeds by hand-scattering them on a field has disappeared from the lives of our people. Thus "broadcasting" now refers simply to the operations of radio and television and never manages to spark the flash of recognition which it once was able to do.

Unfortunately, the same fate has overtaken many liturgical symbols: the term "congregation," with its original sense, not of gathering, but of being gathered; "communion," which has become a name for the sacrament instead of a name for the body which celebrates the sacrament; "baptism," which has long since lost its original sense of being pushed under water. And it is not only words, but the actions themselves which have lost their metaphorical tension: the act of coming together as Church, the act of baptizing, the act of breaking bread, the act of anointing, the act of kneeling—they have all lost their grounding in common human experience to become steno-symbols of otherworldly realities. The other-directedness, if I may so put it, has in the course of time so come to dominate their rootedness in this world as to render them formalized and stereotyped. Paradoxically, the very reverence which their disclosure-potential inspired has resulted in the collapsing of the tension upon which their communicative effectiveness depended. Hence the attempts in modern liturgical reform to simplify the ritual and to allow the major symbols to stand out and speak for themselves. Yet recent controversies, such as that over the composition and appearance of the eucharistic bread reveals that the lesson has not yet been learned. Only when the bread is real bread will it again be possible to be surprised by its metaphoric meaning as body. Only when there is enough water to allow baptism to recover its original contact with drowning and death will its claim to be the sacrament of life grip us as something more than a tired cliché.

The Role of Qualifiers

Yet, for a metaphor to be a metaphor, it is not enough to recover its literal reference, for the literal meaning has simultaneously to be asserted and denied. This is extremely important in religious language, for whereas the inadequacy of a model or metaphor can be fairly obvious in referring to aspects of common experience, that is not always the case in matters of religion. For example, to speak of old age as autumn is clearly a metaphorical usage, but when God is spoken of as "he" or as "Father" or as "Savior" the metaphorical character of such discourse is easily overlooked.

For this reason, Ian Ramsey stresses the role of what he calls "qualifiers." Words such as "infinite," "everlasting," "immortal" and "all-loving" are not words which have any recognizable human experiential referent. In fact, their role is rather to deny any such reference to the words such as "Father," "Lord," or "Savior" which they qualify. Thus to speak of God as an all-loving Father or an all-powerful Savior is to deny any real continuity between God and any human experience of the role of father or savior. In this way, through simultaneous assertion and denial, through the juxtaposition of claim and disclaimer, the transcendence of the reality of which we speak is safeguarded. In Christian ritual, a similarly important function is played by the formalization of human activities into ceremonial acts. Familiar gestures of greeting, embracing, sharing bread, drinking together, bathing and even of gathering together are carried out in such a way as to put them at least one remove from their usual form. This distancing from the purely functional is what lends these actions their metaphorical tension, so that we are prompted to attend more closely and to ask after the meaning of what is done. As Pierre Colin remarks: "It is the very solemnity of the liturgical gesture which prompts us to look for the fullness of its meaning beyond its immediate significance—and that is why it is important to maintain this solemnity."[27]

Yet experience has shown that in the course of time there is an almost unavoidable tendency to exaggerate the role of qualifiers. This happens when the style of the language or the secondary elements of the rite come to be regarded as significant, indeed sacred, in themselves and thus compromise the effectiveness of the primary symbols they are meant to support. The inherent conservatism of the liturgy does not at all mean that it is not in continuous process of development, just as language is. Indeed, that very conservatism becomes an instrument of change when purely functional elements, such as ministerial vesture, or the use of elevated language, or the placing of the bread and wine on the altar come to assume a role of their own and end up by overwhelming the primary symbols. When that happens, interpretations arise which gradually move further and further away from the meaning implicit in the metaphor of the rite, so that its rooting in human experience becomes utterly unrecognizable. This happens when eucharistic eating and drinking become so otherworldly that people leading ordinary lives feel they have to keep their distance, or when the baptismal bath evaporates into a few drops of water sprinkled on the head, or when the sacredness of the Gospel so dominates its content that it ends up being sung in a foreign tongue behind a cloud of incense. By that stage the metaphor has become so otherworldly as to be of no earthly use at all.

Thus we have to be attentive to preserving both terms of the metaphor *and* the logical gap between them. If the gap closes and one meaning assumes the other meaning into itself, we are back to literal statements and prosaic actions. At that point, they have either become totally secularized, or else they have become mere steno-symbols for otherworldly realities. While the Church has always been conscious of the danger of secularization, she has not always recognized that the opposite tendency is equally damaging to the disclosure-function of liturgical words and actions.

I have tried to indicate in this paper some of the problems confronting liturgical participation in our time and to suggest some of the ways in which the study of metaphor, which itself demands participation, can help us to tackle these problems. But the problem is not one which can be solved simply in terms of the liturgy itself. It demands a similar reappraisal of the whole way in which the Christian tradition is handed on in preaching and catechesis. There, too, we need, as Guardini said, to "relearn a forgotten way of doing things and recapture lost attitudes." But the problem, we suggested, is not so much a specifically religious problem as a cultural one. Students and teachers of literature have similarly to struggle against the flatminded literalism of the age.

Conversely, the Christian tradition itself has been kept alive not only by the celebration of the liturgy and the preaching of Christian doctrine, but by the writings of poets and contemplatives who have risen above reading and writing and learned how to look. The gift of the poet is above all the gift of vision; the gift of writing is the gift to be able to share that vision with others, that they too may see.

These are only hints and guesses,

Hints followed by guesses; and the rest

Is prayer, observance, discipline, thought and action.

The hint half guessed, the gift half understood, is Incarnation.[28]

---

[1] *Herder Correspondence* (August 1964) 237–8.

[2] Ibid., 238.

[3] "Addressing God in Faith," in *Concilium* 82 (1973) 62–3.

[4] Though the problem has been posed as a problem of culture rather than of faith, the very act of faith is rendered problematic if it is understood simply in propositional terms. But the cultural dimension of this problem serves to remind us of the necessity of a certain kind of openness to life and its questions and thus reveals the implications for areas of life, such as the appreciation of literature, which go beyond what is ordinarily considered the realm of faith but which are equally threatened by literalism.

[5] "The Second Naiveté: Approach to a Pastoral Problem," in *Concilium* 81 (1973) 110.

[6] *Catechism of the Council of Trent*, trans. J. Donovan (Dublin, 1829) Part II, ch. 1, q. 13, p. 134.

[7] Thus Philip Wheelwright, *Metaphor and Reality* (1962) 23–6.

[8] Susanne Langer, *Philosophy in a New Key* (1960) 21.

[9] *Metaphor and Reality*, 33ff. Also his book *The Burning Fountain: A Study in the Language of Symbolism*, rev. ed. (1968) 14–5 and passim.

[10] Max Black, *Models and Metaphors* (1962) 38.

[11] Ibid., 236–7.

[12] Wheelwright, *Metaphor and Reality* 70–91.

[13] Augustine's *Sermo 227* is of particular interest for the ways in which the participation of the faithful in the liturgy is discussed in terms of its being a *sacramentum*.

[14] I. T. Ramsey, *Models and Mystery* (1964) 54–60.

[15] Ibid., 58.

[16] See Ramsey's *Models for Divine Activity* (1973) ch. 3: "Presence." Attention has frequently been draw to the unresolved ontological problems in Ramsey's work, specifically with regard to his claims concerning the objective reality of the cosmic disclosure. The only study of Ramsey based on the complete corpus of his published and unpublished work is T. W. Tilley's unpublished dissertation *On Being Tentative in Theology: The Thought of Ian T. Ramsey*, G.T.U., Berkeley, 1976. Tilley reports that Ramsey abandoned the quest for a metaphysics after 1960 and argues that Ramsey's contribution lay in elaborating a theory of religious language which would account for the empirical rooting of such language in human life, and clarify its proper use and justification. Similarly, this paper is concerned with the pragmatics rather than the semantics of liturgical metaphor. The use of Ramsey's ideas in the study of liturgy is exploratory rather than explanatory, so that their usefulness is to be assessed in terms of the insight they offer on how to proceed liturgically.

[17] Ramsey, *Religious Language* (1957) 35ff.

[18] We might note in passing the suggestive parallel between this view of metaphorical language as inadequate to that which it bespeaks and Augustine's reflections on "memory" and "recollection" in Book 10 of his *Confessions*. This could, perhaps, serve as the starting point for attempting to relate liturgical celebration to the tradition in such a way as to suggest that the liturgical action "recollects" that tradition, but always inadequately and always subject to correction and amplification by other rituals and other traditions.

[19] Ramsey, *Words About God* (1971) 212.

[20] On the classic and the classical, see H. G. Gadamer, *Wahrheit und Methode* (1960) 269–75.

[21] Wheelwright, *The Burning Fountain*, 120.

[22] Alan Paton, "Meditation for a Young Boy Confirmed," in Massey Shepherd, ed., *Holy Communion* (1959) 149.

[23] Guardini, *Herder Correspondence* (August 1964) 238.

[24] Ramsey, *Models and Mystery*, 61.

[25] Carl Gustav Jung, *Psychology and Religion, East and West*. Collected Works 11 (1969) 105.

[26] Bernard Lonergan, *Method in Theology* (1973) 240–1.

[27] P. Colin, "Phénoménologie et herméneutique du symbolismes liturgiques," in *La liturgie après Vatican II*, ed. J-P. Jossua and Y. Congar (Paris, 1967) 226.

[28] T. S. Eliot, *"The Dry Salvages." The Complete Poems and Plays 1909–1950* (New York: Harcourt, Brace 1952) 136.

J. Frank Henderson

Introduction to
"The Pedagogical Function of the Liturgy"

In "The Pedagogical Function of the Liturgy," Mark Searle presents a vision, a challenge, and a method. The vision has to do both with liturgical reform and renewal and as well, with ecclesial reform and renewal. The challenge is addressed to the entire Church: laity, scholars, clergy, and Church authorities. The method is to apply a particular pedagogical theory to the life, governance and worship of the Church and to its mission in the world, complementing the more commonly used theological, historical, and anthropological approaches. This article was ahead of its time when it was prepared twenty years ago; it remains so today.

As a basis for considering liturgy and Church, Mark Searle chose the pedagogical theory of the Brazilian educator, Paulo Freire, an approach that was related to the liberation theologies of that era. For a variety of reasons, neither liberation theology or Freire's pedagogical theory is as influential now as they once were. Today Searle might instead have chosen to use one of the theories of adult learning that have emerged recently, for example, transformative learning theory or critical reflection theory. These are just beginning to be applied to liturgy and ecclesiology, but may well lead in the same direction as that followed in this article.

From another perspective, one might also say that this article is a study of the full, conscious, active, and fruitful participation in the liturgy that Vatican Council II named as the basic principle of liturgical reform and renewal—and by extension, of Church reform. This, the Council stated, was the right and responsibility of all the members of the Church, based on their baptism and the life of the Holy Spirit in them.

Mark Searle was well aware of the close relationship that exists between liturgy and ecclesiology. Indeed, this article is as much concerned with the life, governance, and mission of the Church as it is with liturgical celebration. He was also aware that liturgy has a dual potential: it could socialize people "into the utopian ecclesia which holds the keys of the Kingdom of God;" it could also socialize them in the opposite direction—"into the dominant culture," whether of Church or society. He recognized that "liturgical practice more often than not fails to realize its critical potential."

Implicit in this article is the view that the liturgical reform and renewal initiated by Vatican Council II has not one but two major phases; and indeed, it is ongoing—not a once-for-all sort of phenomenon. This was the vision of many pioneers of the liturgical movement, but it is not as prominent today as it once was. It would even be denied by some. The first phase of renewal, which was well underway in 1981 when Searle wrote the essay, was to recover the best liturgical traditions of the Church's long history and to set aside unhelpful accretions. This would bring the liturgy up to the twentieth century. The second phase was to move liturgy and Church into the future: the twenty-first century and beyond. The second step is variously spoken of as inculturation, as implementing the insights of feminist theologies or, as here, as the liturgy becoming "critical pedagogy." During the 1970s and 1980s especially, the need to implement the first phase of liturgical renewal meant that there was little time or energy left for the Church as a whole to do much else. Other issues such as the shortage of priests, the place of women in the Church, relations with other Churches and with other world religions, great changes in the political and economic scene, etc., also distracted us from the task of continuing the reform. Though theoretical foundations for the second phase of renewal have been developed, for the most part they have not been implemented.

In the language of this article, the full participation of all in liturgical celebration and in the life of the Church—the goal of Vatican II—requires "critical reflection" and "a critical learning process." Searle speaks of "liturgy as critical pedagogy." He also speaks of moving from the "closed society" of the Tridentine liturgy and Church to an intermediate state of "populism" in which the laity experience greater participation but still really have little influence. The next step is a state of "critical reflection" in which liturgy and the life of the Church are not determined solely by Church authorities or by scholars, but where the voice of the Holy Spirit in all the baptized is truly acknowledged and respected.

Mark Searle does not consider in this essay how these goals might be realized, except in an abstract fashion. How does liturgy become "critical pedagogy"? How does sacrament come to be experienced as "critical praxis"? Certainly the clergy are to have an important role, not as those who supply answers or give directions, but as "enablers" and "facilitators," "seeing themselves as also being in a learning situation. It will be their task to help their fellow Christians to discern the liberating power of the truth in their own lives and to recognize the saving presence of God in the circumstances of their life and times." But this would require that the education and formation of clergy and of lay leaders—indeed all teaching in the Church—be "critical" and not simply the transmission of information from teachers to those who are taught. Toward the end of his article Searle asked "whether the liturgical reforms have really made any significant change in this picture, or whether an interventionist theology still operates, thereby precluding any real interaction between the historical-cultural experiences of the people and the language of faith." This question is still relevant today. Certainly the implementation of Searle's vision will take courage, wisdom, trust in the Spirit of God, and a willingness to walk on new, unmapped paths.

Though Mark Searle did not foresee the tensions and struggles regarding renewal of liturgy and Church that exist at the present time, he was aware that there was resistance to the vision of Vatican II. One of the dangers he names is that the process of renewal might be "subverted from the Right when the power elite, sensing the imminent collapse of their world, acts decisively to protect itself by launching a coup d'état." At the present time some—Church authorities, clergy, and laity alike—have turned their backs on the vision, opportunities, and challenges of Vatican II, with respect both to liturgical renewal and to ecclesial reform. Such an attitude is not open to a "critical" way of doing things, nor is it open to the full participation of all. Others, however—Church authorities, clergy, and laity alike—are still faithful to the basic principles of Vatican II and seek to implement them, sometimes in unfavorable circumstances. For the former, Mark Searle's views are even more irrelevant and threatening than when originally presented. For the latter this article is still a welcome and enlightening challenge.

J. Frank Henderson is a Roman Catholic liturgist who lives in Edmonton, Alberta. He was editor of the National Bulletin on Liturgy and currently teaches courses in liturgy and ecumenism.

The Pedagogical Function
of the Liturgy*

The liturgy and human sciences study group of the North American Academy of Liturgy has set itself the task of looking at the phenomenon of liturgical celebration through the prism of a series of models drawn from the human sciences. In tackling the subject of the pedagogical function of the liturgy, we are using a particular pedagogical model as a heuristic tool in the hope that it might shed some light on the way in which participation in liturgical celebration may be shaping the *Weltanschauung* of the faithful. The educational value of the liturgy has long since been recognized—from the time of the Church's struggle with Gnosticism, through the christological controversies, to the reforms and counterreforms of the sixteenth century. Nevertheless, one's evaluation of the educational potential of the liturgy will in large measure depend upon one's understanding of the pedagogical process.

If education is conceived of in terms of the classroom transmission of information, then a dichotomy is immediately assumed between the teacher (who has knowledge) and the taught (who do not). Education is then conceived to be an exercise in transmitting those educational commodities which the teacher decides the learners need. Correspondingly, the liturgy will be seen as an opportunity for those who claim to understand the things of God to instruct those who do not and to tell them what they need to know. The primary focus will be on such opportunities as the liturgy provides for explicit teaching: introductions, Scripture readings, commentaries, sermons, exhortations. This focus may also be expanded to incorporate prayers and hymns, which can serve as supplementary resources for inculcating moral and doctrinal truths.

Work done in anthropology and sociology has tended to discredit the classroom model somewhat in favor of a broader concept of socializa-

* This article first appeared in *Worship* 55 (1981) 332–59.

tion. As someone once remarked: "We learn to speak, to think, to love, to cure, to feel, to play, to politick and to work without the interference of a teacher." In this perspective, attention will be drawn to the ways in which liturgical celebration operates, as a total experience, to form and shape our Christian identity. So much goes on that is not adverted to, influencing us in unreflected, even subliminal, ways. So viewed, the educational process is somewhat unstructured and unpredictable in its results. This is always so, but in a pluralistic society the formative outcome of Christian liturgy can never be fully relied upon. For one thing, the Christian living in a pluralistic society belongs to a plurality of communities and is consequently subject to a plurality of competing socializations. We are far removed from the "total community" of the medieval village, where the liturgy served to structure people's lives so much more pervasively than can ever be the case today and where, in turn, so many nonliturgical areas of life lent their support to the same "world of meaning." Today, by contrast, the weekly celebration of the liturgy represents for many an isolated oasis of contact with the ethos of the believing community. On the one hand, then, the liturgy becomes extremely important as being—for most people—the sole source of Christian socialization. On the other hand, its "world" into which, it is hoped, the participants are being socialized is always subject to the risk of being relegated to the periphery of their existence or else of being thoroughly subverted by being understood in terms of meanings derived from other "worlds." John Westerhoff and Gwenn Neville have written on the socializing role of liturgy,[1] but they pay insufficient attention to the problems of Christian socialization in terms of whether the values being communicated actually measure up to those of the Gospel. In short, while the socializing power of the liturgy has been recognized, such socializing seems to be fundamentally unreflective and uncritical.

However, it can be argued that the socializing function of the liturgy has become altogether more self-conscious in the past two decades, insofar as the liturgical reform was undertaken precisely in order to communicate Christian values and to shape Christian attitudes more effectively. In other—less neutral—words, what once operated as unconscious or subliminal influences on the faithful is now subject to deliberate, if benevolent, manipulation on the part of the "authorities," whether those authorities be ecclesiastical (the hierarchy) or academic (liturgical experts). As Francis Bacon long ago remarked, "Knowledge is power." This insight is enough to give rise to a hermeneutic of suspicion where liturgy is concerned and to raise the question of whether the liturgy, like other forms of pedagogy where the content is selected by the "teachers," is not in fact an exercise of power. Is the liturgy really neutral? Is it in fact manipulative? More specifically, is the claim that the liturgical reforms have given the liturgy back to the people an accurate reflection of the current state of affairs, or is it simply an example of the way new rhetoric can camouflage old attitudes?

The body of this essay is a working paper presented for discussion by members of the human sciences group, to which has been appended a brief summary of some of the discussion it provoked. The paper utilizes the pedagogical model developed by the Brazilian educator Paulo Freire, and attempts to shed light on two issues: what critical reflection on the liturgical event can uncover in terms of the liturgy being an exercise of power by one group over another; and how the liturgy might be capable of exercising a critical role in the larger life and mission of the Church.

Anthropological Presuppositions

Although Paulo Freire nowhere expounds his anthropological presuppositions in any systematic way, these presuppositions are nevertheless important for understanding his critical approach.[2] His mentors are Marx—as mediated by Althusser—and the Gospel, for Freire is a committed Christian. This double influence is noticeable in his vocabulary and in his moderated Marxism.

In contrast to animals (caught in the cycle of instinctual reaction to sense perception), the human person is open to continual development. It is our "ontological vocation," resulting from the gift of consciousness, with all that that implies of memory and imagination, to be constantly becoming more. We not only know: we *know* we know—and hence we live not only "in" the world, but "with" the world.

Consciousness enables us to transcend nature and the transcendence of nature leads to the creation of a human world of culture. This happens through the triple process of externalization (images of reality separated from reality in thought and imagination: that is, symbolization), objectification (images are translated into reality in turn through human activity and create a new reality which then confronts us as objective), and internalization (the new objectivity of human artifacts then, in turn, shapes and defines our consciousness). In this way, human beings are constantly transforming the world of nature into a world of meaning by interaction with the world. Then the "world" which confronts us is (a) physical: environment, chairs, automobiles, factories, and so on; (b) social: parents, teachers, priests, policemen, soldiers, and so on; (c) abstract: moral principles, philosophy, and abstract concepts like "freedom," "success," "exploitation," and so on. All these "things" have socially constructed meaning for us, and such socially constructed (cultural) meaning defines the object for us, determines the way we see it, prepares the way we act towards it and speak of it. The social construction of reality includes the sense we have of our own reality, insofar as it is defined *ab extra* in defining us in terms of our roles.

Given our "ontological vocation" to grow in consciousness through creative interaction with the "world," it is clear that meaning itself, created through continuing social interaction, should also be in continuous process of reformulation and development. In fact, however, this ideal is not realized. Instead, the human tendency is continually to identify reality with a given meaning assigned to it. Meanings become fixed, as human beings act and react in terms of already established definitions and images of reality. Instead of the response to the world being questioning and reflective, it becomes automatic and conditioned by inherited interpretations. This is what Freire calls "naïve consciousness."

"Naïve consciousness" (akin to what others would call "naïve realism") simply assumes that the way we see things is the way they are. In other words, such consciousness is totally immersed in a predefined world and reacts to "reality" thus perceived more or less instinctively, rather than with critical consciousness of the difference between reality and the social definitions of reality. A more or less coherent system of assigned meanings is what is called "language" in the broad sense of the term. Language already determines for the speaker what is to be spoken about and how; it chooses what is significant, gives it an evaluation, and thereby serves to "construct" reality. "Language," in this broad sense (which includes the narrow sense of a verbal system, but goes beyond it), is a system of identifications, categorizations, and values which mediates reality. Naïve consciousness is the state in which the role of language in constructing social reality is not adverted to. It precludes the acknowledgment of certain kinds of reality as meaningful, tends to absolutize what is relative, and thereby to canonize a given stage in the evolution of a culture.

Given the existence of naïve consciousness in a culture, it is unlikely that people within a culture will be able to recognize that their consciousness is indeed naïve; that is, to acknowledge that things are not simply as we see them and that our way of seeing and speaking about reality is inadequate to reality. It is only when such naïve consciousness is strained and cracked by the influx of experience which cannot be ignored and which the social constructs of inherited language cannot account for (demythologization), or when confronted with the clash of one's own with another's language, that naïve consciousness can be overcome and critical consciousness can (possibly) arise. For Freire, it was a series of economical and social disasters that opened his eyes to the discrepancy between the way things were in Brazil and the way they were officially interpreted.

Freire saw that the history of this discrepancy went back beyond the events of his own lifetime (his father was bankrupted in Brazil as a result of the collapse of Wall Street in the 1930s!) and constituted the history of the country since the early days of Portuguese colonialization. Brazil had thenceforth been a colony, that is, a people whose experience of the world had failed to find expression because of the imposition of foreign language, law, authority, religion, economics, art, and so on: in short, because of the imposition of a social reality-construct which reflected the "world" of the oppressor and not of the colonialized peoples. Hence, Freire talks about "cultures of silence"—ways of experiencing and seeing the world that go unnoticed, even by the oppressed themselves, because the "worldview" of the oppressor becomes normative. The oppressor, in turn, fails to notice any discrepancy: the way he sees things is the way they are, and his very success in the work of colonializing, that is, imposing his system, simply confirms him in this "naïve consciousness." For this reason, "conscientization," the overcoming of naïve consciousness in favor of a critical consciousness, must start among the oppressed rather than the oppressors, among the third world rather than the first; for those who suffer from the discrepancies between reality and official definitions of reality are more likely to notice such discrepancies than those who stand to profit from them.[3]

Yet even here, the overcoming of naïve consciousness is not as easy as one might think. It is not that the oppressed can simply reject another's "language" as alien, because they have in the course of time come to make it their own and thus to accept it as "natural." They live their lives on others' terms in such a way that even their failure to do so is accounted for: they are mere peasants, Indians, laborers, drunkards, lazy, and dirty. They interiorize not only the oppressors' language, but the oppressors themselves, and see this as making progress by imitating the oppressor, rising to approximate his style, language, values, methods, relationships, goals. In short, the oppressed lose touch with their own authentic existence, live the lives of the oppressors, become deeply alienated within themselves. Their work and language (in the full sense) is no longer an "externalization" of their own memories and imagination, but an internalization of the memories and imagination of the oppressor through living and working on his terms. Thus, says Freire, "What in fact is pure interiorization appears in naïve analysis to be imitation."[4] The dominators live inside the consciousness of the dominated. Conversely, the beginning of liberation, of the overcoming of alienation from self, is "distancing." By this he means that the culture which conditions knowledge and subsequent action must itself become the object of knowledge, so that those who have been conditioned by it can recognize its conditioning power. Cultural revolution consists of this "distancing," whereby people can recognize how the "superstructures" of a society—politics, language, religion, the administration of justice, the arts, and so on—define reality.

Naïve consciousness accompanies a "closed society." A closed society is characterized, in turn, by the following traits: a rigid hierarchical social structure and the corresponding silence of the masses; by lack of internal markets (because the economy is geared to the interests of the foreign dominator, not of the native people); by a selective educational system which functions to maintain the status quo; by high percentages of illiteracy and disease; by a high rate of infant mortality and low life expectancy; by high rates of crime. The masses of the people are totally preoccupied with trying to survive, trying to meet biological needs, and are thus incapable of questioning the structures in which they live, or of being able to objectify the facts of problems of daily life and relate them to their structural causes. Confronted with such problems, such people typically attribute them to some super-reality (fate, the will of God, the way life is) or to deficiencies in themselves.

Invariably, the way out of such a closed society, the beginning of a certain critical distancing from the conditioning power of the superstructure, occurs through changes in the "infrastructure," which means, in Marxist vocabulary, in the economic bases of a society. Economic shifts result in the perception of discrepancies between the way things are and the way things are described. This situation is one of what Freire calls "naïve transitive consciousness." It is not a question of sudden total collapse of a world, but of painful readjustments that take place in a context marked by strong ambiguities. On the one hand, new questions are raised and new realities are confronted; but on the other hand, the old consciousness continues to work and adjustments are kept, as far as possible, within the flexible framework of the old system. This is a time of considerable anxiety, not only for the oppressed, but also for the oppressors, as the oppressed begin to claim new freedoms and the oppressors seek to preserve the status quo which they see as "natural" because it works so well to their advantage. Contradictions come into the open and conflicts break out, leading to greater demands creating greater anxieties. In order to salvage as much of the existing "world" as possible, compromises have to be made and this move to salvage through compromise is what Freire identifies as "populism." Populist leadership arises to speak for the experiences of the masses and to represent them in the political process, but failing to overcome the interests of the elite, it ends up manipulating the masses. It does this by winning "reforms" which nevertheless leave the people naïve, because it does not address the structural problem of whose definition of reality will prevail. It works within the (elastic) definitions of reality provided by the "language" of the dominant elite. It remains at that stage unless and until there is critical reflection upon the process of manipulation itself. At this populist stage, peasants may be promoted to foremen, natives may be entrusted with middle and lower management positions. They will be encouraged to work hard and to study hard in the hope of winning promotion. In short, instead of questioning the system, they are encouraged to offer their best people to become part of the running of the exploitative system itself. The areas in which contradictions and conflicts are most painfully felt are the areas in which palliatives are brought to bear by means of pension programs, schooling, health and welfare programs. The symptoms of alienation are eased, but the structural causes remain unaltered in the populist approach.

The only way through the populist impasse is through critical reflection on the populist process and on the contradictions which it masks. Such a move towards critical consciousness, however, is endangered according to Freire—and there he reveals himself as a *critical* Marxist—by its possible subversion from either the Right or the Left. The process is subverted from the Right when the power elite, sensing the imminent collapse of their world, act decisively to protect it by launching a coup d'état. Although such a move often claims the name of "revolution" it is the antithesis of revolution, for it is the attempt to reactivate old behavior patterns in the people and to restore the old ideologies. But the threat from the Left is no less serious, for violent revolution which bypasses cultural revolution (in the proper sense of that word) is likewise the imposition of an ideology. By ideology, or "myth," Freire means a view of reality (a "language") which claims to be definitive, beyond criticism. What happens in both cases is that the future is foreclosed because it is predefined. The future is not seen as open-ended, as continuing discovery and redefining of reality, as something in continuous process of being built on the basis of critical reflection; but as something already known, to be put into effect. (This aspect of Freire's thought is extremely important, as we shall suggest later.) The net effect, in either case, is renewed oppression, as the sustainers of the new (or old) ideology proceed to denounce those who denounce it and to render them silent.

Such, sketchily, is the context of Paulo Freire's proposal for a new pedagogy. He offers a critique of "learning through instruction" and "naïve socialization" in order to propose the need for a critical leaning process. We shall return to this, but, remembering our purpose in this paper, we shall first suggest the relevance of his analysis to the situation in the Christian "world."

Parallels in Roman Catholicism

The cultural situation of the peoples of the Third World offers a number of comparisons with the situation of the laity in the Roman Church.

Given the historical and incarnational character of the Church, it is understandable that the Christian culture of a given epoch should correspond closely to the secular culture, particularly at a time when the latter was considered to be thoroughly permeated by the former. It is perhaps significant, for example, that the post-Tridentine Church took shape at precisely the same time when European nations were discovering and subjugating the New World, and that the cross actually accompanied the sword in effecting such colonialization. The political structure of the colonizing countries was absolute monarchy, upon which the Church consciously modeled itself (cf. Bellarmine). The Church no more considered that the indigenous people had any right to freedom of conscience, to the retention of their own culture, or to having the Scriptures and the liturgy in their own tongue than did the colonializing powers consider that they had any right to civil liberties, to their own political structures, to their own independent economies or to any say in their own destiny. Rare exceptions (for example, the Jesuits in China) prove, by their rarity and their eventual suppression, the strength of religious imperialism. This is not to judge the policies of those days or to condemn them for not being more enlightened, but simply to remember the character of the ecclesiastical structures which have shaped Roman Catholicism into the twentieth century.[5]

Moreover, in the case of the Church (and perhaps of the various nation states as well) the same sort of policy was applied in Europe as much as in the new world, producing the same symptoms of alienation. The history of the Church in Europe is marked by the same control of life and thought as the Church in the "foreign missions." Roughly speaking, what Britain was to the British Empire, and Spain, France, Portugal, and Holland were to their respective empires, Rome was to the rest of the Catholic world in matters of religion.

The cumulative effect of the symptoms of alienation recognizable in a colonialized people is characterized by Paulo Freire as "the culture of silence." The culture of silence is born, as we saw, of the structural relations between the dominator and the dominated, in which the latter are dependent upon the former. This dependence is the source—for both parties—of their respective ways of thinking, expression, and living. It means that the dominated have no voice of their own: their voice is merely the echo of the dominant society.

Put in terms of the Christian life, the dominance of Rome in religious matters has resulted in the silencing of the authentic voices of other Christian churches (that is, local churches). The most obvious indication of this is in the realm of liturgical usage, with the suppression of local rites (Missal of Pius V, Chinese rites controversy, Synod of Pistoia, prohibition of vernacular translation of the Mass, and so on), but the effects were much more wide-ranging, particularly with the growth and development of the Roman Congregations. Again, one is not raising these matters to condemn them, but to illustrate a certain "imperialist" mentality which has left its mark.

The most important consideration here is how the Church saw itself. The supposition was that revelation was something confided to the (hierarchical) Church who thereby had a monopoly of "truth" which it was her duty to "teach" and "pass on" by catechetical instruction and authoritative definition. Passive acceptance and "submission to the truth" were all that was required from the rest of the Church, which was not considered to have any voice of its own. Since what was "true" was identified with what was "taught," and since what was done by the duly authorized ministers was alone considered to be real and ultimate, and since the form in which these things were said and done was alone considered authentic, it was inevitable that people's experiences and knowledge of life were regarded, even by them, as irrelevant to their life of faith, even as unreal. With the "really real" thus taken away from the immediate experience of the people and concentrated in the hands of the "Church"—represented by the hierarchy from pope to pastor—there was created a classic example of the alienation of the masses from the sources of power: *ipsa enim scientia potestas est.*

This whole system rested upon the concept of "sacred truths" and "sacred mysteries"—or grace—standing over against life in the world. Official Roman theology was characteristically "interventionist"; it flourished on the dichotomy between the sacred and the profane, the eternal and the temporal, so that the sacred and the eternal were understood not only to transcend human, historical experience, but to undermine its value as real. The Church and its work withdrew from history, effectively sacralizing salvation and privatizing sin.[6] In this context, something akin to the economic monopolies of the colonizers began to be operative in the Church. In accordance with the laws of supply and demand, the Church-as-hierarchy was able to maintain the dependence of the faithful by persuading them that they had a need for what she alone could provide. This was achieved by imposing Roman patterns of thought, behavior, and expression upon all Catholics and by persuading them that these were more real and more important than their own historical experiences and their own cultural forms. Christian education—by instilling in the faithful the patterns of thought, concepts, vocabulary, and values of an esoteric minority—underpinned the whole sacramental system and the whole complex of ecclesiastical discipline, while the sacramental system and ecclesiastical discipline in turn continued to "socialize" the faithful (and the hierarchy, of course) in this social construct which passed itself off as the way things are (eternally!).

The role of the liturgy in maintaining this whole structure was, in fact, crucial. On the one hand, its obligatory character, together with its being identified as the exclusive source of contact with the otherworldly which was "really real," served to ensure the legitimation of the status quo, the "unchanging" dominance of the elite who ruled, taught, and sanctified—and a denial of the relevance or authentic religious value of the secular experiences of the many. On the other hand, when—as always happens—the individual failed to measure up to the expectations determined by the hierarchical Church (for example, by sin, doubts of faith, or simply by suggesting that religious observance was not very satisfying) then the only recourse such persons might have to resolve their anxiety or frustration was to return to the sacraments—thereby further interiorizing the system. Faced with the situation of "failure," the believer had no option but to explain it in terms of personal inadequacy. There was no realistic likelihood, given the way the Catholic's consciousness was immersed in such a powerful and all-encompassing reality-construct, that such persons could see the ecclesiastical structures as the cause of their malaise. Consequently, individuals were encouraged to absolve themselves of any historical responsibilities to change the world or to change the ecclesiastical situation in which they found themselves. They had no voice of their own, they did what they were told, they thought what they were told to think—even though it was alien to their own language and experience. They simply discounted this worldly experience which did not fit the constructs of religion.

Our present era is often associated with the term *aggiornamento*, with the phenomenon of large-scale changes in Western society which have finally caught up with the Church. Infrastructural changes have created the need for shifts in the superstructure of religion. Among the changes in the infrastructure we might note the affluence which both facilitates and demands mobility, leading to the breakup of traditional Catholic ghettos and the loss of "closed" parochial life. People no longer concerned with simply surviving have the leisure to question the status quo, to pursue new ideas and new experiences. In many ways, Vatican II served to sanction such questioning because it was itself an exercise in questioning. The conciliar rethinking of Catholic life and teaching inevitably created a certain "distancing" from the hitherto unquestioned "reality construct."

The pastoral constitution *Gaudium et Spes* on the Church in the Modern World openly acknowledged "the split between the faith which many profess and their daily lives," saying that it is "to be counted among the more serious errors of our age" (no. 43). In context it is clear that this is not simply a moral injunction to live according to the rules of the Church, but the recognition of an alienation deep in the Christian life between religious belief and secular experience. Consequently, the "split" will be overcome not by more aggressive instruction and disciplining of Christian people, but by giving the faithful back their voice, in the sense of recognizing their life experience as an authentic source of Christian reflection on the world. This, in turn, will diminish the dependency of the faithful upon the structures of the hierarchical Church and lead to a profound transformation of the Christian community in accordance with Jeremiah 31:34. It opens the possibility of critically evaluating not only our Christian lives and aspirations, but the tradition we have received, as a continuing process of claiming the freedom of the children of God and of working to realize the kingdom of God. (We shall return to this point later.)

This process is legitimated by two theological principles that reemerged at the council. The first is the acknowledgment that all Christians, in virtue of their baptism, share the Spirit, who is the ultimate source of the Church's "knowledge" and "power"—otherwise known as "revelation" and "salvation." The second concerns the way in which such "knowledge" and "power" are attainable. Whereas they were previously regarded as the "deposit of faith" and "the treasury of the Church," of which the hierarchs were the custodians—validated by the "orthodoxy" of the Roman theology manuals—now, particularly in the light of the dogmatic constitution *Dei Verbum* on divine revelation, salvation and revelation are both seen as ongoing processes running throughout history and permeating all human experience. Consequently, revelation and salvation are available to all in their experience of life, if only they can recognize it and respond to it.

From this premise, three consequences follow. First, it means that a person's own experience of life in the world is a valid Christian experience and that the "true" and the "really real" are not to be located elsewhere as the monopoly of the few. Second, theologizing, or the articulation of faith-experience, is not the occupation of professionals alone and is not restricted to the manipulation of certain imposed patterns of thought and speech. Third, the sacramentality of grace is no longer to be confined to specific acts confided to the jurisdiction of one class, but escapes the narrow confines of liturgical celebration to permeate all Christian life. In short, all Christians share the functions of Christ as prophets, priests, and rulers, so that these can no longer be conceived as functions simply exercised by some (who have) in favor of others (who have not).

In this perspective, the role of the hierarchical Church is seen quite differently. It is not for the clergy to "give the answers" out of their professional fund of knowledge; nor is it enough for them to say "we haven't got all the answers" (as if certain commodities just happened to be in short supply at the present time). Instead of acting as "suppliers," they will move to the position of *enablers*, seeing themselves as also being in a learning situation. It will be their task to help their fellow Christians to discover the liberating power of the truth in their own lives and to recognize the saving presence of God in the circumstances of their life and times. This implies the corresponding task of discerning and unmasking the untruth that masquerades as truth, and all the false avenues to salvation which beckon to us. In short, instead of being plyers of ideologies and capitalists of grace, they will become *facilitators* of critical theory and critical praxis in the Christian community. In this way, responsibility for the coming kingdom is shifted back firmly to where it belongs, to the Christian people, and not shifted away to a superior being, "God" or "the Church," or dissipated by a fatalistic acceptance of personal incapacity or subjective failure.

In this way, too, the eschatological tension inherent in authentic Christian existence is not nullified by recourse to ritual or evaporated into "life after death." Instead, as we shall suggest more fully below, the liturgical celebration of the Christian community, which is a rehearsal of the reality of the death and resurrection of Jesus as a critical unmasking of ideologies and false salvations, will be an objectivization in the language of the community of the communal experiences of that community. Inseparable, therefore, from such celebration will be the denunciation of whatever is "unreal" and dehumanizing and oppressive (and thus contrary to the God-given reality of human existence) and the proclamation of the Good News of our liberation to a fuller life which is not allowed to remain theoretical but becomes the call to praxis.

Such, at least, was the promise inherent in the critical objectivization of Roman Catholic religiosity that occurred during and after Vatican II. The history of the postconciliar period, however, revealed the same symptoms of anxiety which Freire noted in other societies characterized by what he calls "naïve transitive consciousness." In other words, the advent of such changes found resistance among both the "dominators" and the "dominated," whose attachment to the structures of dependence was deeply threatened by such moves. Consequently, we have seen the ecclesiastical equivalents of both rightist and leftist reactions. The reaction of the Right, attempting to salvage and restore the status quo, is obvious enough. Less easily recognizable, perhaps, is the equivalent of the revolutions mounted by the Left. Here, as in the case of the reaction of the Right, the solution to the anxiety of transition is the imposition of *a predefined future*, which we have seen in various attempts to predefine what the Church should be and what form its life and mission should take. Both responses to the situation are, in that sense, ideological, for they consist of battling to impose a priori ideas instead of allowing the future to be shaped by the whole people through their engagement in critical reflection and praxis.

Neither of these approaches, however, really characterizes the situation of "mainline" Catholics, or of the leadership of the Church. Instead, we seem to be experiencing the phenomenon of "populism." If we focus simply upon liturgical reform, we may entertain the suspicion that contemporary liturgical theory and practice constitute a real, if unconscious, attempt to retain the essentials of the old "structures of domination" by adjusting to the symptoms of "naïve transitive consciousness" among the faithful. For example, does the shift from the "eastward" to the "westward" position of the celebrant really overcome clerical domination of the liturgical event, or does it serve to give it new life? Does the introduction of vernacular texts, revised lectionaries, and liturgical homilies effectively redistribute the "knowledge that is power" or does it simply provide a new and more palatable form of the *potestas docendi*? Is the concept (and practice) of "active participation" a genuine step towards the redistribution of responsibility in the Church, or is it a means to heading off more radical forms of participatory democracy? What are we to make of such phenomena as concelebration, the revised Chrism Mass, and the papal Eucharists in the U.S.? Is the introduction of "lay ministries" a move to acknowledge the value of lay existence, or is it a subtle form of retaining and even extending clerical control? In short, is the revised liturgy serving the pedagogical role of fostering a genuinely new consciousness, or it is a way of perpetuating the old imperialist theology in more attractive packaging? In order to evaluate the liabilities and the possibilities of the revised liturgy, we need to return to Freire and his suggestions for a critical pedagogy.

The Pedagogy of the Oppressed

Starting from Bacon's axiom that knowledge is power, Paulo Freire basically distinguishes two approaches to education: education as inculcation, which is basically one person (teacher) exercising power over another (pupil); and education as liberation or as an empowering of those who learn. Freire combats two widespread assumptions about education.

The first is that education is neutral, that it is merely the transmission of pure information. In fact, he argues, the selection and arrangement of the content and—even more importantly—the mode in which it is communicated prevent education from being neutral. It functions either to indoctrinate students into given reality constructs, established values, and so on; or to enable men and women to deal critically with their experience. In the first case, education is for the sake of the society, whether the educational emphasis be on past knowledge (as arranged in disciplines) or on equipping people to meet the future needs of the society. Only in the second case is education truly liberating, when students have the opportunity to reflect critically on their culture by distancing themselves from it.

Secondly, Freire challenges the assumption that learning presupposes teaching. Here again, the same alternatives appear. Either education is based on a "banking concept" where knowledge is credited to a student's account and then drawn upon in examinations; or else it is based on a concept which holds every student to be a teacher and every teacher to be a student. The first case exemplifies the classical model of the dominator/dominated relationship, where the student is treated as a passive object upon whom the choices made by those "in power" may freely be imposed and the student is supposed to be grateful. In the second case, learning is a common enterprise undertaken as a critical investigation of the world of common experience. The instructor's monologue cedes to the learners' dialogue, so that students are acknowledged as subjects of an activity, not as objects of an activity; where they are naming the world themselves and not just being named; where they are enabled to speak instead of being forced to memorize.

It is this second approach that Freire endorses as necessary for our "ontological vocation" to become ever more human and to escape the "freezing" of the human world in naïve consciousness which identifies the world with the way it is defined. Such a definition of reality, which is a cultural product masquerading as nature, the way things are, is what is meant by an "ideology" or "myth." The term ideology, particularly, points to the fact that such an established a priori definition of reality is in the interests of some members of a society and not in the interests of others. An ideology is a description of reality which claims to describe the way things are, but in fact serves to keep a given class in power. Thus education is a venture of extreme political importance, for it either fosters ideology or it makes people aware of ideology: it is either naïve or critical. On occasion, Freire has pointed to the ideological implications of the Church's claim to neutrality and noninvolvement in politics, showing that to refuse to become involved critically is in fact to support the structures of domination.[7] It would be valuable to consider the role of catechetics and homiletics from this point of view, but since our focus here is on liturgy, and specifically on liturgy as a pedagogical event, we may ask whether the liturgy can ever be neutral. Would it be true of liturgy, as a major form of socialization, that it is either naïve—in which case it tends to support the dominant ideologies of the elites in Church and state—or else it must be critical? And if this suggestion is allowed, then what might be involved in the concept of "critical liturgy"?

The concept of "critical liturgy" really involves two things. First, it means that we need to be critical about how the liturgy itself operates as a medium of socialization: that is, critical reflection upon the liturgy itself. Second, it means that the liturgy could be conceived as a form of consciousness-raising, hence as an exercise in critical praxis. These two are intrinsically connected, as the prophetic critique of worship in the Old Testament reveals. Cult which has lost its connection with the life of justice can be denounced because it does not foster justice, but allows injustice to flourish, and because such worship is itself a perversion of true "obedience." This corresponds to Freire's two stages in the pedagogy of the oppressed: "In the first, the oppressed unveil the world of oppression and through the praxis commit themselves to its transformation. In the second stage, in which the reality of oppression has already been transformed, this pedagogy ceases to belong to the oppressed and becomes a pedagogy of all people in the process of permanent transformation. In both stages, it is always through action in depth that the culture of domination is culturally confronted. In the first stage, this confrontation occurs through the change in the way the oppressed perceive the world of oppression; in the second stage, through the expulsion of the myths created and developed in the old order, which like spectres haunt the new structure emerging from the revolutionary transformation."[8]

The hypothesis here is that the liturgical renewal of the Church requires the development of a critical awareness of how the liturgical event is itself compromised in order that, at a second stage, the liturgy can serve as the focus of the Church's continuing transformation. To see how this might be effected, we need to look at the process of critical pedagogy which Freire proposed and realized in Brazil.

Freire's Critical Pedagogy

The process is dialectical, because the act of knowing is itself dialectical. This has been suggested already in looking at Freire's anthropology, but he makes the point quite explicitly: "The act of knowing involves a dialectical movement which goes from action to reflection and from reflection upon action to a new action. . . . As an event calling forth the critical reflection of both the learners and the educators, the literacy process must relate *speaking the word to transforming reality*, and to man's role in its transformation. . . . On the other hand, as an act of knowing, learning to read and write presupposes not only a theory of knowing, but a method which corresponds to the theory."[9] It is such a method, corresponding to the theory that knowing is a dialectical act, that Freire has developed. We will present it here in brief outline.

1. *Selection of a "generative word"*: Such a word represents a "generative theme," while a "generative theme" is one that clusters together a number of experiences in the life of the people concerned which are felt as central and which touch on the more or less explicit contradictions in their lives, for example, employment, slum living, alcoholism. These "themes" are not selected by the educators so much as thrust upon their attention as they live among the people by their constant reappearance in conversation, and so on.

2. *Codification*: In order to be able to facilitate discussion of the "generative theme/word," an image of the theme has to be provided, to "objectify" the situation, so that the participants can transcend the "theme" that they are usually quite immersed in. This "objectivization" or "codification" can take any number of forms: a photograph or film can be shown, a story told, and so on. The point is to have "a knowable object mediating between knowing subjects."[10]

The participants describe the kinds of experiences and feelings they associate with the "image" and thus list the elements which make up the total experience ("surface structure").

3. *De-codification*: In discussing the "image," participants verbalize their thematics and so have the opportunity to "perceive their perceptions" by reflecting on why they felt or acted the way they did in such situations. Thus they "distance" themselves from their "naïve consciousness" and learn to put things together in new ways, to make new associations through calling their accepted ways of thinking and acting into question and replacing them with more critical understandings ("deep structure").

This process encounters resistance to the degree the "oppressed" have internalized the "oppressor."

4. *Announcing and Denouncing*: Freire calls his pedagogy "utopian" because it is an exercise in denouncing what is dehumanizing in a situation and announcing what can realistically be done (that is, what exists as the seed of a more human future). "[D]enunciation and annunciation in this utopian pedagogy are not meant to be empty words, but an historical commitment. Denunciation of a dehumanizing situation today increasingly demands precise scientific understanding of that situation. Likewise, the annunciation of its transformation increasingly requires a theory of transforming action. However, neither act by itself implies the transformation of the denounced reality or the establishment of that which is announced. Rather, as a moment in an historical process, the announced reality is already present in the act of denunciation and annunciation."[11]

This process is perpetual (cf. the two stages above) while there is hope, but hope becomes impossible if (a) the future is predetermined (thus simply to be awaited): Marxism; (b) the future is an extension of the present: the Right. Hence critical praxis defines itself over against both Left and Right as a praxis of genuine hope, in which human beings come to express themselves and to transform the world. (For Freire the destructuring and restructuring of words in learning to read and write is paradigmatic for the decodification and reconstruction of a culture.)

5. *Pre-project and Project*: the annunciation of humanizing realities, or of the possibility of transforming dehumanizing realities constitutes a "pre-project," that is, people's recognition of their capacity for intervening in a situation and actually transforming it.

In mass societies, the problem is not so much naïve consciousness itself, as the complexity of those societies which demand such specialization that no one has much sense of the whole picture and consequently new mythologies arise.[12] In either case, the pre-project is the acknowledgment that we can change things, that we can humanize our world. But this is not enough: it must lead to commitment to a specific project, chosen and defined in the process of denouncing and announcing, as a praxis.

6. *Critical Praxis*: Both the project itself (as carried out) and the process of coming to it must become the object of critical reflection.

In this brief résumé of Freire's pedagogical process, certain things stand out: (a) it is based on the present experience of the participants;

(b) it takes past and future seriously as part of the present and does not allow them to become "ideologized"; (c) it provides a structure which, in theory at least, provides for continual "cultural revolution" in keeping with our "ontological vocation" to be more, and thus should preclude the "fixing" of the world in new ideologies.

Liturgy as Critical Pedagogy

Word as Critical Theory. Thierry Maertens has suggested[13] that the Christian *ecclesia* was self-consciously modeled, in its origins, on the *qahal* of the Old Testament. He shows that the Old Testament assemblies were convoked by God through prophets, priests, or kings to hear his word anew and to commit themselves anew to this alliance and to the future it promised. Key examples are Sinai (Exod 19:1-24:11), the Deuteronomic reform (2 Kgs 22-23), and the return from Exile (Neh 8–10). In each instance, the word confronts the assembly as historically present, as judgmental, and as calling for a commitment to action ("praxis") for the realization of a future. The life and mission of Jesus, with his work of ingathering the new *qahal*, may be understood in the same light. Likewise, the role of baptism and Eucharist in the life of the early Church had a strong critical, moral, and eschatological flavor which was lost once the Church became "established" and her relationship to time, change, and history was changed. The Constantinian era saw the Church surrender her critical role (which was maintained and deformed by the monastic movement) and become the chief means of mythologizing the status quo. Nevertheless, even while abandoning her responsibility for the future in favor of ideologizing the past, the Church continued to celebrate a liturgy which, despite all the accretions of new interpretation it acquired, still retained its critical potential. Perhaps this can be indicated in a suggestive series of parallels between liturgy and what Freire calls "cultural action":

leiturgia	*cultural action*
a public undertaking; an office or benefaction assumed at private expense for the public benefit *opus dei*, work of our redemption, sanctification,	a shared enterprise, as opposed to educational systems which promote personal work, competition, and personal gain as motive for freedom, full humanization, de-mystification of reality

freedom of the children of
God, liberation from bondage
to the powers

eucharistia/eulogia/exomologesis acknowledgment of reality in all its dimensions as call and gift	"conscientization," de-mystification of reality, critical awareness. Silence is overcome in speech
apotaxis and *syntaxis*, recognition of sin and grace, as constitutive of call to conversion and to work for kingdom	denouncing and announcing as process of discernment leading to commitment to a project
transformation of people, of relationships, of material world (through acknowledgment of their sacramental potential)	transformation of reality through critical praxis, especially the transformation of the subject from passive object to active recipient
double function of two-edged word (cf. Deut 29:28ff.; Heb 4:12) and sacramental act which is already an anticipation of the eschatological kingdom and a means to its realization	double function of theory and praxis, of knowing and doing understood dialectically; the past is appropriated critically in the creative speech and activity of the present for the future as an exercise of hope.

One major problem confronting our use of the "conscientization" model for an interpretation of Christian liturgy is that in Freire the past hardly figures at all, except as something to be overcome. Any positive evaluation of the past would seem to run the risk of appearing "ideological." This obviously created problems for a Christian liturgy that is so essentially constituted by Scripture and tradition as normative.

One important attempt to overcome this problem, retaining the *traditum* as normative without allowing it to become ideological, is represented by the work of Thomas Groome[14] whose "Christian religious education" is profoundly influenced by Freire's concern that education should be about building a future which is not just an extension of the present. The way Groome reconciles the normative past with a real present and a real future is through the twofold concept of "Story" and "Vision." We shall use his insight in what follows, without attempting to give a presentation of his total educational process.

Sacrament as Critical Praxis. Not all action, all practice, is "praxis": only that which is undertaken with critical consciousness. Another way of putting this: "praxis" is action accompanied by *exomologesis*, for the building of the coming kingdom whose shape is discerned in critical assessment of the present. Some examples:

bathing, oiling, touching: given self-consciously new meaning through renunciation of Satan, profession of faith, recapitulation of salvation history, prayer formulae;

eating and drinking: eucharistic prayer situates the present critically by reference to past (anamnesis), present (epiclesis), and future (intercession). Eucharist then becomes not only memory or "real presence," but utopian task;

anointing the sick: human weakness, failure, mortality are critically evaluated in light of scriptural Story and Vision, thus giving the "patient" a redescribed future as dimension of the present;

social grouping: both affirmed and negated in the liturgical assembly insofar as the assembly finds itself under the judgment of the word which promises a universal assembly without any divisions of sex, status, etc.;

sexuality: both denunciation of dehumanizing relationships and annunciation of the potential of man-woman bonds are more or less explicit in the liturgy of marriage;

leadership: perhaps one of the most ambiguous areas of human life as lived in the Christian community. The history of ordination rites shows how the ritual itself has been ideologized to sacralize developments which are denounced in the scriptural Story and Vision.

In all these instances, people are engaged in actions which are consciously expressive and, more than merely expressive, which create a new "world" of meaning. In each instance, the participants commit themselves to a particular set of attitudes, to values which are not those of the social majority and are therefore constitutive of a cultural revolution. They commit themselves to a praxis which is utopian, that is, an act of hope in a genuinely alternative future, one which is not just an extension of the present, and yet which is not automatic or inescapable. On the contrary, the participants in such activity know themselves thereby committed to working for the realization of the future which they celebrate and anticipate in the relationships they realize in the sacramental actions. As Freire remarked about his own program, this critical praxis is realized in concrete historical circumstances in which the future is known, not as something theoretical, but as a real dimension of the present; and it is realized as a sociocultural activity, not as the action of individual subjects. In other words, a sacramental act is an act engaged in by a community and mediated by the (material) world, in which both the world and the participants are transformed. The "word of faith" constitutes a "re-description" or reality that is inevitably critical of the ways in which that same reality is culturally defined by current ideologies. Moreover, as we have seen, that "word of faith" is characteristically narrative, thus relating such sacramental acts to a larger Story and challenging the participants to undertake such "projects" as will realize the Vision of the kingdom of God. Hence the "word of faith" takes the structure of prayer—anamnesis, epiclesis, and intercession.

Ideologized Liturgy

Unfortunately, as Marx recognized in his denunciation of religion, liturgical practice more often than not fails to realize its critical potential. When that happens, it becomes the medium whereby people are socialized, not into the utopian *ecclesia* which holds the keys of the kingdom of God, but into the dominant culture. Tissa Balasuriya, among others, has illustrated the way in which the Eucharist can and has become an ideological tool for colonializing powers.[15] What this suggests is that, for the liturgy to fulfill its critical role in the life of the Christian community, the Christian community has itself to become critically conscious of how the liturgy operates in the present. The vision of a critical liturgy itself serves as a "codification" around which we can develop an awareness of how liturgy, in our experience of it, can become an ideological tool. Because of the length which this paper has already reached, I shall be content here simply to indicate some symptoms of such "alienation." These are given in somewhat random order, for they are all interconnected and any one of them could be taken as a starting point.

1. *Individualism*: Christianity and Christian liturgy began as a cultural phenomenon, but is now largely interpreted as being about the salvation of individual souls, rather than about establishing the rule of God in human society. Sin and grace are spoken of as interior realities,

evil and salvation are mythologized through projection outside the historical process. Consequently, the collective dimension of sin and grace is not incorporated into the Christian "reality construct." Although the liturgy bears vestiges of its collective character, it is itself reinterpreted in an individualistic sense. For example, who is the subject of the sacramental action? Is the contemporary search for "meaningful liturgies" really dealing with the problem, or is it continuing to mask the radical isolation (and consequent disempowerment) of the individual in contemporary society?

2. *Dehistoricization*: The Christian liturgy has strong historical and eschatological dimensions, but these are mythologized as a distant past (which is recounted only to validate present structures) and an unhistorical future ("Kingdom come!") which thereby loses any real claim on the present. This is connected with the individualism: the Constantinian Church gave up its orientation to the future (as critique of present structures) in order to assume the role of sanctifying social structures. When this happened, eschatological references in the Christian story were gradually depoliticized by being interpreted in terms of each individual's eternal future. But it has to be recognized that the loss of eschatological tension means the loss of the sense of historical task because, without a real future to work for, the need to transform present cultural and social realities goes unrecognized. Conversely, it permits the uncritical acceptance of the past which is regarded as normative simply because it is the *past*. Yet the past itself is not recognized as past, that is, as the subject of critical historical investigation, because it is ideologized in support of the status quo. Christian art depicting the sacraments reveals this to be so (the Virgin Mary receiving the Eucharist from St. John, Peter in baroque pontificals, Christ in priestly chasuble, etc.). Much of the sermonizing and catechizing concerning the sacraments reveals the same lack of historical awareness and consequent lack of vision concerning the future as task.

3. *Reification of the real*: By this I mean that the "really real" is projected outside the historical, social process into another world, seemingly parallel to this one yet disengaged from it. The absolute reality attributed to the other world, and the necessity of access to it through the limited channels of esoteric revealed "truths" and narrowly circumscribed "channels of grace," clearly operates to keep the majority in a relation of dependence upon a small but powerful elite. Such concepts as "God," "the revealed word," "sacrifice," and "grace" are predefined as in the hands of the few and not as being immediately accessible to the many.

This is connected, in turn, with dehistoricization and individualization. It has been pointed out by some that the encounter of Christianity and Hellenism meant translating the temporal categories of the Judeo-Christian tradition into the spatial categories of the unhistorical Greeks. The kingdom of God is located "up there" instead of "ahead," which plays into the hands of a static, hierarchically structured society and negates the reality of the historical process in which power changes hands.

One has to ask whether the liturgical reforms have really made any significant changes in this picture, or whether an interventionist theology still operates, thereby precluding any real interaction between the historical-cultural experiences of the people and the language of faith.

In short, Christianity is faithfully understood as "utopian praxis" insofar as it is about the Kingdom of God being "at hand" and thereby calls all other kingdoms ("reality constructs") into question. However, history shows that Christianity is always in danger of being subverted by other views of what is real which claim to be "natural," thereby masking their cultural relativity which the Gospel message and evangelical liturgy should proclaim. The result is that liturgical celebrations provide a forum for "naïve socialization" into these cultures and not into the Christian community with its own vision and task.

Some Questions

The use of models requires that one be attentive to the discrepancies as well as the fit between the two realms of experience which are brought together, for the differences may be as important as the similarities and what is not accounted for may in the end turn out to be what is most significant. Some of this has been hinted at in the body of the paper, but the discussion which followed its presentation raised two further important questions for consideration.

First of all, given that the liturgy is about our encounter with God, it was questioned whether liturgy could ever be reshaped in a way which would make it a truly democratic undertaking. In particular, the symbolic function of the reading of Scripture and of the presidency of an ordained priest would seem to require a teacher-taught relationship as an intrinsic structure of the rite. On the other hand, it could also be argued that Jesus' pedagogical method largely avoided this polarization. Although the Gospels do present him as a teacher and master, still enough of his own characteristic pedagogy comes through to suggest that his originality and his authority as a teacher came precisely from the sort of nondirective approach represented by his signs and parables. In other words, he taught with authority, not by laying down the law or communicating new information, but by raising questions and telling stories which enabled people to confront the truth in their own lives and to find themselves inescapably faced with a decision for praxis. In short, he taught more as a prophet who subverts people's world view than as a sage who is content to transmit and expound some prior wisdom. Once again, it would seem that Christology is the touchstone for what is considered normative in the liturgy, which would seem to suggest that the political dimensions of different christological models would be worth investigating.[16]

A second point raised in discussion is closely related to the first, though its starting point is more anthropological than theological. Ritual, it was argued, is characteristically resistant to change, largely because of its nature as an activity engaging social interaction. Social interaction requires recognizable patterns of expected behavior and recognized patterns of behavior produce habits of mind. Thus ritual behavior and critical praxis would seem mutually incompatible. Responses to this objection took off in two different directions. It was pointed out on the one hand that the ritual of the Church is not Christian praxis in Freire's sense, but merely the objectification which permitted a critical appropriation of reality and thus made praxis possible. It would be a criticism of certain forms of Christianity precisely that they identified Christian praxis ("the practice of faith") with sacramental practice. On the other hand, it was also argued that there is a kind of dialectical relationship between rite and praxis, habit and creativity, the established and the new—as there is between *stasis* and ecstasy, for example. Neither of these lines of thought was exhaustively pursued. They are presented here so that, together with the paper, they may serve to encourage critical thinking about the pedagogical ambivalences of liturgical practice.

---

[1] John H. Westerhoff III and Gwenn Neville, *Learning Through Liturgy* (New York: The Seabury Press, 1978).

[2] Freire's main writings available in English include: *Cultural Action for Freedom* (Cambridge: *Harvard Educational Review*, Monograph Series, no. 1, 1970; Penguin edition 1972 cited here). *Pedagogy of the Oppressed*, trans. Myra B. Ramos (New York: Herder & Herder, 1970; Penguin edition 1972 cited here). *Education for Critical Consciousness* (New York: Seabury, 1973). "Conscientization," in *The Month* 7 (1974) 575–8; and *Cross Currents*

24 (1974) 23–31. *Pedagogy in Process: The Letters to Guinea-Bissau*, trans. Carman St. John Hunter (New York: Seabury, 1978). See also, *Paulo Freire*. LADOC. Keyhole Series, no. 1. Division for Latin America, USCC, Washington, D.C., n.d.

[3] The terms "oppressor/oppressed" and "dominator/dominated" should therefore not be identified *simpliciter* with good or evil. The polarization is a structural one, not a moral verdict: to be identified as belonging to one or other class says nothing about personal moral qualities but only locates one in a system which is itself unjust. If the oppressed and the dominated appear to be favored in Freire's thinking, it is because he looks to them as the ones most likely to recognize the inequities of the system and thus to begin a process which is to lead to the liberation of all.

[4] *Cultural Action for Freedom*, 35.

[5] Modern Catholicism is the more direct result of the nineteenth-century tensions between faith and reason, culminating in Vatican I and the Modernist crisis. Nevertheless, liturgical uniformity and centralization were early products of the tendency to Romanize the Catholic Church which reached its apogee in the late nineteenth and early twentieth centuries. If it has become customary to date the pastoral liturgical revival from the initiatives of Pius X, it should be remembered that the encouragement of popular participation and frequent Communion were part of the same attempt to consolidate the loyalties of the faithful as the letter *Pascendi*. Both were pastoral reactions to what was felt to be a critical and irreligious age.

[6] Gregory Baum, *Religion and Alienation* (New York: Paulist Press, 1975).

[7] "The Educational Role of the Churches in Latin America," in *Paulo Freire* (note 2 above) 15–28.

[8] *Pedagogy of the Oppressed*, 31.

[9] *Cultural Action for Freedom*, 31.

[10] Ibid., 85.

[11] Ibid., 40.

[12] Ibid., 71ff.

[13] Thierry Maertens, *Assembly for Christ* (London: Darton, Longman and Todd, 1970).

[14] Thomas Groome, "The Crossroads: A Story of Christian Education by Shared Praxis," *Lumen Vitae* 32 (1977) 45–70. "Christian Education: A Task of Present Dialectical Hermeneutics," in *Living Light* 14 (1977) 408–32. *Christian Religious Education. Sharing our Story and Vision* (San Francisco: Harper & Row, 1980).

[15] Tissa Balasuriya, *The Eucharist and Human Liberation* (Maryknoll: Orbis Books, 1979).

[16] Behind this comment, and behind the paper as a whole, there lies the question of revelation and salvation, which would need far more careful consideration than we can provide here.

Gerard Austin, O.P.

Introduction to
"Reflections on Liturgical Reform"

Mark Searle's article, "Reflections on Liturgical Reform," is extremely timely today due to the recent liturgical changes brought forth by the new *Missale Romanum* of 2002 with its introductory *Institutio Generalis*.[1] Searle's article was occasioned by a Notre Dame Symposium on the Catholic Parish, during which he attempted to bring into focus the liturgical renewal in the American parish resulting from the Vatican II liturgical reforms. He surveyed the American parish over a time period of the twenty previous years. Now we revisit his remarks another twenty years later. We discover that the underlying question he posed back then needs to be reiterated today: "Have the liturgical changes brought about 'a new order' or have they merely been assimilated into previously existing structures without transforming them?"

How we answer this may cause us to situate better in our own time just what is meant by the urgent question: What is the renewal that awaits us?[2] Another way to phrase the question would be to ask: Do we need to reform the reform (of Vatican II)? Indeed, many people today are asking that question. It has been answered astutely by Bishop Donald W. Trautman of Erie, Pennsylvania, recent chair of the United States Bishops' Committee on the Liturgy: "We do not need to reform the reform. We need to revitalize the reform. This is my thesis: *To revert to a liturgical practice and style before the Second Vatican Council, rather than to progress with vision for the millennium, sins against the reform and restoration of the liturgy accomplished at Vatican II.*"[3] Mark Searle would be in agreement.

Searle wrote his reflections on liturgical reform twenty years after the Vatican II renewal. At that time very few wanted to "reform the reform." Today, many want to do so. Looking back twenty years to Searle's analysis can help us more clearly focus on the task ahead of us. Searle divided his observations on the reform into three parts: the dilemmas involved in the program of liturgical reform; the mixed fortunes of its implementation; prospects on areas of pastoral liturgical concern which seem to demand immediate attention.

The Dilemmas of the Reform

Searle rightly praised the council's decision to combine practical measures of liturgy with theological exposition. This pattern was continued after *Sacrosanctum Concilium* in the particular reforms by prefacing each of the *ordines* (the rites) with theological explanations of the "why" of the changes (the *Praenotanda* or in the case of the Mass or Liturgy of the Hours, the *Institutio Generalis*). As Mark Searle writes, "It was the council's intent that these two processes should move in tandem, so that theological principles would help people understand the reforms and the reforms would deepen the people's understanding of the liturgy." But unfortunately, it proved difficult to pour new wine into old wineskins. The greatest difficulty proved to be the disconnect between the message itself and the mindset of those for whom the new message was intended. Searle quotes Congar as saying that the Vatican II reform was a reform made from above, which was not prepared from below. "The irony of Vatican II, however, was that the message being passed down this time was that the laity, too, are the Church and that their active participation was urgently requested." He shows how some did get the message, but unfortunately vast numbers did not. That does not mean that they did not implement the liturgical changes, and indeed surveys showed they were happy with the changes; but as Searle notes they "loyally introduced the changes with little comprehension of the principles behind them or of how those principles offered a coherent and rather different vision of the life and mission of the parish." What was desperately needed was often not provided: a thorough liturgical catechesis and a whole new way of being local church, one much more attuned with the life of the early Church. Searle's grasp of the situation of the early 1980s reveals a rather negative assessment, but today, in light of such strong pressure to "reform the reform" on the part of so many, one sees how correct his analysis was, albeit a pessimistic one. Had his analysis been more widely heard and acted upon, perhaps the present situation would be a more balanced one.

The Fortunes of Reform

The implementation of the liturgical reforms of Vatican II met with mixed fortunes. Searle underscored three successes and two failures.

As successes he lists (leaving aside the important General Norms of *Sacrosanctum Concilium* and the norms governing cultural adaptation and liturgical experimentation): the successful introduction of the vernacular; the people's sense of ownership of the liturgy; and the "overall experience of the liturgy." Immediately, however, he perceived that each of these successes brings with it a new set of problems. The vernacular introduced on the part of most people a painful lack of understanding of the language of Scripture and liturgical prayer. Certainly some heeded this cry for needed catechesis, but not the vast majority. The second success (the people's sense of ownership of the liturgy) revealed "that active participation in the liturgy on the basis of baptism is something of a sham if it does not mean active participation in the whole life of the local church and the assuming of the wider responsibilities of the Church towards its members and larger society which flow from the liturgy." This may well be Searle's most key and prophetic point of the article. Active participation at Sunday Eucharist presumes and calls out for active participation in the entire life and mission of the Church. Twenty years after Searle's article, partially resulting from the recent sexual scandals in the Church, there is a mounting cry for a far greater participation in the total life of the Church.

Searle's third success (the "overall experience of liturgy") expressed itself in deeper encounters with Christ in the celebration of the assembly. He warned, however, that "this is sometimes confused with a strong sense of togetherness in which the horizontal rather than the vertical dimension of liturgy predominates." Today that seems to be less of a problem, but it still remains with us, and certainly we are still paying the price in that a fear of any inculturation of the liturgy is on the upspring, especially on official levels.

Searle also identifies two failures: failure of leadership and failure in the area of spirituality. Under the first, he involves over-centralization and fear of loss of power. Under the second, he laments that the majority of our people have not used the liturgy as a source of genuine, deep, ecclesial spirituality. "The result is widespread disillusionment and a hunger for meaning among American Catholics." Again, he could have been describing the situation of today.

Prospects

Searle concludes his reflections on liturgical reform by underscoring developments that truly signal hope: "In each of these three developments—recognizing the objectivity of the liturgy, the mystery (as opposed to mystification) which we celebrate, and the paschal mystery as a reality for the whole race—lie the seeds of the future evolution of the renewal begun at Vatican II." This reveals the vision of someone who spent his entire life as a servant of the liturgy.

Searle ends by summing up that vision with one word: "reverence." But note well, it is very different from the "reverence" being urged by many today. He writes, "let it be a reverence that goes beyond a preoccupation with sacred things. Let it be a reverence for the word as well as the sacrament, for the world as well as the Church, for the people of God as well as for the ordained and the vowed." Yes, Searle's vision was a *total* vision! It is a vision much needed today as we implement the new *Missale Romanum* of 2002 with its introductory *Institutio Generalis*.

Rev. Gerard Austin, O.P., is professor at the Rice School for Pastoral Ministry, Diocese of Venice in Florida.

---

[1] *Missale Romanum ex decreto sacrosancti oecumenici Concilii Vaticani II instauratum auctoritate Pauli Pp. VI promulgatum Ioannis Pauli Pp. II cura recognitum. Editio typica tertia.* (Urbs Vaticana: Typis Vaticanis, 2002).

[2] A helpful source is Nathan Mitchell, "What Is the Renewal That Awaits Us?" in *The Renewal that Awaits Us*, eds. Eleanor Bernstein and Martin F. Connell (Chicago: Liturgy Training Publications, 1997) 18–31.

[3] Most Rev. Donald W. Trautman, "On Receiving the Michael Mathis Award," in *The Changing Face of the Church*, eds. Timothy Fitzgerald and Martin F. Connell (Chicago: Liturgy Training Publications, 1998) 6.

Reflections on Liturgical Reform[*]

It is extraordinarily difficult to bring the tumultuous history of litur-gical renewal in the American parish over the last twenty years into any kind of satisfactory focus.[1] Perhaps the best way of grasping what has happened would be to go into almost any parish church in the land, built before the middle or late sixties, sit about halfway back and allow the environment to tell its own story. Chances are that the struc-ture itself remains essentially what it was. The old altar against the back wall is probably still in place, but stripped of its mass cards, its candles, and maybe its tabernacle. The sunlight continues to filter through the same stained-glass windows upon the same worn pews. The same plaster madonna continues her serene and steady gaze upon the passersby, though it may be that a portable font has edged out the old votive light stand in vying for her modest smile. The altar rails may still be in place, but the gates have been removed and the starched linens which used to adorn them have long since been folded up and abandoned to some inaccessible sacristy cupboard. The interior of a Catholic church was never very tidy, but the litter problem seems to have worsened over the years. The sanctuary, in particular, has suf-fered. The once intimidating sweep of steps up to the high altar is now broken with a second, portable counterpart, invariably looking makeshift and out of place. The pulpit, if it remains, goes largely un-used: a spindly lectern, with a colored cloth and a microphone at-tached, has replaced it. Chairs of undetermined vintage, rescued from the monsignor's hallway, take up the remaining spaces. One has the sense that in half an hour all that has come about in the space of twenty years could be cleared away and the old order restored. It has not died, it has not even faded away. It merely sleeps.

* This essay first appeared in *Worship* 56 (1982) 411–30.

One wonders about those who have occupied these pews over the years. What has changed for them? Have the "changes" awoken them out of their sleep? If so, has the eye-opening been one of insight or disillusionment? Have their Christian convictions been renewed, or has it all been borne in more or less patient submission to the whims of ecclesiastical authority? Surveys claim to show that the overwhelming majority of Catholics pronounce themselves in favor of the reforms, but it is hard to know what that means. Liturgical change has meant so many things to so many parishes, to so many people. It may be little more than a code word for a low-tremor earthquake which shook the pictures off the wall, caused a momentary thrill of anxiety, provoked a short-lived storm of commentary and gossip, but left the foundations intact in most parts of the country. There are really no tools available for conducting an empirical study of the impact of the reforms upon the lives of American Catholics. We are left with impressions of what has been happening and guesses as to what it all means, but if the parish church described above is in any way typical, then it is probably a safe bet that liturgical reform has meant the introduction of changes which were, for the most part, assimilated into existing structures—physical, managerial, and conceptual—without transforming them. So far, it has meant not the arrival of a new order so much as the calling into question of the old.

The process continues, however, and it remains an open question whether the Church will continue to move, however slowly and awkwardly, toward the realization of a new vision of itself and its worship. In the meantime we can attempt to plot our present position by reference to the dilemmas involved in the program of liturgical reform, to the mixed fortunes of its implementation, and to the areas of pastoral liturgical concern which seem to demand our most immediate attention.

The Dilemmas of the Reform

The Constitution on the Sacred Liturgy (*Sacrosanctum Concilium*) was the first of the conciliar documents to be debated and the first to be promulgated. There was a certain appropriateness in this, as Paul VI noted at the end of the third session of the council: "for it is our conviction that God must be given the first priority, that it is our first duty to offer up prayers to Him, that the sacred liturgy is the primary course of that divine interchange in which the very life of God is given us; that the liturgy is the primary school of the spirit; that this should be the first gift we offer to the Christian people . . . and the first invitation to the human race to unloose its mute tongue in true and heartfelt prayer and to discover the wonderful power, which restores the soul, of singing the praises of God and the hope of humankind with us through Jesus Christ and in the Holy Spirit."[2] The document itself broke with the style of encyclical letters to return to that of previous councils.[3]

In its decision to combine practical measures with theological exposition, the preconciliar commission developed a format which was to serve as a precedent for other commissions and other documents. This was extremely important, for by giving theological principles as well as directives for reform, the council assumed its responsibility for helping the Church to come to *think* of liturgy differently and not merely *do* different things (though, as we shall remark later, the directives proved easier to put into effect than the change of thinking). It was the council's intent that these two processes should move in tandem, so that theological principles would help people understand the reforms and the reforms would deepen people's understanding of the liturgy.

Time has shown how optimistic such expectations were. Certainly there were many in this country for whom the document came as vindication: people who had learned from the liturgical movement to draw their spiritual sustenance from the liturgy of the Church. But they were a very small minority and it is probably true to say that most parishes in the United States were living and moving in patterns of thought and devotion which were so far removed from those of the Liturgy Constitution as to render the latter something altogether alien to their religious sensibilities. Garry Wills has described as pungently as anyone the echoes of preconciliar American Catholicism: the anti-intellectualism, the suppression of doubt "for the sake of the children," the ragtag network of devotions and theological clichés which set us off from other Americans, mediocrity disguising itself as moral superiority, and above all the total lack of any historical sense which sustained the otherwise unsupportable conviction that the Church never changes.

> Robbed of its past, the church existed in a present of precarious immediacy. Faith bound one's whole life up in ties of communal teaching, habits, discipline, authority, childhood assumptions, personal relationships. The church was enclosed, perfected in circular inner logic, strength distributed through all its interlocking aspects; turned in on itself, giving a good account of itself to itself—but so vulnerable, so frag-

ile, if one looked outward, away from it. It had a crystalline historicity; one touch of change or time could shatter it—and did. No wonder we protected it as long as we could, with a latent sense of its brittleness, and wept when it broke.[4]

In moving to reform the liturgy, the council moved to disturb the most sensitive area in Catholic life. So much of Catholic identity was tied up with the Mass, in particular. Not merely an attachment to the simplified Tridentine theology of the catechisms—for who had an intellectual attachment to that anyway?—but a whole world of memories, associations, feelings, and values whereby Catholics, even if "fallen away," had learned to identify themselves. Enthusiasts for the liturgy were right to recognize that the theology sustaining this system was out of step with the theology implicit in the texts and rites of the liturgy itself. They were right to recognize that this experience of Eucharist was far removed from that of the early centuries of Christianity. They were right to see that this in turn had produced a style of Catholic life that, being far removed from the spirit of the Gospel, was in urgent need of reform. It is true that the biblical and patristic perspectives of the Liturgy Constitution offered a more complete and more dynamic picture of the Christian life and vocation and that the reforms enacted in the council brought our liturgical practice closer to its authentic form. But it came like a different religion to the priests and people of St. Bridget's, St. Adalbert's and St. Odile's. As it turned out, it was all equally bewildering to their diocesan bishop who had listened to the Latin debates and voted a loyal "placet" at their conclusion.

Given the need and urgency of the reform, it is hard to know how things might have been done otherwise, yet the very process of reform was riddled with contradictions from whose unresolved frustrations we still suffer. Perhaps the central contradiction consisted of the fact that an institutional Church was trying to adopt a community style by the use of institutional means. Richard McBrien points to two fundamental errors of judgment on the part of Church leadership: first, in trying to maintain the unity of the Church before the council by suppressing free discussion of issues; and secondly, after recognizing the need for institutional change, by thinking "that it could introduce change under entirely controlled circumstances, by imposing conciliar reforms from above, without adequate preparation of those whom the changes would most immediately affect."[5] Yves Congar, quoted by Gerard Noel, says the same thing: "The Vatican II reform was a reform made from above . . . which was not prepared from below."[6] But this was the way the Catholic Church was used to operating. The irony of Vatican II, however, was that the message being passed down this time was that the laity, too, are the Church and that their active participation was urgently requested. It was a message that centuries of conditioning and the very form of the injunction made unintelligible to most. In the short run, at least, the only people who stood to gain were those whose cause was at last vindicated. So Garry Wills can comment: "Vatican II was a theologians' rebellion, that of the *periti* (expert consultants) against the Curia."[7] It was a blow for progressive elites over the hierarchical bureaucracy.

This reading of the council certainly makes sense in terms of the liturgical reform. It not only accounts for various attempts to sabotage the Constitution on the Liturgy before and during the council (e.g., *Veterum Sapientiae* in 1962)[8] but also explains the extraordinary attack on the validity of the 1970 *Ordo Missae* by some curial officials.[9] More importantly, though, it accounts for the very mixed reception accorded the liturgical reforms in the parishes of English-speaking Catholicism. They were accepted in some places with great enthusiasm, but in most the reaction was one of bewildered obedience to the wishes of the Holy Father. The new rites thus came to be celebrated in the old Church. The directives were obeyed, but the theological principles were not much grappled with by clergy or people. Undoubtedly, the major change introduced into the liturgy was the very idea that change was possible.

Of course, there were bishops and pastors who, skilled in the Scholastic distinction between substance and accidents, hastened to reassure their people that nothing had really changed; but even conservative Catholics, conditioned in the old fideism, found this reversal of the transubstantiation motif hard to swallow. On the other hand, the dismantling of liturgical practices long thought immutable served for some as a license to change anything and everything in the name of progress and "pastoral need."[10] Thus the pace of "reform" quickly gathered momentum and began to outdistance the measured gradualism of the official program of renewal. Polarization set in as some parishes became redoubts of minimalism and others set out to gain a reputation for "creative" liturgy. For the most part, however, American parishes did their best: that is, loyally introduced the changes with little comprehension of the principles behind them or of how those principles offered a coherent and rather different vision of the life and mission of the parish. What Gerard Noel says of the American Church at official levels is equally applicable to the same Church at the parish level: "It has merely kept pace and rendered many improvements innocuous by allowing them to become respectable."[11]

In short, the expectations of Vatican II have not been realized for several complex reasons. These reasons have to do with the upheavals in civil and political life in the West and especially in the United States; they have to do with the weaknesses in American Catholic religious and community life which the reforms succeeded in revealing rather than curing; and they have to do with contradictions within the process of reform itself. All these problems were unforeseen and, indeed, unforeseeable back in 1963, but they contributed mightily to the upheavals of the intervening years and account for the very mixed situation which prevails liturgically at the present time.

The Fortunes of Reform

The history of the last twenty years alone should serve to confirm the fact that the state of the liturgy reflects the general state of health of the Church, which makes it difficult to isolate the story of liturgical renewal from the broader context of American Church life in this period. Moreover, the task of drawing up a balance sheet for the reform is further complicated by the fact that it is difficult to distinguish its successes from its failures. What succeeded, it now appears, succeeded in raising new problems. What failed was in turn a source of insight. Among the many surprises that lay in wait for us in the postconciliar era was the fact that the reform should produce such surprises.

Successes. In numbers 21–40 of *Sacrosanctum Concilium*, the council laid down the general principles upon which the reform would be undertaken. The general norms (22–25) concerned regulation of the reform by Rome, the organic development of new forms from the old, the centrality of Scripture and the revision of liturgical books. Numbers 26–32 emphasized the role of the community as celebrant of the liturgy and the different ministerial roles that involves. Under the heading of "Norms Based Upon the Educative and Pastoral Nature of the Liturgy," numbers 33–36 take seriously the role of communication within the liturgy, adopting the principles of simplicity and intelligibility, permitting the use of the vernacular "in the first place [for] the readings and directives, and [for] some prayers and chants." The fourth set of norms governs cultural adaptation and liturgical experimentation, an area of liturgical renewal which, for various reasons, has hardly begun to be considered in this country. If we leave aside the

General Norms and those governing cultural adaptation and focus on those derived from the communitarian and pastoral character of the liturgy, we can point to some genuine successes in the implementation of the Liturgy Constitution in this country.

The introduction of the vernacular has undoubtedly been well received. In the early days, at least, the shock of hearing the readings and prayers proclaimed in English was a wholly salutary one. There were, of course, complaints in some quarters about the quality of the translations being used, but that hardly detracted from the overall popularity of the move. The reading of the Scriptures in English, especially once the new Lectionary was introduced, has given Catholics a new appreciation of the role of the Bible in the life of the Church and has exposed them to a hitherto unparalleled encounter with biblical texts. Perhaps the single most significant indicator of the impact of the introduction of the vernacular was the pressure which built up so quickly to extend its use far beyond what the council fathers had envisaged, until the final traces of the Latin liturgy had disappeared within a very few years. It would surely be a mistake to attribute this pressure to an animus against Latin, or simple desire to follow the path of vernacularization to its logical conclusion. What was also involved was a growing sense that the very idea of a macaronic rite was theologically flawed, as if the Liturgy of the Word was a period of instruction to be followed by a sacred action preserved in an ancient tongue. A growing sense of the inner dynamic of the liturgy made it inevitable that "sacred moments" could not be fenced off by switching back to Latin. If for no other reason than this, the introduction of an English liturgy must be accounted a success and it is clear that it is now so firmly rooted in the life of the American Church that there can be no going back on it.[12]

However, the very success of the vernacular—a success easily guaranteed by the mere stroke of a legislative pen—revealed a new set of problems that were not so easily resolved. In a sense, the criterion of intelligibility enunciated by the council aroused expectations which could not immediately be met, for it soon became clear that the problem of understanding the liturgy lay not in the language in which the texts were written, but in the texts themselves and in the people to whom they were addressed. The reading of the Scriptures in English brought us to painful awareness of the lack of biblical understanding among priests and people. Similarly with liturgical texts which, once translated from the Latin, appeared to lose the richness for which they had hitherto been cherished. After the initial excitement of the English liturgy, the new texts proved no more engaging than the old and the poverty of our grasp of the native language of Scripture and liturgical prayer was revealed. The result was banal, listless liturgies in many churches and the introduction of nonscriptural readings and improvised prayers in others. The newly established liturgical industry began cranking out "experimental liturgies" in an effort to revive the flagging interest of parochial congregations and a torrent of liturgical ballads to keep parishioners from settling down to think what it was all about. Since these new products, too, largely shared the common ignorance of the native language of Scripture and liturgy, they proved gimmicky and ephemeral. But it is important to notice that they flourished, while they flourished, in the name of intelligibility.

A second area of success, closely related to the success of the vernacular, is what is often identified as "the people's sense of ownership of the liturgy." The council had laid down as a principle that "liturgical services are not private functions, but are celebrations of the whole Church. . . . Therefore liturgical services pertain to the whole body of the Church; they manifest it and have effects upon it . . ." (no. 26). The primary consequence of this principle, of course, has been the canonization of the liturgical movement's primary goal: the active participation of the faithful in the liturgy of the Church. By and large this has been extraordinarily successful, especially given the equally extraordinary emphasis on hierarchical authority and the powers of the ordained in modern Catholicism. What may have started in many places as mumbled responses read off missalettes has grown to a familiar and accustomed habit of dialogue between priest and people. Hymn singing, if not yet all that it might be, has made tremendous strides in most parishes. Moreover, Catholic laypersons have taken with astounding ease to the unfamiliar roles of ministers of Word and Eucharist. Their role in the planning of liturgies and in the shaping of the overall prayer life of their communities is still minimal or nonexistent in many places, indicating that they have run up against limitations in the conciliar invitation to active participation.

Two areas where they have quickly moved into the opening provided are the kiss of peace and the frequent reception of Communion. The latter case is especially interesting. Since the Council of Trent, popes have been urging people to frequent Communion and yet it never caught on until after Vatican II. One reason for this is surely that the invitation was contextualized in a much broader series of liturgical changes wherein people saw their own relationship to the Mass and the community quite differently. Thus a whole complex of changes is involved in this phenomenon, which still awaits adequate study. Andrew Greeley's reminder that 80 percent of those going to Communion so regularly are in disagreement with the Church's official teaching on birth control[13] suggests that an important ecclesiological shift has occurred, whereby people are no longer content to have their status defined for them by the Church authority, but claim their right to demur and communicate in virtue of the fact that the Church and its liturgy belong to them as much as to the hierarchy. Greeley warns of "do it yourself Catholicism," and of the breakdown of confidence in ecclesiastical leadership, but from the viewpoint of liturgical renewal it would seem to justify claims that the laity have asserted, to this degree at least, their ownership of the liturgy and their refusal to consider themselves as participants simply in virtue of someone else's permission.

But here, too, there are frustrations. Since the council, ecclesiastical authority in general and Rome in particular has shown itself fearful of the full and logical consequences of the adopted principle of active participation. What those consequences imply is a recovery of the congregation's sense of itself as a local church, with its own particular identity, continuity, vocation, and mission. Rome's strict insistence on the universal oversight of every last detail of liturgical reform works in practice against the conciliar vision of local churches. This is replicated at the local level by tokenism in lay involvement in areas, including liturgy, which used to be the priest's preserve. At every level, it is revealed in the nervousness with which the involvement of women in liturgical ministry is regarded. Once again, the council seems to have opted for a liturgical principle whose full consequences were not foreseen. It has become increasingly clear that active participation in the liturgy on the basis of baptism is something of a sham if it does not mean active participation in the whole life of the local church and the assuming of wider responsibilities of the Church towards its members and the larger society which flow from the liturgy being merely the source and summit of Christian life. The faithful will not be able to make the desired connections between liturgy and daily life if their participation in the life of the believing community is restricted to liturgical role-playing.

A third area of success might be said to be in the overall experience of the liturgy. The conciliar reforms aroused the expectation that with the new rites there would be a new experience of the presence of Christ among his people and a deeper sense of encountering the paschal mystery. While it would be difficult to measure the extent to which people have become immersed in the paschal mystery, the revised liturgy has certainly exposed people to a new discovery of the presence of Christ in the word and in the assembly, as well as in his eucharistic presence. This has often proved true in the other sacraments, such as the anointing of the sick and, on occasion, penance, especially communal services. More generally, it has been the experience of most Catholics that, when the liturgy is done well, they find themselves drawn into an encounter with Christ in the celebration of the assembly. One suspects that this is sometimes confused with a strong sense of togetherness in which the horizontal rather than the vertical dimension of liturgy predominates. This was especially true in the early days of the reform, when the novelty of house Masses and coffee-table Eucharists sometimes overwhelmed participants with a sense of their oneness in Christ.

Today such experiences seem less frequent, the result perhaps of a growing familiarity with the new rites and a growing maturity among the faithful. What worked in the sixties is less likely to work today, as people seem to have tired of high-spirited liturgies and begun to look for something more substantial and more sustaining. In fact, there is something of a crisis facing the liturgy today, precisely in the realm of religious experience. Having been led to expect liturgies to be "meaningful" and engaging, the faithful find themselves frustrated by celebrations which are dull and listless or full of the distractions of forced bonhomie. It is as if we have had to work a number of things out of our systems, to discover the shallowness of some of our earlier understandings and expectations, and to emerge from it all with a real hunger for the life of the Spirit mediated through the liturgy of the Church. For many, though, that hunger goes unsatisfied. "I don't get anything out of it," people say. "I just keep going for the sake of the children." Such attitudes are uncomfortably close to those which Garry Wills would claim as symptomatic of the hollowness of preconciliar Catholicism. In the meantime, however, the revised liturgy has given most people at one time or another a taste of what might be and has shaped their expectations of what should be in directions quite different from the preconciliar Church.

Failures. The chief failure in the liturgical renewal has undoubtedly been the failure of leadership. This is said without any desire to assign blame, for the clergy and the bishops, indeed Rome itself, are as much victims of their history as anyone else. Nevertheless, it has to be acknowledged that at every level, from parish to Roman congregation, there has been a profound lack of conviction about the meaning and direction of liturgical reform. In some ways this is already built into the Liturgy Constitution itself, where the insistence that not even local conferences of bishops can act without submitting their proposals ahead of time to the scrutiny of Rome has created a process in which those who were to implement the reform were continually looking over their shoulder for higher approval instead of looking to the needs of their own people. The criterion has been, not whether it is in the spirit of the reform and to the pastoral advantage of the people of God, but whether we would get into trouble if we do it.

The result is that the sheep look up and are not fed. One of the most common complaints about the new liturgy is the abysmal quality of Catholic preaching: it lacks spiritual depth and religious conviction, it is out of touch with the joys and struggles of Christian people. The same lack of authentic faith comes across in the inability of most priests to recognize what is required of them in their new role as presidents of the liturgical assembly and leaders of prayer. They either resort to gimmicks and pseudo-intimacy or withdraw into "saying Mass."[14] At the present time, only a minority of priests show themselves capable of performing the liturgical roles for which they were ordained. Nor is the new, postconciliar generation a notable improvement. Recent studies[15] have shown that the conciliar exhortation to upgrade the status of liturgical studies in seminaries and to make it the focal point of all studies for the priesthood has been given a mixed reception. Seminarians emerge with skills in counseling and the transcendental method, but often lacking the spiritual maturity and leadership skills required for the very function for which they were ordained: to lead the people of God in prayer and celebration.

At the root of the problem is the issue of power, according to Andrew Greeley. Certainly this is a hypothesis that would explain Rome's unwillingness to allow regional churches to be responsible for their own prayer lives, the bishop's unwillingness to rock the boat, and the priest's profound insecurity as he finds himself called into question on all sides. Basically, it is a fear of losing control. Hence the more or less profound disillusionment which has set in among once enthusiastic priests and people, as they discover that the theological principles and practical directives of Vatican II run aground on the shoals of unreconstructed authoritarianism. It becomes daily more clear that the failure of Church leadership to sustain and promote a new, more evangelical vision of Church—with all the changes in order and polity that would imply—seriously compromises the liturgical life of the people of God.

A second area of failure is in the area of spirituality. For many people in the preconciliar years, the liturgical movement was not merely a bandwagon, but a source of genuine, deep, ecclesial spirituality. The hope of the council was that this would become true for the whole Church, but that has patently not happened: witness the impact of the charismatic movement, of the Cursillo, and of other spiritual renewal movements which owe little or nothing to the liturgy of the Church. The introduction of liturgical changes without much appreciation of the theological vision informing them—and, as we have just seen, without the sustaining leadership of the Church authorities—has led to confusion among many and to superficial and undirected enthusiasm among others. The result is widespread disillusionment and a hunger for meaning among American Catholics. Perhaps it was inevitable that the reaction against the negativity of preconciliar Catholic spirituality should have provoked a giddy swing towards affirming everything as good and celebrating resurrection as if we already lived it. The *Allelu* sounds hollow now. In the Church, and in the sociopolitical events of the last two decades, we have been through too many traumas.

Perhaps we are now ready to read the Liturgy Constitution anew and to hear the Lenten Scriptures with fresh ears. The constitution situates the liturgy of the Church within the context of a sweeping panorama of salvation history, whose climax is the paschal mystery of Jesus dead and risen. This mystery gives meaning to suffering as well as joy, to conversion as well as fellowship and, above all, it gives meaning to time and to change. Perhaps we are more realistic than in those years immediately after the council. Perhaps history itself has prepared us to take another, more sober look at the deeper meaning of the mystery of faith. Perhaps we can learn from the charismatics and cursillistas that what we are about is not fulfilling obligations or passing an hour together in church, but finding meaning and hope in life itself.

Unexpected Developments. No review of the liturgical reform would be complete without an acknowledgment of developments that were quite unforeseen. Some of these are well known or have been mentioned already: the disillusionment which set in during the late sixties and early seventies; the falling away of Catholic laypeople and the mass resignation of priests; the enormous reversal of Catholic practice concerning the frequency of Communion. Here we shall touch briefly on four other significant surprises.

First, the experience of being "massed out." Since the council we have witnessed the widespread decline of devotions and exercises which once played so strong a role in Catholic life: Benediction, Stations of the Cross, novenas, Holy Hours, and so forth. Every occasion came to be celebrated with a Mass. Perhaps this is more a problem for the Church's "professionals" than for most of the laity, but in any case a severe imbalance has arisen in the prayer life of the Church as a whole. It had been the halfhearted expectation of the council that the liturgy of the hours might be restored as the regular prayer of the people of God (*Sacrosanctum Concilium* 84), but the reform of the breviary was compromised from the very beginning. Once again, the cause was the tension between keeping control (insisting that the clergy recite the breviary) and radically revitalizing the prayer life of the Church. Hamstrung by the council's directives, the postconciliar Commission on the Liturgy of the Hours produced a document that satisfied no one. The result is that large numbers of priests in the United States appear to have virtually abandoned the daily prayer of the Divine Office. That, plus the multiplication of Masses at all hours of day and night, may well destroy any rhythmic pattern of prayer among them. The laity, for their part, have little or no knowledge of the tradition of daily liturgical prayer. Attempts to promote such prayer though adaptations of the Divine Office have run up against the disapproval of ecclesiastical authority (for example, the Collegeville *Book of Prayer* and an abortive ICEL project to adapt the Liturgy of the Hours for popular use). Thus people are left to their own resources, join prayer groups, and turn out in unexpected numbers when some old-fashioned devotion is announced (95 percent of the congregation in a nearby parish remained for the blessing of the throats after Sunday Mass following the feast of St. Blaise!). We need to discover what needs such devotions meet and try to satisfy them in more substantial ways.

A second surprise lay in store for us with the revision of the sacrament of penance. This was one of the later reforms (1973) and one which had an extremely troubled history in its preparation.[16] Once again, it was a case of whether the Church would move to discover people's spiritual needs and meet them, or whether it would cling to the previous balance of power. The result was a severely compromised document in which the power of absolution fought to regain the ascendancy over a biblical approach to penance as conversion of heart. It contained the supreme irony of a rite for general absolution which was hedged around with even tighter restrictions than had governed such a celebration of penance before the council. When some bishops moved to use the rite they were swiftly rebuked by Rome, despite the fact that it appeared to have had quite remarkable impact upon their people. Of course the danger of "cheap grace" is there, but how can a viable discipline ever be developed if the use of the rite is forbidden? In the meantime, the two other forms of penance are largely ignored outside the captive audience situations of convents and schools. Once again, one must be careful not to rush to hasty conclusions. The staggering decline in the practice of "confession" is remarkable only against the equally remarkable frequency with which it was practiced in the preconciliar Church and it would surprise no one but a 1950's Catholic to know that Catholic life in the first half of the twentieth century was by no means typical of the longer tradition. Still, the fact remains that, in the present situation of American Catholicism, the sacramental celebration of penance is not something most Catholics engage in with any regularity, leaving a vacuum of repentance and reconciliation that cannot long be ignored without danger to the health of the Church.

Perhaps a third unexpected development was what might almost be called the bankruptcy of catechetics. This was one area that American Catholicism really believed in and which grew even more important and powerful in the era following the council. The council, in fact, generated a whole new upsurge in the catechetical industry. Publishing boomed. The new Church meant that adults, too, were now fit subjects for instruction and catechesis and renewal programs. Yet, the complaint was and is that the laity were not sufficiently catechized! It is probably true that, even with the explosion of books and programs, a large proportion of American Catholics went untouched, apart from the more or less helpful "instructions" on the revisions of the liturgy given from the pulpit. Despite all the money the Church poured into catechesis and religious education, its impact has been disappointing. It is perhaps only with the belated welcome being given to the Rite of Christian Initiation of Adults (1972) that the realization is beginning to dawn that the mystery of Christian existence is not something that can be explained or made the topic of instruction. Of course, the attempt can be made, but the point of encountering the Gospel, the Church and the sacraments is that they require initiation, not elucidation, the adoption of a lifestyle of conversion, not the accumulation of ideas or credit hours. Unfortunately, the RCIA, like the rest of liturgy, has in many places fallen among religious educators and is being turned into a program of instruction. But there is still hope that we will learn from the liturgy and from the Scriptures—as well as from the faith of the faithful themselves—how to pray, celebrate, be converted, and live.[17]

Finally, it was never in anyone's dreams that, twenty years after the council, many of the most devout and active of the faithful would look for sustenance in their religious lives to sources outside the Church, finding themselves alienated from the liturgy they once loved. Such, however, is often the case. Many whose vocation is to prayer either suffer parish liturgy or avoid it. They take up the medieval mystics and disciplines of the East, they search for a guru or a counselor and live their inner lives and pursue their inner search without any liturgical anchorage. What should be rich with symbolic meaning appears shoddy, mass-produced, and uncaring. At the other pole, activists who once perhaps drew their inspiration from men like H. A. Reinhold, Virgil Michel, and other liturgists who saw an intrinsic connection between liturgy and social order, between common prayer and common justice, now feel increasingly alienated from self-serving, visionless parochial liturgies. We are in danger of being left with those of the faithful who have neither the sense of conviction nor clarity of vision to go anywhere else. This has to change.

Prospects

This may appear to be a gratuitously negative assessment of the state of liturgical renewal in these United States. Everyone will have instances which prove happy exceptions to this judgment; many perhaps will quibble with the criteria being implied. Nevertheless, the goals and aspirations of liturgical reform were clearly set forth by the council in the opening words of the Liturgy Constitution:

> It is the goal of this most sacred Council to intensify the daily growth of Catholics in Christian living; to make more responsive to the needs of our times those Church observances which are open to adaptation; to nurture whatever can contribute to the unity of all who believe in Christ; and to strengthen those aspects of the Church which can help summon all mankind into her embrace. Hence the Council has special reasons for judging it a duty to provide for the renewal and fostering of the liturgy.

These, then, are the criteria by which the performance of the Church in North America is to be judged, twenty years after the promulgation of the program of liturgical renewal.

On the evidence considered here, we are still a long way from realizing those objectives in most of our parishes. *Stalemate* is perhaps not too strong a word to characterize our present liturgical situation. We have lived through turmoil of high expectations dissolving into sad disillusionment, through surges of newly released energy and unexpected conflicts, through gimmicks and craziness and patient, plodding dullness. Liturgically, the Church seems now largely quiescent, for the most part untroubled by the distant cries of feminists, ecumenists, and other discontents. Yet there are new dreams stirring even as we sleep, new realizations which may draw us on toward a deeper comprehension of the mysteries we celebrate.

There is growing respect for the objectivity of the liturgy. For a long time such a concept seemed outdated: the monolithic structures of the past, venerable and untouchable, had seemed to give way to a new apostolic age in which everything was in process of being created anew. Liturgy was to express the faith of the Church, which was interpreted to mean (since we *were* the Church) that it was to be the medium of our self-expression. Our faith bubbled up in song, our love in tearful protestations of mutual acceptance, our hope in the cult of spontaneity. Now that seems to have passed, by and large. Once is less likely to encounter improvised eucharistic prayers and nonscriptural readings. There is a growing sense that the liturgy is a tradition that must shape us and discipline us if we are to be able to enter into it fully. For all the subjectivity of our celebrations, we were caught in the critical distance which the council had opened up for us all in even venturing to reevaluate and to reform the rituals we had received. Once a few things could be changed, everything could be changed. New expectations once aroused, we were continually watching ourselves to see if our faith was stronger, our love more real, our experience more genuine, our liturgies more authentic. Such concern for the quality of the experience, of course, militated against our very involvement in the rite. Perhaps we have learned that the role of the liturgy is not so much the cultivation of feeling-experiences as the quiet disciplining of Christian attitudes toward God, self, and world. Out of the disappointments of the recent past, a new appreciation for the objective givenness of the liturgy may be coming to birth.

Similarly, we are undergoing a revaluation of the principle of intelligibility. Once the problem was thought to be in the rites and texts, so that the search was on for new forms that might be more "meaningful." Once the texts were translated and still made no sense, they were rejected in favor of others. Similarly with rituals deemed archaic and unredeemable: they were to be dropped and new symbols created. It was a barren quest. Pinning our sins to the cross on Good Friday to guitar accompaniment proved no substitute for the ancient ritual of veneration and the challenge of grappling with the Reproaches. Now we are coming to realize that ritual has its own forms, that its language is that of poetry and image, that it does not simply convey obvious meaning to all who attend but inducts into mystery those who participate. Moreover, Christian liturgy, the celebration of God in Jesus Christ, requires conversion to life in the Spirit of God. Its meaning becomes only gradually intelligible to those who live within it in a spirit of humility and openness. It can be understood, not through historical and theological explanation, but through evangelization and initiation into the whole Christian way of life. Of immense importance has been the restoration of Scripture to its proper place in the life of the Catholic community, for it is from Scripture chiefly that the stories and images in which the liturgy engages us are drawn. But the Scriptures are opened to the believer, not through exegetical commentary so much as through their proclamation in catechumenal groups and in the assembly of the faithful. We are recovering the meaning of mystagogy.

Similarly, despite all the ups and downs of the past two decades and the rise and fall of clichés about community, the reformed liturgy has begun delicately to reshape our self-understanding as Church. Where once we put our hopes in facile communitarianism, we are coming to recognize that our bonds to one another in the Spirit of Christ are a mystery not so easily realized nor so easily dispensed with. It depends not upon frequency and intensity of contacts so much as upon a sober realization of our common brokenness and need of redemption. This, in turn, enables us to look quite differently upon the wider society of humankind: not with the condescension of a preconciliar Church that knew it was right; not with the thoughtless affirmation of postconciliar Catholicism embracing the world's agenda; but with a profound sense of compassion for a world gone awry and a more sober and determined confrontation with the mystery of evil. Perhaps our experience of dissent and disillusionment within the Church will make us more open to the reality of the paschal mystery as it unfolds in the life of the world and is celebrated in the liturgy of the Church.

In each of these three developments—recognizing the objectivity of the liturgy, the mystery (as opposed to mystification) which we celebrate, and the paschal mystery as a reality for the whole race—lie the seeds of the future evolution of the renewal begun at Vatican II. We shall surely continue to be plagued by symptoms of preconciliar attitudes that refuse to die, but events are overtaking such attitudes. The dwindling number of priests will bring about radical changes in local Catholic community life, changes prepared for by the new sense of "ownership" engendered by the reformed liturgy. Social and political developments will continue to force Catholics, perhaps even more urgently, to ask what it means to be called to be Christian in the world. New thresholds are being reached in the development of music and texts which will respect the process they are meant to serve, the mystery of Christ among us, our hope of glory (Col 1:27).

Perhaps, if there is one word that can sum up the direction in which we need to go, it is "reverence." Reverence is one of the things that many thought had disappeared from the liturgy after the reform. If that was so, it is time to cherish it again. But let it be a reverence that goes beyond a preoccupation with sacred things. Let it be a reverence for the word as well as the sacrament, for the world as well as the Church, for the people of God as well as for the ordained and vowed. Let it be a reverence which shows itself in mutual service, and above all, in sensitivity and respect for the faith-life of ordinary Catholics, for the burdens they carry and for the testimony they can bear to the joys and struggles of the Christian life.

---

[1] I am indebted to my colleagues at the Center for Pastoral Liturgy and to a number of the associates of the Center for stimulating these reflections, though responsibility for the positions adopted is, of course, entirely my own.

[2] Allocution of Paul VI, 4 December 1963, in R. Kaczynski, ed., *Enchiridion Documentorum Instaurationis Liturgicae*, vol. I (Turin, 1975) 133.

[3] P.-M. Gy, "The Constitution in the Making," in A. Flannery, ed., *Vatican II: The Liturgy Constitution* (Dublin: Scepter Books, 1964) 11–20.

[4] Garry Wills, *Bare Ruined Choirs: Doubt, Prophecy, and Radical Religion* (Garden City, New York: Doubleday, 1971, 1972) 32–3.

[5] Richard McBrien, *The Remaking of the Church* (New York: Harper and Row, 1980) 68.

[6] Gerard Noel, *The Anatomy of the Catholic Church: A Roman Catholic in an Age of Revolution* (Garden City, New York: Doubleday, 1980) 51.

[7] *Bare Ruined Choirs*, 71.

[8] See Herman Schmidt, *Die Konstitution über die hl. Liturgie* (Freiburg: Herder, 1965) 72–7.

[9] *A Critical Study of the New Order of the Mass (Novus Ordo Missae)*. By a group of Roman Theologians (London: Lumen Gentium Foundation) n.d.

[10] As my colleague Gerald Lardner has pointed out, the new antinomianism was a true offspring of the old legalism. Before the council, law was the sole restraint; when law fell, it appeared there were no constraints. It was to take time before a sense of the tradition, theological consistency, a more refined appreciation of the aesthetic and communicative dimensions of liturgy and so forth would begin to replace law as the sole factor in shaping response to pastoral needs.

11 *The Anatomy of the Catholic Church*, 99.

12 See the recent survey of the world's bishops taken by the Congregation for Sacraments and Divine Worship, *Notitiae*, no. 185 (December 1981) 589–611; reported in *Origins*, National Catholic News Service, Washington, D.C., vol. 11, no. 35 (February 1982) 556–69.

13 Andrew Greeley, "The Failures of Vatican II After Twenty Years," *America* (6 February 1982) 86.

14 Unfortunately, both these reactions directly affect people's perception of what the "new liturgy" ought to be insofar as they are justified by those responsible by appeal to Vatican II and/or other official documents. It is probably significant, however, that ecclesiastical authority has generally been more zealous in reining in those deemed to go too far than in spurring on those clergy who offer passive resistance to liturgical and ecclesial renewal.

15 Thomas Krosnicki, "A Survey Report on the Teaching and Celebration of Liturgy," CARA Seminary Forum 3 (September 1974) 1–8; Nathan Mitchell, "Liturgical Education in Roman Catholic Seminaries: A Report and an Appraisal," *Worship* 54 (1980) 129–57. A more recent survey of the liturgical training of seminarians of various denominations in the U.S. is offered by James F. White, with responses by Nathan Mitchell and Frank C. Senn in *Worship* 55 (1981) 304–32.

16 See James Dallen, *A Decade of Discussion on the Reform of Penance, 1963–1973: Theological Analysis and Critique* (Ann Arbor, Michigan: University Microfilms International, 1976), esp. 300ff.

17 It would be better to speak of the formative, rather than the didactic, function of the liturgy in Christian life. Here Edward Fisher's remark is apropos: "Religious educators need to work harder at communicating the idea that the *way* something is done is at the very foundation of religious life. No activity is religious if it lowers life, and none is secular once it lifts life. *How* a thing is done is rock-bottom communication that goes beyond all words and turns an act into one of worship or into a blasphemy." *Everybody Steals From God* (University of Notre Dame Press, 1977) 124.

Gilbert Ostdiek, o.f.m.

Introduction to "New Tasks, New Methods: The Emergence of Pastoral Liturgical Studies"

Two decades have passed since Mark Searle delivered the vice-presidential address at the annual meeting of the North American Academy of Liturgy. The address was entitled, "New Tasks, New Methods: The Emergence of Pastoral Liturgical Studies."[1] The vision for the future of liturgical studies which he voiced remains as compelling now as it was then.

The heart of Searle's vision lies in his proposal that a third branch of scholarly research be added to the field of liturgical studies. As Searle notes in his introduction, historical research had long been the predominant approach to studying the liturgy. In the first half of the twentieth century, under the influence of the liturgical movement, the study of the theology of the liturgy took its place alongside history as the second branch of liturgical study. It was these two already established disciplines, the history and theology of the liturgy, that shaped the liturgical renewal launched by Vatican II. Restoration of the role of the assembly and recovery of the importance of the whole complex of symbolic words and gestures in engaging the worshiping community create the need, in Searle's view, for a third branch of scholarship which he names "pastoral liturgical studies."

As Searle envisions it, the discipline of pastoral liturgical studies is distinguished from the history and theology of the liturgy in that it focuses on the actual worship life of the Church today. This new discipline will have three tasks. First, its *empirical task* is "to attend to what actually goes on in the rite" and to describe what is happening. Second, the *hermeneutical task* is to study "how symbols operate and how symbolic language communicates." Third, the *critical task* is to compare the previous two sets of findings "with the historical tradition and with the theological claims made for the liturgy" and to draw appropriate theological and pastoral conclusions. Pastoral liturgical studies, as Searle envisions it, engages in a scholarly and critical study of the liturgical event with the help of methods and findings of the social sciences. The first task will have to rely especially on the "use of self-conscious methods of enquiry developed in the social sciences."

Searle was not the first to recognize what great benefits the study of liturgy could gain by drawing on the work of the social sciences. Some discussions and efforts toward that end were already underway in Germany, France, and the United States.[2] What made Searle's proposal unique was that he foresaw the need to gather these fledgling attempts into the framework of a new academic discipline. The focus and formal object of that discipline is the event of worship. But because the liturgical event is multidimensional, the new discipline will have to draw on appropriate social science methods of research, within limits he carefully noted; its approach must therefore be interdisciplinary, or multidisciplinary.

In the years that followed, others took up the discussion about whether and how to use the methods and findings of the social sciences in the study of the liturgy,[3] and Searle's article has become a standard reference for interdisciplinary courses offered at various graduate schools.[4] Searle himself continued both to equip himself in social science disciplines and to partner with scholars in those fields. In particular, he worked with sociologist David Leege on the Notre Dame Study of Catholic Parish Life ("The Notre Dame Study of Catholic Parish Life," 1986) and with semioticians (e.g., "Semiotic Analysis of Roman Eucharistic Prayer II," 1992; *Semiotics and Church Architecture*, 1993, which resulted from his sabbatical work with semioticians at Tilburg and was coauthored with Gerard Lukken). He was also a conversation partner with anthropologist Martin Stringer who has studied liturgical performance.[5] Despite these individual initiatives of Searle and others, few programs of graduate liturgical studies seem to have taken up Searle's proposal of establishing a full set of curricular offerings in pastoral liturgical studies. Perhaps the most promising work in the multidisciplinary study of the liturgy is being done in an ongoing collaborative research program sponsored by several universities in the Netherlands and Belgium.[6]

Searle's vision for pastoral liturgical studies is fully consistent with the larger vision of the liturgy he drew from Vatican II. Elements interwoven in that vision include the following: "Assembly: Remembering the People of God," 1983; "Renewing the Liturgy—Again," 1988; "Forgotten Truths about Worship," 1988. The paschal mystery lies at the heart of Christian worship. That mystery sums up Christ's life of total self-giving in service of the coming of God's reign, and it has brought him before the throne of God, where he remains the one and only liturgist (Heb 12:2), always living to offer praise and make intercession on our behalf. The essential activity of the liturgical assembly, then, is to remember, to keep the memorial of that mystery, to be joined to Christ's action as his Body, to embody his presence and action in word and symbolic gesture. Gathered Sunday after Sunday, the worshipers rehearse that mystery until they have assimilated it and can live it as fully as possible in daily life.

Several convictions follow in the mind of Searle. Because worship is a public, corporate act, it is important that the choice of how liturgy is celebrated not be left to the whim or personal taste of presiders and planners. Because human words and actions are made to be the sacramental symbols and bearers of God's saving presence and deeds, it is important to attend to the concrete yet subtle ways in which they communicate to worshipers in the actual liturgical event, to bring all our scholarly resources to bear in seeking to understand what they say and how they work. Liturgical scholars must come to that study with what Searle calls the "prior theological commitment" that "the mystery of grace [is] sacramentalized in the words and actions of the congregation." He is equally convinced that they also need to study the human dimensions of the words and actions which form that sacramentalization. It is there that his vision for the future of liturgical studies finds its cogency. To a large extent it is a vision that still awaits fulfillment.

Rev. Gilbert Ostdiek, O.F.M., is professor of liturgy at the Catholic Theological Union, Chicago, Illinois.

---

[1] Mark Searle, "New Tasks, New Methods: The Emergence of Pastoral Liturgical Studies," *Worship* 57 (1983) 291–308. The ideas he expressed took shape and were honed over a period of fifteen years in the lively discussions of the NAAL seminar group devoted to bringing the methods and findings of the social sciences to bear on the study of liturgy. It has been a great privilege to count Mark Searle not only as mentor and colleague in those discussions, but as a loyal friend.

[2] In this country most notable was the work done by Mary Collins at The Catholic University of America. See the collected essays in her *Worship: Renewal to Practice* (Washington, D.C.: The Pastoral Press, 1987).

[3] Martin D. Stringer, "Liturgy and Anthropology: The History of a Relationship," *Worship* 63 (1989) 503–20, criticized how liturgists use anthropology. For a more positive position on using the social sciences, see: Theodore W. Jennings, "Ritual Studies and

Liturgical Theology: An Invitation to Dialogue," *Journal of Ritual Studies* 1 (1987) 35–56; Margaret Mary Kelleher, "Liturgy: An Ecclesial Act of Meaning," *Worship* 59 (1985) 482–97; "Liturgical Theology: A Task and a Method," *Worship* 62 (1988) 2–25; "Hermeneutics in the Study of Liturgical Performance," *Worship* 67 (1993) 292–318; Nathan D. Mitchell, *Liturgy and the Social Sciences* (Collegeville: Liturgical Press, 1999); John D. Witvliet, "For Our Own Purposes: The Appropriation of the Social Sciences in Liturgical Studies," *Liturgy Digest* 2:2 (1995) 6–35.

[4] For example, such courses are offered at the University of Notre Dame, where Searle taught, at Catholic Theological Union, The Catholic University of America, and Sant' Anselmo. These courses typically focus on symbol and ritual, and occasionally on liturgical methods.

[5] Martin D. Stringer, *On the Perception of Worship* (Birmingham, Ala.: University of Birmingham Press, 1999).

[6] The focus of the first project has been the processes of change in relation to Christian rituals. See Paul Post, "Liturgical Movements and Feast Culture: A Dutch Research Program," in *Christian Feast and Festival: the Dynamics of Western Liturgy and Culture*, eds. P. Post et al. (Leuven: Peeters, 2001) 3–43.

New Tasks, New Methods:
The Emergence of Pastoral
Liturgical Studies[*]

Ever since liturgiology became something more than the study of rubrics, the study of the liturgy has been regarded as a predominantly historical discipline. In the last fifty years or so, however, largely in response to the demands of the liturgical movement, a historical and systematic approach to the theology of liturgy has reflected upon and complemented the work of historical scholarship. The massive reforms of the Church's actual practice of worship were both promoted and made possible on the basis of liturgical history and a newly recovered theological understanding of the liturgy of the Church. To this day, the field of liturgical scholarship is properly dominated by the historians and theologians among us. Nevertheless, in the past fifteen years, new developments have been taking place in the work of members of this Academy and of scholars elsewhere, which, for all their diversity of focus and method, have this in common: that they attempt to grapple with the question of how the liturgical celebrations of the Church actually operate today in the worship life of local congregations.

What I would like to propose in this paper is that these attempts to come to terms with newly perceived problems, using newly developed methods mostly borrowed from the human sciences, deserve our serious attention. A new area of liturgical studies is beginning to emerge, to take its place alongside the historical and theological approaches to liturgy, an area about which we could be much more deliberate and self-conscious and which, for purposes of identification, I shall call the area of pastoral liturgical studies. In proposing that we should acknowledge the emergence of this new branch of liturgical scholarship, I wish to indicate the need for such studies, suggest their scope, make some remarks upon their method, and indicate what I consider to be

* This paper first appeared in *Worship* 57 (1983) 291–308, and was presented at the 1983 North American Academy of Liturgy meeting.

their relationship to the historical and theological approaches that have already established themselves in the field of liturgical studies.

The Need for Pastoral Liturgical Studies

There is no need to emphasize here the enormous impact which liturgical scholarship has had upon the worship life of all the Churches in the last thirty years. Liturgists, as Walter Burghardt reminded us some years ago,[1] have wielded enormous power. Yet there are many, both members of the churches at large and even liturgists themselves, who have wondered about the propriety of so much influence being given to liturgical scholars. A recent complaint, which, if it be untypical, is untypical only because of its moderation, runs as follows: "To paraphrase Clemenceau, the liturgy is too precious to be left to the liturgists. We know now that, as a result of the Council, the Church's liturgists gained too much power. Despite their good intentions, they de-mystified our worship, including its cornerstone, the Mass. Something vital, if intangible, was lost with the changes, and thus far apparently no one knows what to do about it. . . ."[2] Those who have promoted liturgical reform and renewal in other Churches will no doubt recognize the gist of this accusation.

Looking back over our accomplishments, we liturgists can rightly claim to have achieved a success beyond the wildest dreams of the early pioneers of the liturgical movement, especially at the structural level. Where the effects of such structural changes are concerned, however, the verdict is not quite so unanimous.[3] It must be admitted that the liturgical pioneers who pressed for change had no special competence to foresee what the results of those changes would be. Whereas they were equipped with profound knowledge of the liturgical tradition and a deep insight into the centrality of the liturgy in the life of the Church, theologically understood, the conviction that reforms would generate renewal was based on little more than a hunch, validated by the enthusiasm of some monastic communities and of lay and clerical followers who, in the words of Miss Jean Brodie, "like that kind of thing." In short, historical awareness and theological depth were enough to persuade Church authorities to reform the liturgy, but they were insufficient to ensure any controlled connection between the reform of the liturgical books and the renewal of Christian life.

Moreover, the experience of implementing the liturgical reform has raised a whole series of new questions that are not in the competence of historians or theologians alone to answer.[4] Some examples will illustrate the point. Among questions confronting us now are matters such as: the polyvalence of the term "community" as applied to parish or congregation in contemporary American society; the various forms of interaction which might correspond to the term "active participation"; the various definitions of the terms "sign" and "symbol" and their relative usefulness for understanding the expressiveness and operativity of liturgical functions; the kind of religious imagination extant in our congregations through which the hearing of the word and the experience of the rites are filtered; the compatibility or incompatibility of aspects of American culture or subcultures with the "world" of the liturgy and what in fact happens when they conflict; the relative importance of what is *said* and what is *done* in liturgy, in terms of their impact upon participants; the role of such factors as age, sex, psychological type, education and social status in the way different people relate to different styles of liturgical celebration.[5]

Given that these are genuine problems for the Church's celebration of the liturgy today, and given that our ultimate loyalty is to the service of the worship life of the Church, it is surely not permitted to us to absolve ourselves of all responsibility and to return to the contemplation of our palimpsests. If confronting such questions lies beyond the limits of our competence as historians or theologians, then it is for us to extend our competence. I am not suggesting that every member of the Academy switch to pastoral liturgical studies, but merely that the Academy as such recognize the urgency of the undertaking and its valid place within the field of liturgical studies as a whole.

It would seem to me, in the end, a matter of vocation. Who else, if not we, can be entrusted with the crucial task of identifying, analyzing and responding to the critical problems of Christian worship today? The field cannot be abandoned to the social sciences. After all, the study of liminality in Ndembu ritual does not offer a better qualification for dealing with the problems of contemporary Christian worship in America than does the study of the Roman sacramentaries. Even if the liturgical scholar as such is presently unequipped to analyze the contemporary sociocultural situation, he or she is at least uniquely familiar with the tradition with which we are entrusted. The anthropologist *as* anthropologist is qualified to speak neither of the tradition nor of the situation facing the Church today.

In short, I am arguing that the study of the liturgy in the life of the Church today is too important to be entrusted to anyone else but liturgists, but that we as liturgists have the responsibility to recognize the limitations of our traditional resources and to see the need to address new problems in new ways. Alongside liturgical history and liturgical theology there is room and need for a third branch of scholarship, that of pastoral liturgical studies, or pastoral liturgy for short.[6]

The Object of Pastoral Liturgical Studies

In attempting to circumscribe more exactly the formal object of pastoral liturgical studies, we could do worse than return sixty years to Guardini's definition of the object of *Liturgiewissenschaft* as "the living, offering, praying Church, which accomplishes the mystery of grace, considered in terms of her actual worship in practice and her statements concerning it."[7] This definition presupposes an incarnational view of Church and recognizes the ritual words and gestures of the Church's liturgy as the "flesh" in which the mystery of grace is actualized for believers today. The specific focus of pastoral liturgical studies is on the sacramental or communicative potential of the human words and actions which constitute both the form of the mystery of grace and simultaneously the human response to that mystery. The methods used, then, will be those appropriate to describing and analyzing the human functions involved, and the approach will be scientific or scholarly in the sense that it will use the paradigms developed in the human sciences and apply them in methodical and responsible ways.

Nevertheless, it has to be recognized that the use of the terms "pastoral liturgical studies" and "pastoral liturgy" is not without its problems.

In the first case, the term "pastoral liturgy" is generally used in English to translate the French phrase, *pastorale liturgique*. Insofar as *pastorale liturgique* implies, as in Vagaggini's definition,[8] that the ministers of the Church are regarded as the dirigents and the faithful as the objects of such an approach to the liturgy and the larger life of the Church, pastoral liturgical studies are not the same as *pastorale liturgique*. The proper starting point for pastoral liturgical studies is the liturgical activity of the whole assembled community. It is concerned to study the various forms and degrees of engagement exemplified by all the participants, to analyze the claims made for such participation by the participants themselves as well as by the Church's authorities and by theologians, and to identify whatever discrepancies may be occurring between what the rites and texts are supposed to communicate and what they may actually be communicating. But it is not, per se, dedicated to the implementation of existing liturgical forms, for reasons that should become clear later on.

A second and related source of confusion is that we use the term "pastoral liturgy" to refer to the supervision or actual carrying out of worship in our Churches. As such, pastoral liturgy is something of a practical art, a set of skills required of all participants, and stands in much the same relationship to pastoral liturgical studies as married life stands to family systems research. The one is a research discipline, the other the object of research. While one would hope that liturgy, like marriage, would benefit from the findings of such research, neither one is a substitute for the other. On the other hand, liturgy, like marriage, suffers from the attentions of a lot of uninformed opinion and unscholarly punditry. It is precisely to protect the worship life of the church from ill-advised experimentation and unhelpful advice that the development of scholarly research under the umbrella of pastoral liturgical studies is so important.

In short, pastoral liturgical studies will be distinguished from other forms of scholarly study by its focus on the actual worship life of the contemporary (American) Churches, as its formal object, and from other activities that claim the name of "pastoral liturgy" by its scholarly and critical approach to worship.

Three Tasks of Pastoral Liturgical Studies

The suggestion that liturgists should undertake serious and methodical study of the human dynamics operative in the Church's worship, and should do so using the findings and methods of the human sciences, is nothing new. A number of proposals in this direction have already been made by members of this Academy[9] and, more explicitly, by recent German literature.[10] Even more significantly, a review of liturgical literature in recent years confirms the experience of this Academy in revealing a growing openness toward the consideration of contemporary liturgical problems and the corresponding development of new paradigms for use in liturgical studies.[11]

Yet the very proliferation of proposals and approaches, a proliferation that results from the multidimensionality of the liturgical event itself, seems to suggest a pluralism, if not a confusion, in the area which might make it too unwieldy to form a coherent field of endeavor. Nevertheless, it is important to attempt some sort of framework in terms of which the various kinds of work being done can be related to one another. It is toward this end that I make the modest proposal of envisaging the fledgling discipline of pastoral liturgical studies in terms of three sets of tasks: the empirical, the hermeneutical, and the critical. By focusing on the tasks, it should be possible to relegate questions of method to a subordinate place and to avoid the confusion that arises when similar methods are used in different paradigms. It should also become apparent that, while these tasks need to be distinguished formally, they cannot be entirely separated.

The Empirical Task. By the empirical task of pastoral liturgy, I mean simply the function of describing what is going on in worship. Of course, the question of what is going on in worship can be answered at any number of different levels, each of which has to be identified and described in appropriate ways. The use of the self-conscious methods of enquiry developed in the social sciences, or the use of paradigms drawn from the study of language, does not itself replace the role of hunches and guesses we are all accustomed to make, but instead goes on to examine and test those hunches empirically, by paying close attention to the collection of data. There are three points I would like to make concerning this empirical task.

First, while it may involve the use of procedures to which historians and theologians are unaccustomed, the empirical task is not at all dissimilar to the first task of the historian and the theologian, which is the establishment of the text to be studied. The reason for this is that, while we have defined the formal object of pastoral liturgy as the event of celebration, the event itself, as a fleeting temporal phenomenon, is simply not available for study. Just as human discourse is only available for study insofar as it is registered as text, so the event is only available for study insofar as it leaves a record of itself which is more or less permanent and thus retrievable.[12] Hence the whole apparatus of field studies, participant observation, documentation and interviews: their function is to retrieve the event from its temporal dimension and to make it available for analysis.[13]

Thus the pastoral liturgist's preoccupation with the data is not dissimilar from the historian's concern to reconstruct and interpret the past on the basis of the different kinds of records left behind by the liturgical celebrations of the past, although it must be said that the task of pastoral liturgy has the inestimable advantage of being able to determine ahead of time which aspects of the event it wishes to record for subsequent study.

As far as the interpretation of the data is concerned, the rules governing sociological evidence or the case studies of psychology are not all that different from those which guide the historian or the theologian in the interpretation of their texts.[14] A given text, or, in this instance, a collection of data, offers a multiplicity of possible interpretations which jostle one another in their claim to be accepted. As Ricoeur puts it, in the procedures of literary criticism and in the human sciences, what is at stake is not verification along the lines of the physical sciences but validation, and "the procedures of validation have a polemical character."[15] Out of the series of conflicting interpretations, we give our allegiance to that which, at this time, appears to have the greatest probability. But it always remains just that, a claim to greater probability, a claim that may, as further evidence becomes available, be consequently challenged and overcome by another interpretation. But my point here is not to encroach upon the quagmire of methodology so much as to suggest that the empirical task of pastoral liturgy has a number of parallels with the problems of establishing and interpreting a text with which we are already familiar.

A second point to be made about the empirical function of pastoral liturgy is that, in describing what is going on in worship, it will be particularly attentive to what Roy Rappaport calls "the obvious aspects of ritual."[16] Both our actual participation in liturgical worship and our theological study of it tend to make us overlook the surface elements of the rite in our concern to reach for the meaning behind the signs. Of the need for what might be called a more shortsighted approach, Roy Rappaport writes: "If an expedition into the obvious calls for justification, it may be suggested that in their eagerness to plumb ritual's dark symbolic or functional depths, to find in ritual more than meets the eye, anthropologists have, perhaps increasingly, tended to overlook ritual's surface, that which does meet the eye. Yet it is on its surface, in its form, that we may discern whatever may be peculiar to ritual."[17]

Rappaport goes on to suggest that, in attaining the depth of meaning inherent in ritual, we find ourselves in a realm which ritual shares with other expressive forms such as art, mythology, and poetry, or, we might add, with preaching, theology, and private devotion. It is only in attending to the surface form of ritual that that which is specific to ritual, that which makes ritual indispensable, can be grasped. That observation alone should commend the empirical study of the liturgy to all of us who feel it incumbent upon us to remind our coreligionists of the indispensability of ritual to the Christian Church! Thus the study of the liturgical event will imply the careful description of what is actually done before conclusions are drawn as to what it all means.

Lastly, it might be worth remarking again that the attempt to describe what goes on in liturgy must include not only what happens at the altar or in the pulpit, but also what is going on from the perspective of the congregation and what is happening to them. We are far too glib in making theological claims about what liturgy is or does. Yet, if those claims have any substance to them, they can be verified. Grace cannot be measured with any precision, of course, but grace, like fleeting events, leaves its mark on people's lives and that mark is as available to the investigator as is the shadow of nuclear war. In other words, if the claim that liturgy is not only of the Church but for the Church is true,[18] then liturgical celebrations should, in the course of time, at least, make some perceptible difference to those who take part in them. People's attitudes, outlooks, lifestyles, and behavior are all open to investigation, as are also their understanding of what liturgy is for, the motives with which they participate, and the account they give of the place it has in their lives. All these are dimensions of what is going on in and through the liturgy. They are all susceptible to empirical research. They are all part of the descriptive or empirical function of pastoral liturgy. On their basis, comparisons can legitimately be made between the theological claims that are made for liturgy and the actual experience of Christian people. How the results of such comparisons are to be evaluated and what use is to be made of them then becomes a matter for theological reflection and for critical praxis.

The Hermeneutical Task of Pastoral Liturgy. The term "hermeneutics" has become so slippery in contemporary usage that I hesitate to contribute to the confusion by using it in this context. What I mean by it here is the study of how the symbolic words and gestures of the liturgy operate when they engage the believing community. This corresponds roughly to Charles Peirce's "pragmatics," though that term, too, is open to misunderstanding.[19] In any case, under this heading, I would wish to include all the kinds of questions that refer not so much to what the liturgy means but to how it means. How can the word of God be proclaimed as word of God and how can it be heard as such? How are the texts converted into prayer? How does the contemporary believer enter into the rite and become engaged by it?

To some degree these are new questions. The dominant model in the liturgical movement and in subsequent reforms has been that which Stephen Happel has identified as linked to a classicist view of culture.[20]

Just as "culture" was once identified with a particular, elitist way of being in the world, yet regarded as something to which all should aspire, so there has been a similar "trickle-down theory" (to use another metaphor) where popular understanding of the liturgy is concerned. It has been assumed that some people—Church leaders, liturgists and theologians—knew what it meant, and that they were to instruct the clergy so that the clergy could instruct the people as to what the liturgy was really about. The difficulty with this approach, apart from its apparent relative lack of success, is that it bypasses the liturgical medium itself. It is rather like reading to illiterates instead of teaching illiterates to read for themselves.

The hermeneutical function of pastoral liturgy, then, is not to be identified with catechesis, as that term is usually understood. Instead, it will undertake a study of how symbols operate and how symbolic language communicates. On the basis of such broad studies, it will be able to examine (a) the effectiveness of the contemporary presentation of liturgical symbols in communicating the mystery of grace and (b) the capacity of modern people for receiving such communication.

It is under the heading of the expressiveness of liturgical symbols today that concerns for the quality of the liturgy can best be addressed. These concerns for quality would go beyond the merely aesthetic to raise substantive questions about how the rites are celebrated, about the kinds of music admitted to the liturgy, about the capacity of its texts to engage the believer, about the viability or nonviability of inherited rites and gestures. This concern for quality, Guardini points out, must mean something different today than it did to "the priest of the late nineteenth century who said: 'We must organize the procession better, we must see to it that the praying and the singing are better.' He did not realize that he should have asked himself quite a different question: how can the act of walking become a religious act, a retinue for the Lord progressing through his land, so that an 'epiphany' may take place."[21] That is what is meant, in this context, by a hermeneutical question.

On the other hand, the capacity of contemporary American Christians for engaging in the symbolic language of the rite must also be explored. Is the average North American Christian *liturgiefähig*? Among the features of our culture which might call for particular study as possible obstacles to people's ability to "read" the liturgy properly might be mentioned the following: our cultural experiences of time; our relationship to place and to the physical universe; the structures of social life and the forms of belonging which exist today and which are so different from those in which the liturgy developed; the functionalism or pragmatism of our culture; expectations about how authority should be exercised and about the freedom of the modern individual to create his or her own world and lifestyle through personal choices; the related privatization of religion and the corresponding pluralism of beliefs, practices and lifestyles.[22] Obviously, these factors have an impact on Christian and ecclesial life far beyond the liturgical celebration, but they become particularly crucial there. Nor do I wish to suggest that everything in contemporary society constitutes an obstacle to symbolic communication in the liturgy, or that there may not be elements which need to be incorporated into our symbol system. But that is precisely what the hermeneutical dimension of pastoral liturgical studies needs to explore.

On the basis of such research, it might be possible to develop forms of catechesis and mystagogy in which direct communication through the medium of the liturgy's symbolic complex might once again become possible. Perhaps the empirical study of what goes on in liturgy will help us see how to proceed. Perhaps work done in language theory and in literary criticism will help us see better what is involved. Perhaps a phenomenology of symbols will enable us to relate the symbols of the liturgy more obviously to the limited situations of human life.[23] But the research will have to be done before the catechesis can be developed, and it is this research that is properly the task of the hermeneutical dimension of pastoral liturgical studies. It is by attention to form rather than to content that pastoral liturgy will contribute to the liturgy's ability to communicate effectively as both expressive of the faith of the community and formative of it.

The Critical Task. If the empirical task of pastoral liturgy is to attend to what actually goes on in the rite, and if the hermeneutical task is to reflect upon how the symbolic complex we call liturgy operates, the findings of those two sets of undertakings will continually have to be compared with the historical tradition and with theological claims made for the liturgy. By accepting the normativity of history and theology, or rather of the tradition which they make available, pastoral liturgy both differentiates itself from the other, nontheological, disciplines whose methods and findings it uses and also acknowledges the sacramental character of the economy of salvation. It is thus quite different from the sociology of religion, or the psychology of religion, for however much its procedures may approximate to theirs, it remains ultimately a theological enterprise and moves from a purely neutral, descriptive stance to make recommendations about pastoral liturgical practice. Although the critical and prescriptive roles of liturgical studies have all been well addressed by others, it would be important here at least to indicate four areas which will require the pastoral liturgist's critical attention.

First, pastoral liturgical studies will be scholarly only to the extent to which they are self-critical. In particular, they will have to be attentive to the way models drawn from other disciplines are used and to the kind of conclusions that may legitimately be drawn, if they are to avoid what David Power has rightly called "the false rationality of much theoretical explanation."[24] In other words, the more attractive a model is in terms of the insight it generates and the practical applications it suggests, the more its limitations are likely to be overlooked and the more danger there is of a reductionist explanation of the liturgy.[25] We shall return to this briefly below.

Second, because it takes the present moment seriously as being not only the context within which the Church works, but the very flesh in which the grace of God is to be incarnated—and thus as presenting the Church not only with a challenge, but with its very vocation[26]—pastoral liturgical studies will have to undertake a critical evaluation of contemporary culture. It will rely on sociocultural studies of contemporary society to identify the dominant features of our age, but it will then proceed to subject them to theological criticism, particularly with a view to their possible impact on contemporary celebration. Talk about cultural adaptation of the liturgy to North America has hitherto been largely meaningless, because those aspects of the culture to which adaptation might be made have not been identified and scrutinized. Conversely, it is also true that the same lack of a developed cultural critique is probably permitting considerable cultural assimilation to go on unconsciously and therefore unchecked.

Third, there needs to be a critical evaluation of the various forms of religious imagination that exist among North American Christians, because it is through the imagination rather than through professed beliefs and conscious attitudes that religious understanding and behavior are filtered.[27] This implies that the understanding of Scripture and liturgy not merely form the religious imagination, but are themselves filtered through it and are understood accordingly. Thus it could be extremely important to compare the imaginative world projected by the liturgy with the imaginative world out of which North Americans operate. On the basis of such comparison and of theological reflection, it might be possible to identify certain common distortions that occur while also identifying those elements of the contemporary religious imagination which lend themselves to incorporation into the liturgy itself. For example, the quasi-linear concept of time might be found to be dominant in the American religious imagination, thus creating problems for the way the liturgy is related to past events, but also offering a basis for understanding the eschatological dimension of the liturgy which the official Church has not made much of.

Fourth, pastoral liturgical studies will exercise an important critical role insofar as they are able to identify the various ways in which contemporary liturgy may be alienated and alienating.[28] By alienation is meant the reservation of the right to define what is real to a small and powerful elite at the expense of the majority's sense of reality. In short, where the experience and capacities of the many are excluded in favor of the authority of the few there is alienation. The language and symbols of the rites then take on an alienated, and to that degree, unreal quality. What is said to be done is no longer what is actually done; what the rite is claimed to mean is at the same time a cover for other meanings. An obvious example would be the rhetoric of "active participation" and "Church as community" which covers over the real restrictions imposed on participation in Church life and real divisions existing in the community. Conversely, what the Marxist critique does to raise our consciousness about the social dimensions of liturgy, the Freudian critique of ritual does for the personal psychological dimension. To what extent can liturgical and sacramental worship foster the various kinds of alienation which deserve the name of neuroses? Once again, in accepting the Gospel as the living criterion of acceptable and unacceptable practice in the Church, pastoral liturgy will exercise a critical and prescriptive function. Precisely because of this final critical function, it should be obvious that pastoral liturgical studies cannot lend themselves to the agenda of implementing official liturgical reforms, for its task must include a critical evaluation both of the official reforms and of their mode of implementation.[29]

Some Remarks on Method

The delineation of these three areas or functions of pastoral liturgical studies, sketched here only in broadest outline, may serve to suggest the range and scope of this fledgling approach to liturgical studies. While each set of tasks presents its own range of issues, each requiring appropriate methodologies, what they all have in common is the requirement of interdisciplinary or multidisciplinary research, a requirement deriving from the multidimensionality of the liturgical event itself. There are obviously risks involved, but these risks may be reduced to the degree that we are able to extend our range of competence or are able to engage in joint research with experts in other fields. But, whether we equip ourselves to work with other methods, or whether we enter into partnership with other scholars, it is useful to adhere conscientiously to certain guidelines.

First, it is important to recognize that when we borrow the methods or the findings of other disciplines for our work in liturgy, what we are usually doing is using those methods and findings, developed elsewhere, as models for the study of liturgy. They are useful insofar as they enable us to gain new insights into what goes on in liturgy and enable us to be more articulate about the human dimensions of the rite. But they remain models whose specific limitations need to be acknowledged.

Second, since every model carries with it something of the prejudices of its original discipline, it is important to be acquainted with the original context in which it was developed and deployed, the particular problem it was used to elucidate in its own field, and the standing it enjoys in its own field (for every discipline has its blind alleys and its fads). For example, Freud's theory of the neurotic character of ritual behavior needs to be seen in its own proper context: its place in Freud's own work, its subsequent modification by later Freudians and, not least, the conflict model of the human psyche from which it derives and which has been recognized in psychology itself as having only limited usefulness.

Third, whether the pastoral liturgist begins with a liturgical problem and looks for appropriate models to elucidate it, or whether the liturgist comes across some theory which appears to shed light on certain aspects of human behavior and then asks what its application might be, the area of applicability needs to be clearly defined in order to avoid unlawful generalizations. It is here that the use of more than one model is useful, so that a certain conflict of interpretations is generated. Without such a conflict of interpretations, the way is left open for the sort of reductionist claim that takes a narrowly based hypothesis as its starting point and then proceeds to draw unwarranted inferences about liturgy in general.

Fourth, we need to remember that the formal object of pastoral liturgical studies is the actual worship life of the "living, offering, praying Church which actualizes the mystery of grace." However much we may utilize the findings of other disciplines and however closely we may approximate to them in our methods, we retain our primary loyalty as liturgists to the mystery of grace which we believe to be sacramentalized in the words and actions of the congregations we study. This means that we have a prior theological commitment that guides our hunches about what is worth investigating and offers us both a critical vantage point from which to scrutinize the evidence and a critical standard by which to evaluate possible conclusions.

Fifth and last, the incarnational understanding of the Christian economy requires that we not separate the divine from the human, the theological from the anthropological, but it also requires that we take care to respect the autonomy of each order and not confuse them. They represent different levels of discourse, different ways of looking at the liturgical event which nevertheless remains a single event. What I have in mind here is the sort of docetism that appeals to concepts such as "grace" or "Spirit" while trying to offer an empirical account of a liturgical action, or, its opposite, the claim to be able to account exhaustively for sacramental efficacy in a way that makes talk of grace redundant.

The introduction of a third branch of scholarly research into the field of liturgical studies—a development I believe to be justified both by the demands of the times and by the incarnational character of the Church and its worship—will not be without its impact on the other two branches which currently enjoy their proper recognition: liturgical history and liturgical theology.

First of all, the synchronic approach to liturgy represented by pastoral liturgical studies will make new demands on historians of the liturgy. Whereas liturgical history has largely been concerned up to now with a diachronic approach, reconstructing the evolution of liturgical forms, the questions raised by pastoral liturgy will require of historians that they, too, attend to the larger ecclesial and sociocultural context of the evolution of the rites. More attention to social and cultural history, and particularly to the history of the liturgy as the history, not just of the rites, but of the people who used them and more attention to the place of specific rites in the lives of ordinary people, would be most helpful.

Secondly, pastoral liturgical studies will tend to generate a new agenda for liturgical theologians. Romano Guardini, in the definition of liturgical studies already cited, provided the impetus that led to liturgical theology taking its rightful place alongside liturgical history. Yet his call to focus on the "actual worship (of the Church) and her statements concerning it" gave birth to a liturgical theology which has suffered two serious limitations. In the first place, the statements of the Church concerning the liturgy which were subjected to theological commentary have almost exclusively been the official statements of the Church, not the statements of the faithful at large. Hence a certain divorce between theological claims for the liturgy and popular experience of it. Secondly, the study of the actual worship life of the Church has likewise been largely restricted to the study of the texts employed in worship, to the neglect of nontextual elements. This was inevitable as long as there were no satisfactory methods available to theologians to render the "actual worship life" of the Church into a form suitable for study.

As pastoral liturgical studies develop, then, more and more data concerning the actual worship of the Church should become available for reflection, as well as a whole range of theological problems relating to the anthropological, sociological, and psychological structures and preconditions which constitute the "flesh" in which the mystery of grace is incarnated in the worship life of contemporary communities.

Furthermore, the successful development of pastoral liturgy as a discipline should go some way toward relieving historians and theologians of the burden of having to undertake tasks, at the request of the Church, for which they feel they lack the requisite competence, specifically those I have indicated as providing the agenda for pastoral liturgical studies.

Finally, in bringing this whole matter to the attention of the Academy, I am making two proposals. The first is that the work of those members of the Academy already engaged in this field—specifically, the group working on liturgy and the human sciences, but many others besides—should be acknowledged as essential to our discipline and that we encourage the highest standards of scholarship in this area. Secondly, I propose that we make an effort to recruit to the Academy people whose work in other fields is of proven worth and who have demonstrated an interest in applying their research to the liturgy. At the moment there are not too many, but some there are, and we should invite them to join us in ongoing conversation.

In the last analysis, my major concern is that, as members of the North American Academy of Liturgy, we accept the responsibility of putting our expertise at the service of the churches particularly in regard to those new problems that are surfacing in the wake of the liturgical reforms. And by serving the Churches, I mean serving not only the interests of the official leadership, but attending to the experiences, frustrations, and hopes of the Christian people as a whole, committed as we are to the proposition that the sacred liturgy is the worship of the whole Church and that its benefits are intended even for the least of God's people.

---

[1] Walter J. Burghardt, "A Theologian's Challenge to Liturgy," *Theological Studies* 35 (1974) 240.

[2] Dan Herr, "An Agenda for Vatican III," *Notre Dame Magazine* (October 1982) 25.

[3] See my article, "Reflections on Liturgical Reform," *Worship* 56 (1982) 411–30; also Angelus Häussling, "Liturgiewissenschaft zwei Jahrzehnte nach Konzilsbeginn," *Archiv für Liturgiewissenschaft* 24 (1982) 1–18.

[4] So Mary Collins: "Basically, what complicates the problem today is that we do not have enough knowledge or control of the contemporary historical data we presume to deal with. Until we can devise better methods to remedy this failing, we will either flounder in our formal theological study or redirect all our energy to immediate pastoral concerns." "Liturgical Methodology and the Cultural Evolution of Worship in the United States," *Worship* 49 (1975) 85.

[5] For a preliminary survey of the questions for which the use of the human sciences holds promises, see François Morlot, "Le colloque de Louvain: Questions posées," *La Maison-Dieu* 91 (1967) 152–62.

[6] The use of the term "pastoral liturgy" is obviously coined on the basis of the affiliation of the program proposed here to the larger agenda of pastoral or practical theology, though it is to be hoped that the more clearly delimited object of pastoral liturgy will save it from the crisis of purpose and identity which has afflicted pastoral theology.

[7] Romano Guardini, "über die systematische Methode in der Liturgiewissenschaft," *Jahrbuch für Liturgiewissenschaft* 1 (1921) 104.

[8] Cipriano Vagaggini, *Theological Dimensions of the Liturgy* (Collegeville: Liturgical Press 1976) 808. Something of the same approach lingers in Joseph Gélineau's definition of *pastorale liturgique* when he speaks of it as the implementation of the revised rites. See *Dans vos assemblées: Sens et pratique de la célébration liturgique*, vol. 1 (Paris: Desclée 1971) x.

[9] See Collins, "Liturgical Methodology and the Cultural Evolution of Worship in the United States," and David Power, "Unripe Grapes: The Critical Function of Liturgical Theology," *Worship* 52 (1978) 386–99.

[10] Angelus Häussling, "Die kritische Funktion der Liturgiewissenschaft," in H. B. Meyer, ed., *Liturgie und Gesellschaft* (Innsbruck, 1970) 103–30; K. H. Bieritz, "Ansätze zu einer Theorie des Gottesdienstes," *Theologische Literaturzeitung* 100 (1975) 721–37; P. Cornehl, "Theorie des Gottesdienstes—Ein Prospekt," *Theologische Quartalschrift* 159 (1979) 169–77; Iso Baumer, "Interaktion—Zeichen—Symbol. Ansätze zu einer Deutung liturgischen und volkfrommen Tuns," *Liturgische Jahrbuch* 31 (1981) 9–35; H. W. Gärtner and M. B. Mertz, "Prologomena für eine integrative Methode in der Liturgiewissenschaft," *Archiv für Liturgiewissenschaft* 24 (1982) 165–89.

[11] Mention should be made, in this context, of the contribution of the CNPL in Paris, together with the Institut Supérieur de Liturgie. Though not advancing any program-

matic proposals, the French have nevertheless made the most significant contributions to the dialogue between liturgical studies and the human sciences. See *La Maison-Dieu*, esp. nos. 91, 93, 114 and 119, as well as the volumes appearing since 1975 in the series "Rites et Symboles."

[12] Paul Ricoeur, "The Model of the Text: Meaningful Action Considered as Text," in Ricoeur, *Hermeneutics and the Human Sciences*, ed. and trans. J. B. Thompson (Cambridge University Press 1981) 197–221, esp. 203 ff.

[13] See Gärtner and Mertz, 177–86.

[14] Ricoeur, 209ff.

[15] Ibid., 215.

[16] Roy A. Rappaport, "The Obvious Aspects of Ritual," in Rappaport, ed., *Ecology, Meaning and Religion* (Richmond, Calif.: North Atlantic Books 1979) 173–222.

[17] Ibid., 174.

[18] Gärtner and Mertz, 175–6.

[19] See G. V. Lardner, "Communications Theory and Liturgical Research," *Worship* 51 (1977) 299–306.

[20] Stephen Happel, "Classicist Culture and the Nature of Worship," *Heythrop Journal* 21 (1980) 288–302.

[21] Romano Guardini, "A Letter from Romano Guardini," *Herder Correspondence* (August 1964) 239.

[22] See Martin Odermatt, "Humane Voraussetzungen der Liturgie," *Liturgische Jahrbuch* 31 (1981) 55–64.

[23] See Power, "Unripe Grapes: The Critical Function of Liturgical Theology."

[24] Power, 394. See also, Angelus Häussling, "Die kritische Funktion der Liturgiewissenschaft," in H. B. Meyer, ed., *Liturgie und Gesellschaft* (Innsbruck, 1970) 103–30.

[25] Given the particular importance of communications studies to liturgy, the special bias of the approach to such studies in the United States should be noted. See J. W. Carey, "Communication and Culture," *Communication Research* 2 (1975) 173–91 and, in a slightly different vein, Gerald M. Phillips, "Science and the Study of Human Communication: An Inquiry from the Other Side of the Two Cultures," *Human Communication Research* 7 (1981) 361–70.

[26] See Heinz Schüster, "Die Methode der Pastoraltheologie als praktische Theologie," in F.-X. Arnold, ed., *Handbuch der Pastoraltheologie*, Bd. 1 (Freiburg: Herder 1964) 105–6.

[27] No one has done more to draw attention to the significance of the imagination in human and religious life than Andrew Greeley. See his book, *The Religious Imagination* (New York: Sadlier 1981) and also *The Mary Myth* (New York: Seabury 1977).

[28] See Häussling, "Die kritische Funktion der Liturgiewissenschaft." Also C. Vogel, "An Alienated Liturgy," in Herman Schmidt, ed., *Liturgy: Self-Expression of the Church*, *Concilium* 72 (New York: Herder and Herder 1972): "The progressive alienation of liturgy from the community has been recognized not primarily by professional historians but by those engaged in pastoral practice."

[29] Häussling, "Die kritische Funktion der Liturgiewissenschaft."

Margaret Mary Kelleher, o.s.u.

Introduction to "Images and Worship"

Mark Searle was a man of vision and this is apparent in the article he wrote in 1984 entitled "Images and Worship." What he has to say about the Christian imagination is as relevant today as it was then, perhaps even more so. His topic has significance for many areas within the contemporary field of liturgical studies. In the following pages I will indicate why I think this article would be of interest to persons engaged in the study of liturgical/sacramental theology, liturgical inculturation, liturgical spirituality, and liturgical catechesis. While the whole article has significance for all of these areas of study, I will draw attention to those topics or issues that are particularly pertinent for each.

Central to the study of liturgical/sacramental theology is the question of the nature of liturgy, sacrament, worship. Searle addresses this issue at the very beginning of his article with the provocative statement that "worship is, above all, an act of the imagination." What would a book or course on the nature of liturgy and sacrament look like if it took this principle as its starting point? It would certainly have to include a serious study of the nature and operations of the imagination. Searle was convinced that the absence of such a study from the work of the liturgical renewal and the lack of awareness that liturgy is an activity of the imagination had provoked a liturgical crisis for the Church.

How do sacraments work? This is another question that is central for those engaged in doing liturgical/sacramental theology, and Searle's critique of literalism is particularly relevant for this matter. It is widely accepted that sacraments operate as symbols, a particular kind of sign. However, if those who are participating in liturgical worship have a naïve and literal way of thinking, in which the sign and signified are collapsed into one another, there is no hope of grasping the sacramental nature of such realities as the Eucharist or the ordained priesthood. Mark Searle was convinced that the current educational system plays a major role in shaping individuals with such a literal way of thinking. He concluded that such literalism was a significant cause of the liturgical crisis that was faced by the Church, and he called for an intellectual conversion that would allow people to move beyond such literalism.

Those who attempt to understand or promote the inculturation of the Church's liturgy within diverse cultural contexts must have some knowledge of the nature of culture. There are many different theoretical approaches to this topic, but many would agree that images and rituals play a significant role in the mediation of culture. Searle's recognition of the role played by culture in shaping the imagination suggests that any attempt to study a particular cultural context would have to include attention to the ways in which images and symbols operate within that culture. His awareness of the role played by ritual action in shaping ecclesial identity is relevant for those who study the relationship between liturgy and culture in various places throughout the world, as well as in the situation of cultural pluralism that exists within the United States.

There are at least two major dimensions to the study of liturgical spirituality. First, there is a public vision of what it means to live as a Christian that is manifested in the liturgical performance of various local assemblies. Second, there is the personal appropriation of parts or all of this vision in the spiritual lives of members of each ecclesial community. Images and imaginative activity are central to both. In his article, Mark Searle states that a major goal of the liturgical movement was the renewal of the Christian imagination. However, he notes that this goal has yet to be attained and suggests that a conversion of the imagination is required for such a renewal to occur. He was convinced that a significant step would be to attend to the gathered congregation itself as a visible sign of invisible realities. Among the suggestions he offers to foster such an awareness is the promotion of a contemplative approach to liturgical participation. His attention to the role of ritual repetition in liturgy as a way of rehearsing certain interactions and attitudes is also very pertinent for any exploration of liturgical spirituality. A lived spirituality is a way of life, and Searle is clear that the goal of reawakening the religious imagination is conversion of life.

There is a close relationship between liturgical spirituality and liturgical catechesis. Catherine Dooley has identified three aspects of the one process of liturgical catechesis.[1] There is the phase of preparation for the sacramental celebration, the formation that takes place in and through the liturgy, and the ongoing reflection on the mystery cele-brated in the liturgy. The anticipated outcome of the whole process is a deepening of faith that reveals itself in participation in the Church's social mission. All the topics treated by Mark Searle in "Images and Worship" are pertinent for liturgical catechesis understood in this manner. In fact, his article is required reading in Dr. Catherine Doo-ley's graduate course in "Liturgical Catechesis" at The Catholic Uni-versity of America.

How do we prepare people to participate in liturgy understood as an activity of the imagination? Clearly, we need to have an understanding of the way in which the imagination develops and is transformed, and Searle calls for more studies in this area. As a way of getting beyond the literalism that is so much a part of contemporary education, Searle calls for the development of a "hermeneutical catechetics." By this he means "a catechesis geared less towards content than towards the proper de-velopment of the religious imagination in older children and adults." His attention to the way in which liturgical ritual action rehearses cer-tain behaviors in persons shows how aware he was of the formative na-ture of liturgy. In his article he refers to the discipline of the liturgy, a discipline of learning to listen, look, and gesture in ways that help people become receptive to the actions of the Spirit. In treating the rela-tionship between preaching and catechesis, Searle holds up, as a model, the mystagogical preaching of the Fathers of the Church. His criticism of a sacramental catechesis that does not use the ritual as a major source is still quite pertinent almost twenty years later.

In "Images and Worship," Mark Searle was not offering any final word or systematic statement on the topic of the imagination. Instead, he was calling for some serious scholarly and pastoral work to be done in order to bring the goal of liturgical renewal to a further degree of realization. While there has been some attention to the kinds and qual-ity of images that are made available in the liturgy in recent years, Searle's questions go beyond this. He does want attention to be given to the images that are made available in word and action, but he does not want us to stop there. He is inviting scholars to try to understand the imagining subject, to study the dynamics of human imagination, to become sensitive to the ways in which imaginative activity is nurtured or stifled, to discover the role of images in the processes of human knowing and living.

In his article, Searle refers to the work of theologian David Tracy as one important source for studying the religious imagination. Years after Searle wrote this article, Andrew Greeley published a book on *The Catholic Imagination.*[2] He, too, identifies Tracy's work as fundamental for his own. Greeley writes with conviction of the presence of a liturgical imagination among American Catholics despite the work of "liturgists."[3] While it is unfortunate that Mark Searle is not here to engage in dialogue with Greeley's work, it would be interesting to explore the relationship between the work of Searle and Greeley on the imagination since both share a common source.

Mark Searle was very clear that liturgical renewal and ecclesial renewal go hand in hand. If, as he claims, ecclesial renewal means a renewal of the Christian imagination, then questions about the development and transformation of corporate imagination will also have to be included in future studies. While he does not make this task explicit, it certainly is implied in the attention he gives to the ecclesial nature of liturgical worship and to the assembly as primary signifier in the liturgy. His primary concern in this article is one that is familiar to all those who have read his other works. Ultimately, he was concerned with promoting a kind of academic research and pastoral praxis that would free people to be with one another in liturgy in such a way that they would transcend both individualism and a superficial sense of togetherness and come to experience themselves as the corporate Body of Christ. Then there would be reason to hope that each liturgical assembly might go forth to live as the corporate Body of Christ.

Margaret Mary Kelleher, o.s.u., is associate professor in the School of Religious Studies at The Catholic University of America, Washington, D.C.

---

[1] See Catherine Dooley, "Liturgical Catechesis: Mystagogy, Marriage or Misnomer?" *Worship* 66 (1992) 386–97.

[2] Andrew Greeley, *The Catholic Imagination* (Berkeley and Los Angeles: University of California Press, 2000).

[3] Ibid., 45–6.

Images and Worship*

It is difficult to speak of images and worship without conjuring up visions of image-worship, or to speak of liturgy and imagination without appearing to detract from the seriousness of the liturgy. Yet it will be the contention of this article that religion is inescapably the honoring of images and that worship is, above all, an act of the imagination. Conversely, it will be suggested, the problems faced by religion in our culture and by liturgy in our churches spring largely from habits of literalism which have wasted our powers of imagination.

It is not difficult to agree that the liturgy is full of images: verbal images of Scripture, prayer and hymnody; musical images; visual images in the form of art, but more importantly in the form of the very presence of the participants, their differences of dress, the roles they enact; there are the ritual images of the postures and gestures we are invited to adopt as the ritual unfolds; there are even smells and tastes that are integral to the rite and tend to linger in the memory. Liturgy is obviously a multimedia event, a cornucopia of imagery poured out upon the gathered congregation. This is not to say that it is always well presented, or that it is always as impressive as it sounds. But is it not the aesthetic dimension of the liturgy that we will focus on here as much as the problem of the function of the image to present something more than itself. An image is a copy, a reproduction, a reflection of some original; it is not itself original. It serves to point beyond itself to that which it serves to present. For this to happen, though, it is not enough that the image be good; it is also necessary that those who come into contact with the image have the imagination necessary to go beyond it or to be put in contact with that which the image presents.

* This article first appeared in *The Way* 24:2 (1984) 103–14, and is reprinted with permission.

It is clear, at least in retrospect, that the liturgical movement was a movement for the renewal of the Christian imagination. It originated in a Church that envisaged sacraments simply as causes of graces administered by the few to the many; in which liturgy was thought of as a set of more or less dispensable ceremonies designed to honor the sacrament and edify the observant; and in which devotion was identified with exercises of individualistic interiority. When Pius X wrote that he wished to restore "the true Christian spirit" whose "primary and indispensable source" was "active participation in the holy mysteries and in the public and solemn prayer of the Church,"[1] he was inaugurating (perhaps unwittingly) what would later become known as a "paradigm shift."[2] What the liturgical movement worked for was not so much change in the liturgy itself (though pressure for such change built up as the movement progressed), as an alteration in the way people related to the liturgy and, ultimately, in the way they saw themselves as Ch Liturgical renewal was, from the beginning, a function of ecclesi newal, and ecclesial renewal meant a renewal of the Christian ima tion. "Body" was to replace "institution" as the dominant mo metaphor; "we" was to replace "I" in the language of prayer; "co nity celebration" was to replace "private administration," "par tion" was to replace "attendance" in sacramental rites.

Yet, despite all of this, the imagination itself was never mad subject of conscious and critical reflection, and this may be part reason why, after all the changes that have occurred, the expecte newal of Church life has come to something of a stalemate. The fa to attend to the imagination itself, and not just to the images, is under-standable, for the imagination is invisible. The imagination is not what we see or think: it is rather the lens through which we see, the very patterns within which we think. Consequently, it is only in confronting the mixed effects of liturgical reform that we have begun to take seriously the anthropological conditions under which rites and ritual language flourish or decline. It is only recently that we have become aware of what Ray Hart has called "the sedimented imagination,"[3] a condition in which the imagination goes flat, substitutes translation for contemplation, forfeits signification for function:

> The crisis of our time, as we are beginning
> slowly and painfully to perceive
> is not a crisis of the hands
> but of the hearts.
> The failure is a failure of desire.

It is because we the people do not wish—
    because we the people do not know
    what kind of a world we should imagine,
    that this trouble haunts us.
The failure is a failure of the spirit;
    a failure of the spirit to imagine,
    a failure of the spirit to imagine and desire.[4]

The crisis of our time, liturgically, is not a crisis brought about by poor texts and shoddy ceremonial. These are mere symptoms. The crisis is a crisis provoked by our not desiring, not even knowing, the kind of activity liturgy is: an activity of the imagination. In Romano Guardini's words:

> [T]hose whose task it is to teach and educate will have to ask themselves—and this is all-decisive—whether they themselves desire the liturgical act or, to put it plainly, whether they know of its existence and what exactly it consists of and that it is neither a luxury nor an oddity, but a matter of fundamental importance. Or does it, basically, mean the same to them as to the parish priest of the late nineteenth century who said: "We must organize the procession better; we must see to it that the praying and the singing are done better." He did not realize that he should have asked himself quite a different question: how can the act of walking become a religious act, a retinue for the Lord progressing through his land, that an "epiphany" may take place?[5]

The point of Guardini's warning is that the reform of texts and rubrics, while overdue, is not enough. It is not merely a revision of the images presented in the liturgy—use of the vernacular, congregational participation, simplification of the rites—but a renewal of the Christian imagination which we bring to liturgy, that is called for. What is needed is what Lonergan calls "intellectual conversion . . . the elimination of an exceedingly stubborn and misleading myth concerning reality, objectivity and human knowledge." This myth has to do with what we see and how we see it; "the myth that knowing is like looking, that objectivity is seeing what is there to be seen, and not seeing what is not there, and that the real is what is out there now to be looked at."[6] Such mythical thinking fails to distinguish between the world that meets our senses and the world mediated by meaning: it ignores the sign character of the sensible world and fails to see how "objective realities" mediate a world of meanings within a cultural community. It forgets the caution of Thomas Aquinas's *fides terminatur non ad enuncia-*

bile, sed ad rem—faith moves from the sign to the signified, from what meets the senses to that which transcends immediate knowing. The purpose of revising the signifiers is to call them into question so that they can no longer be taken literally, matter-of-factly, but must yield before the meaning they serve.

Development of the Imagination

Developmental studies of thinking, morality and faith have had enormous impact in our time and this impact will undoubtedly make its mark in catechesis. Yet to be thoroughly studied is the matter of the imagination's development or successive transformations. Dominic Crossan[7] has sketched an outline of a theory which, while based on clinical studies, remains to be tested. Nevertheless, his sketch is of sufficient interest to make its consideration worthwhile here.

The way Crossan poses the problem of the imagination situates it in terms of metaphorical and literal language. Preschool children reveal enormous creativity in the invention of metaphor: the pencil is a rocket, the table is a castle. Yet the abundance of metaphor at this stage is characterized by two things which must caution us against idealizing the childish imagination. For one thing, while the production of metaphors is astounding, not all the metaphors are appropriate: successful and unsuccessful identifications are all jumbled up together. For another thing, the metaphorical transaction between contexts, the identification of one thing with another, is so complete that it represents a veritable metamorphosis. The signifier and the signified become one and the same. In short, one is really not dealing with metaphor proper, but with that characteristic of naïve thinking which Lévy-Bruhl called *participation mystique*: a collapse of the two levels of sign and signified into one, in which the signifier is simply transformed into the signified. One can hardly avoid the question of the extent to which this happens in the liturgy, particularly with regards to the Eucharist as sacrament, the effect of the "words of consecration," and the role of the priest "as representing Christ." Crossan suggests that in this, as in other areas of life, childhood is not so much left behind as incorporated into one's adult life. But do the sacramental system and the authenticity of the liturgy require a regression to naïve, magical thinking? Can they survive growing up?

The second stage in the development of the imagination coincides, Crossan suggests, with the early years of school. Between the ages of

seven and eleven, particularly, children show a serious concern for literal meanings. This is altogether to be expected, since they are being
taught to order and categorize the universe in reading, writing, and
arithmetic. But Crossan's point is that we have to be educated to literalism; it does not come naturally. On the contrary, our habitual, unreflected mode of discourse is heavily laden with allusion and metaphor.
It is speaking univocally, precisely, which requires care and effort, not
speaking allusively and metaphorically. But a person's education in literal language may well be a necessary stage in the development of a
proper understanding of the relationship between the *enuntiabile* and
the *res*, between signifier and signified. For it is only by overcoming
the naïve and childish tendency towards magical identification, where
anything can be anything else, by adopting its antithesis (the literal
mood: this is not that), that a more careful and sophisticated use of
metaphor becomes possible. The problem, however, is that the literalism to which we have been culturally acclimatized by the educational
system has become a prevailing and unexamined habit of mind, even
in religious matters. Paradoxically, magical thinking is highly literal
and can therefore survive in a literalist culture: the sign is taken for
granted as identical with the reality and no further thought need be
given to the matter—whether it be consecration, eucharistic presence,
or the doctrinal definitions learnt in the catechisms.

Lonergan's intellectual conversion, or something akin to it, would
appear to be the only way forward. Enough has already been done by
people like Tracy, Crossan, and Ricoeur, building on Heidegger, Ramsey, Austin and others, to begin to develop some experiments in "hermeneutical catechetics," that is, a catechesis geared less towards
content than towards the proper development of the religious imagination in older children and adults. It will be more concerned with the
fides qua (in its sociocultural context) than simply with the *fides quae
creditur* . . . and it will have to be closely related to the practice of liturgical participation. It is the liturgy which, as a complex of ritual acts
and symbolic speech, suffers most from the "myth of objectivity" and
from the collapsing of sign and signified. What is required is a new
mystagogy of faith aimed at converting the way we see, listen, and act
liturgically. In this sense, what is required is a conversion of the imagination, a reawakening of the imagination as a desire for the "Reality"
mediated by the words, signs, and gestures of the rite.

Liturgy with Imagination

The call for allowing more room to the imagination in liturgy is one that can be (and has been) misunderstood. My point is not that we need to come up with imaginative alternatives to the rites we have received (in the manner of so-called "creative liturgies"), but that we need to recognize that the language of the rite is primarily directed to the imagination, and that we need to let the imagination go to work on the texts and rites we have, to discover anew their twofold level of discourse. Perhaps, by way of example, we might take the most basic sign upon which the rest of the liturgy is predicated: the liturgical assembly. Although theologically the liturgical assembly has been revindicated as a primary sacrament of the presence of Christ and as the primary celebrant of the liturgy, it is not at all clear that in catechesis and practice we have been taught what to make of this, or how to make anything of it. For centuries the sign value or sacramental quality of the congregated faithful has simply been ignored, and much contemporary effort at encouraging "active participation" seems intent on continuing to ignore it. The question is: does "active participation" merely mean joining in, doing what everyone else is doing? Is loud singing and a boisterous exchange at the kiss of peace really what we are after? On the other hand, many who decry the changes in the liturgy seem locked into a religious individualism which makes even less of the congregation as sacrament. C. S. Lewis described this temptation well:

> One of our great allies at present is the church itself. . . . All your patient sees is the half-finished, sham-gothic erection on the new building estate. When he goes inside, he sees the local grocer with a rather oily expression on his face bustling up to offer him one shiny little book containing a liturgy which neither of them understands, and one shabby little book containing corrupt texts of a number of religious lyrics, mostly bad, and in very small print. When he gets to his pew and looks round him he sees just that selection of his neighbours. Make his mind flit to and fro between an expression like 'the Body of Christ' and the actual faces in the next pew.[8]

The Christian imagination must find some way forward between the individualism which prevailed so far as to make the congregation dispensable without noticing any significant difference between "private masses" and "public masses," and the new sociability which is more often successful in destroying private prayer than in cultivating public prayer. Both are forms of literalism. The first step must surely be to make the gathered congregation an object of reflective awareness as a visible sign of invisible realities, instead of being just the context within which (or to which) things are done. I shall try to spell this out a little under four headings.

1. Contemplation

"Our problem," wrote Romano Guardini, "is to rise above reading and writing and learn really to look with understanding."[9] He was referring to the liturgy in general, but his remark applies *a fortiori* to the assembly itself and to the act of participating in an action of the community. So what would it mean "to look with understanding"?

> The condition of all valid seeing and hearing, upon every plane of consciousness, lies not in a sharpening of the senses, but in a particular attitude of the whole personality: in a self-forgetting attentiveness, a profound concentration, a self-merging which operates a real communion between the seer and the seen—in a word, in *contemplation.*[10]

Given that the prayer of the liturgy, even if articulated by the priest, nevertheless arises from the community as a whole, it is necessary, if one is to be part of that prayer, that one come to that "real communion" of which Evelyn Underhill speaks. Often it is assumed that congregational singing will produce such communion and under certain circumstances that may well be true. But it is important that those responsible for liturgical music know the difference between the praying community and the cup-final crowd. In both instances, singing is introduced to forge solidarity, but the kind of togetherness that is appropriate, the kind of consciousness that needs to prevail, is vastly different in each of the two cases. If the liturgy really is the prayer of the Spirit of Christ in his Body, the assembly, then the assembly's song needs to be perceived as functioning as a sign or image of that other prayer.

More study needs to be made of the role of music and song in the liturgy, but the point here is that if such music does not foster "a self-forgetting attentiveness, a profound concentration, a self-merging" into the unity of the one body, then it is mere distraction, whatever its aesthetic qualities. In the meantime, the role of silence should not be overlooked: not the silence of mute withdrawal, but the deep ground of silence in which we find ourselves at one, and in which the Spirit of Christ dwells. Out of that silence, the silence of our common humanity, sinful yet redeemed, where the faithful are not only collected but recollected, the prayer of the Spirit of Christ can rise up before the throne of

God, articulated in the words and gestures of the community. As Taizé has shown, music and song can foster such recollection, but it is rare. It requires a discipline of which most congregations and their leaders are pitifully unaware.

2. Discipline

Discipline might be defined as the kind of self-control which frees one from distraction and preserves one from dissipation. Ritual behaviour is a prime example of such discipline. By putting us through the same paces over and over again, ritual rehearses us in certain kinds of interaction over and over again, until the ego finally gives up its phrenetic desire to be in charge and lets the Spirit take over. The repetitiousness of the liturgy is something many would like to avoid; but this would be a profound mistake. It is not entertainment, or exposure to new ideas. It is rather a rehearsal of attitudes, a repeated befriending of images and symbols, so that they penetrate more and more deeply into our inner self and make us, or remake us, in their own image.

Kneeling, for example, is not an expression of our humanity: it is more an invitation to discover what reality looks like when we put ourselves in that position. The texts of Scripture and the images of the liturgy are not didactic messages wrapped up in some decorative covering which can be thrown away when the context is extracted. They are images and sets of images to be toyed with, befriended, rubbed over and over again, until, gradually and sporadically, they yield flashes of insight and encounter with the "Reality" of which they sing. Their purpose is not to give rise to thought (at least, not immediately), but to mediate encounter. As Heidegger said in another context: "The point is not to listen to a series of propositions, but to follow the movement of showing."[11]

So there is a discipline of listening, looking, and gesturing to be learnt: ways of standing, touching, receiving, holding, embracing, eating, and drinking which recognize these activities as *significant* and which enable us to perform them in such a way that we are open to the meaning (the *res*) which they mediate. In terms of the assembly, the primary signifier, there is a way of being together with others in the liturgy—a way of which all these ritual activities are a part—that goes beyond mere juxtaposition of bodies and beyond the pain or pleasure of orchestrated responses, and that leads to the loss of self in favor of profound union with the Body. One acts without acting, speaks without speaking, sings without singing: for it is Christ who prays, blesses, touches, and sings in the Body to which my own body is given over.

3. Preaching and Catechesis

From all that has been said it must be obvious that preaching and catechizing are crucially important. Do they foster what Guardini calls "the liturgical act"? Do they know that there is such a thing? They must both become exercises of the imagination which foster the religious imagination of those to whom they are addressed. The accusation has often been made, and sometimes on good grounds, that the postconciliar liturgy is too didactic, that it has destroyed the mystery by explaining it all away. This is not true of the liturgical reforms themselves which, for the most part, have actually restored the symbolic dimension of the liturgy rather than diminished it. A liturgical reform that has restored Communion under both kinds, fostered a diversification of ministries, restored the kiss of peace at the Eucharist and the signing of the child by parents and godparents at baptism—not to mention the whole elaborate drama of the Rite of Adult Initiation—can hardly be accused of iconoclasm! But the revised books are not always finding their ideals met in practice, while the freedom allowed to the celebrant, and the encouragement to preach, have often resulted in a barrage of words less chosen and measured than one would have liked.

In one particular way we continue to suffer from the inadequacies of our past, and that is in our preoccupation with teaching people the meaning of things. Thus arguments fly back and forth over whether the Mass is a meal or sacrifice. Parents and teachers are often at odds over the meaning of confirmation. Would it be too much to ask that we temporarily lay aside our preconceptions and begin to attend to the language of the liturgy? Just as in our youth we were catechized as to the meaning of the sacraments without reference to the actual celebration of the rites (that, after all, was how theology itself proceeded); so in our own day preachers continue to read preconceived meanings (whether progressive or reactionary, it makes no difference) into the texts of scripture, and catechists take their cue for teaching the sacraments from any place other than the ritual itself. In either instance, we have a survival of the idea that images are merely the wrappings of "truth" and that they can be dispensed with, explained in other terms, and then reintroduced as illustrations of the teacher's remarks. It is an exact parallel to, and perhaps a symptom of, the understanding of metaphor which regarded it merely as a decorative rhetorical device. But in an age where the indispensability, even the priority, of the image has once again been recovered, can preaching and teaching continue unaffected? The fourth- and fifth-century Fathers only taught about baptism and Eucharist to those who had already been initiated by these sacramental rites. Their preaching was not an explanation of what the rites meant, but a commentary on the experiences of the neophytes. Far from defining the meaning of Eucharist and baptism, they multiplied the associations evoked by the ritual and prayer, showing how the image opens on to a larger world of reality than meets our eye or ear. The role of preaching and catechesis today must be the same: practical demonstrations of how, by befriending the image—whether it be word or gesture, or even the congregation itself—and by working with it lovingly, it will yield a glimpse of the world invisible, a snatch of the song of the angels and saints, a momentary awareness of myself and the grocer as one Body, one Spirit in Christ.

4. Conversion of Life

The importance of this reawakening of the religious imagination goes beyond having better liturgies to what really matters: better living. "To the extent that he is altered in the recesses of his imagination, indeed of his being, to that extent he must act differently in daily life."[12] The imagination is not just some gift possessed by some and not by others; nor is it a particular compartment of the personality, along with intellect and will and so forth. It would seem, rather, to be the very way we grasp our existence in the world, the very form of consciousness itself, and thus the foundation of the activities of intellect and will. To shatter, or even to stretch, the horizons of the imagination is to challenge the intellect and to set new desiderata before the energies of the will. To transform the working of the religious imagination is to enable people to situate themselves differently in the world, to challenge their values, to bring them to question their accepted patterns of behavior.

From this perspective, it can be envisaged that the liturgy might operate in Christian life rather like the parables of Jesus, indeed as enacted parable. By opening oneself to be receptive to the symbols of the liturgy, whether verbal or nonverbal, one risks discovery and encounter in confronting the True and the Holy. One risks growing in wisdom and holiness by developing a contemplative attention to words and actions even outside the liturgy. One risks losing one's comfortable ideas and familiar patterns of prejudice by learning really to listen and to act in the Spirit.

It has often been remarked that the renewed liturgy has not proved as effective as some might have hoped in renewing Christian life in general. If the thesis of this article is correct, then the fault is not so much in the renewed liturgy as in what we have made of it. Were there more widespread awareness of the kind of activity liturgy is, and of the discipline it requires of those who would participate in it, it might yet contribute to a renewal of our self-understanding, or rather of the images we have of our place in the world.

Conclusion

To call for a renewal of the Christian imagination in order for the liturgy to be more effective may sound altogether more utopian than the call for the reform of rites and texts sounded at the beginning of this century. If it is thought of in terms of a program to be imposed upon all the faithful, that would certainly be true; but, in fact, it is less of a program than mere "hints and guesses." Unlike the reform of the liturgy, it is something which we can each undertake for ourselves: an exploration of the possibilities of a more contemplative approach to liturgical participation. While it would be fostered by "good liturgy," it is not dependent upon it (indeed, the criteria by which one judges liturgy good or bad tend to waver somewhat in these circumstances). All that it requires is that one strive to relax and center oneself before the liturgy begins, and to maintain the attitude of attentive receptivity to everything that happens in the rite as it unfolds. Though it helps to have some theoretical knowledge of language and sign theory, and though it helps even more to have some training in meditative or con-templative prayer, one can train oneself. The only important thing is to trust the liturgy and the presence of the Spirit, allowing them to pray through one. This will affect the way one sings, stands, responds, sits, participates in the sacrament, uses the silence, and so forth.

In fact, it is essential that one practice such recollection oneself before attempting to turn it into a program for improving parish liturgy. If those responsible for liturgy—the celebrant, the musicians, those re-sponsible for the readings, the selection of songs, the composition of the bidding prayer—themselves come to the liturgy this way, the effect will register itself in the celebration without a word being said. We probably do not need more programs or more explanations: it may be enough if the images of the liturgy—of which our very presence and participation are constitutive parts—are allowed to speak for themselves.

---

[1] *Tra le sollicitudini, Motu proprio* on the restoration of Church music, 22 November 1903.

[2] Thomas Kuhn, *The Structure of Scientific Revolutions* (Chicago, 1970).

[3] Ray Hart, *Unfinished Man and the Imagination* (New York, 1968).

[4] Archibald Macleish. *Listen to Love,* quoted by Patrick Collins, *More Than Meets the Eye* (New York, 1983) 11.

[5] "A letter from Romano Guardini," in *Herder Correspondence* (August 1964) 238.

[6] Bernard Lonergan, *Method in Theology* (New York, 1973) 238.

[7] John Dominic Crossan, "Stages in Imagination," in C. E. Winquist, ed., *The Archeology of the Imagination*, in *Journal of the American Academy of Religion, Thematic Studies*, XLVIII/2 (1981) 49–62.

[8] C. S. Lewis, *The Screwtape Letters* (London, 1942) 15–6.

[9] "A letter from Romano Guardini," 238.

[10] Evelyn Underhill, *Mysticism: A Study in the Nature and Development of Man's Spiritual Consciousness* (New York, 1930) 300.

[11] Martin Heidegger, *On Time and Being* (New York, 1972) 2.

[12] Ihab Hassan, *Paracriticisms* (Chicago, 1975) 6. Cited by Crossan, "Stages in Imagination," 60.

Maxwell E. Johnson

Introduction to "Infant Baptism Reconsidered"

When I set about to edit my 1995 ecumenical collection of essays on Christian Initiation, *Living Water, Sealing Spirit: Readings on Christian Initiation*,[1] there was no question in my mind but that the final essay simply had to be Mark Searle's "Infant Baptism Reconsidered." This essay had appeared eight years earlier in Searle's own edited volume, *Baptism and Confirmation*, volume 2 in the series entitled *Alternative Futures for Worship*,[2] and had quickly become required reading for those concerned both academically and pastorally with the celebration and theology of infant initiation in the ecumenical Church. In 1995 I said the following about this essay:

> Mark Searle's "Infant Baptism Reconsidered" provides a brief history of infant initiation and offers a brilliant defense of its continuation in the Church "less as a problem to be grappled with than as an opportunity to be grasped." Indeed, the name of Mark Searle († 1992) has been synonymous with concerns related to infant initiation in the American Catholic Church as well as, through his numerous ecumenical students, in other communions. It is thus highly fitting that he should have the last word on the subject in this collection.[3]

"An opportunity to be grasped." The title of Searle's essay, "Infant *Baptism* Reconsidered," is, of course, a misnomer, for unlike his earlier 1980 study of infant baptism, *Christening*,[4] his concern in this essay is with the *full* Christian Initiation of infants and children. As he states near the end of his study:

> At a time when the Church is so intent on rescuing the humane values of Christianity and is concerned to do greater justice to the role of the family and to the Christian vision of sexuality, and a time when the role of the nonrational and prerational dimensions of the life of faith is being recovered, perhaps infant *initiation* ought to be seen less as a problem to be grappled with than as an opportunity to be grasped. Far from barring

children from the *font, the chrism, and the altar, the Church should welcome their participation in these sacraments* as a reminder both of the catholicity of the Church and of the fact that, no matter how informed or committed we might be as adults, when we take part in the sacramental liturgies of the Church we are taking part in more than we know.[5]

Searle's concern for the full Christian initiation of infants and children, especially within the contemporary Roman Catholic Church, still presents a serious challenge awaiting serious consideration by the proper ecclesiastical authorities. But clearly in line with Searle's own concerns, and undoubtedly inspired by them, the 1992 national meeting of the Federation of Diocesan Liturgical Commissions (FDLC), held in Miami, Florida, certainly moved in this direction by adopting the following position statement:

> It is the position of the delegates . . . that the Board of Directors of the [FDLC] and the Bishops' Committee on the Liturgy urge the National Conference of Catholic Bishops to take the initiative to propose to the Apostolic See a discussion on the restoration of the ancient practice of celebrating confirmation and communion at the time of baptism, including the baptism of children who have not yet reached catechetical age, so that through connection of these three sacraments, the unity of the Paschal Mystery would be better signified and the eucharist would again assume its proper significance as the culmination of Christian initiation.[6]

And, interestingly enough, both within the Episcopal Church, U.S.A., and the Evangelical Lutheran Church in America, "First Communion" is now, at least theoretically, reconnected to the reception of baptism at all ages, including infancy.[7]

If Searle is concerned in this essay for the full Christian initiation of infants and children, however, it is not because of some kind of ahistorical romanticism on his part; nor is it an attempt at repristinating early Christianity or copying Eastern Christianity. Rather, as a first step or prolegomenon to writing a complete theology of infant initiation, one of the abiding values of this essay is that it approaches the question of infant initiation from a multidisciplinary methodology, combining liturgical-sacramental history and theology with the social sciences, something Searle was especially adept at doing. As such, this essay is important not only for what it says about infant initiation but for what it says theologically about family as "domestic church" and about the development of a "theology of childhood" within the context of contemporary culture and society.

Many important issues are noted in this study. Against those who would make adult initiation "normative" and would, therefore, only enroll infants and children in the catechumenate until such time that they could be fully initiated through the process of the *Rite of Christian Initiation of Adults*, Searle notes:

> In actual fact while enrolling the child in the catechumenate is often promoted on the grounds that the rite of enrollment is itself a kind of sacrament, the desire to delay the baptism of children until they are old enough to take part actively in their own initiation is itself associated with a "low" view of sacraments. . . . There is, in other words, a possible inconsistency in subjecting the helpless infant to the "sacramentality" of enrollment in the catechumenate but refusing to submit it to the "sacramentality" of the complete rite of initiation.

Similarly, he underscores that the practice of infant *baptism* alone in Western Christianity actually has an interesting theological parallel with the Anabaptist approach to *adult* initiation alone. Regarding the separation of the three initiation sacraments he writes:

> What is not always recognized is that with this unwitting change of policy, the Western Church gave up trying to initiate infants. Once infant baptism is recognized as a form of clinical baptism—an emergency measure—it has to be acknowledged that, with the move to defer confirmation and first Communion, *Christian initiation was in fact deferred until the child was old enough to be catechized*. Instead of initiating infants, as had been the universal policy of the first millennium or more, the Church now put them on hold—baptizing them as a *precautionary measure*—until they came of age. . . . The net result is that, beginning in the late thirteenth century and universally from the sixteenth, the Roman Catholic Church has really only initiated "adults," even though it continued to baptize the newborn as a precautionary measure within a few hours or days of birth.

And, equally helpful, he invites us to embrace other images of Christian initiation beyond the paschal death and burial imagery of Romans 6:

> The dominant image, especially in Syria, was not Calvary but the Jordan, not the death of Jesus, but his baptism and manifestation as Son. Around the image of the baptism of Jesus and his messianic anointing being shared by those being baptized, there clustered a whole range of images much more congenial to the baptism of infants: adoption, divinization, sanctification, gift of the Spirit, indwelling, glory, power, wisdom, rebirth, restoration, mission, and so forth.[8]

Perhaps most intriguing and compelling, however, is Searle's emphasis not only on the Incarnation of Christ as having "sanctified" childhood itself (i.e., the patristic principle that "what is not assumed is not redeemed"), but that infants and children are not merely passive recipients of adult ministry. Rather, they have a ministerial role to play—a ministry—within the Church:

> Children bring both joy and the Cross. Children will test the sacrificial self-commitment, the self-delusions, and the spurious faith of those with whom they come in contact for any length of time. They summon parents particularly to a deeper understanding of the mystery of grace and of the limitations of human abilities. They probe the ambivalences of their "way of leaning into life." But they also evoke a spirit of wonder and benediction and become messengers of unsolicited consolation. All this is merely to suggest that in their own way children in fact play an extremely active, even prophetic role in the household of faith.

Finally, as should be obvious, this essay remains as relevant today as it was in the late 1980s. Many of the issues regarding infant initiation that Searle raises herein are issues still needing to be addressed in detail today. And while one must certainly lament the fact that he was unable to accomplish the larger work of which this was the prolegomenon, this essay clearly sets the agenda for the study and practice of the Christian initiation of infants and children. The full initiation of infants and children in Western Christianity is *not* a problem. It remains a joyful and life-giving "opportunity to be grasped." And we all remain indebted to Mark Searle for this continual reminder of this opportunity in our midst.

Maxwell E. Johnson, an ordained minister of the Evangelical Lutheran Church in America, is professor of liturgical studies in the Department of Theology, University of Notre Dame, South Bend, Indiana.

---

[1] Maxwell E. Johnson, ed., *Living Water, Sealing Spirit: Readings on Christian Initiation* (Collegeville: Liturgical Press, a Pueblo Book, 1995) 365–409.

[2] Mark Searle, ed., *Alternative Futures for Worship*, vol. 2, *Baptism and Confirmation* (Collegeville: Liturgical Press, 1987) 15–54.

[3] Johnson, xix–xx.

[4] Mark Searle, *Christening: The Making of Christians* (Collegeville: Liturgical Press, 1980).

[5] Emphasis added.

[6] *FDLC Newsletter* 22:4 (December 1995) 45.

[7] See Evangelical Lutheran Church in America, *The Use of the Means of Grace: A Statement on the Practice of Word and Sacrament* (Minneapolis: Augsburg Fortress, 1997) 41–3.

[8] This invitation to explore alternative baptismal imagery, along with Romans 6, was taken up by me in my *Images of Baptism* (Chicago: Liturgy Training Publications, 2001).

Infant Baptism Reconsidered[*]

"What the value of baptizing infants might be is an extremely obscure question. But one must believe there is some value in it" (St. Augustine. *De quantitate animae*, XXXVI, 80).

During the past twenty or thirty years sacramental theology has undergone an enormous transformation. Undoubtedly the leading indicator if not the cause of this transformation is the abandonment of the questions and vocabulary of Scholasticism in favor of more existentialist and personalist approaches to understanding what sacraments are and how they function in the Christian life. What began as a recovery of the ecclesial dimension of the sacraments quickly led to further shifts: from speaking of sacraments as "means of grace" to speaking of them as encounters with Christ himself; from thinking of them primarily as acts of God to thinking of them mainly as celebrations of the faith community; from seeing sacraments as momentary incursions from another world to seeing them as manifestations of the graced character of all human life; from interpreting them as remedies for sin and weakness to seeing them as promoting growth in Christ.

Such shifts have been prompted in part by theological developments, but also by the influence, both on theology and pastoral practice, of a growing awareness of the radically altered sociocultural circumstances in which the Christian life is lived in the second half of the twentieth century. Yet while the practice of infant baptism has been particularly challenged in this "post-Christian" era, it has remained strangely neglected in the work of theological reconstruction. Instead,

---

* This essay first appeared in Mark Searle, ed., *Alternative Futures for Worship*, vol. 2, *Baptism and Confirmation*. Collegeville: Liturgical Press, 1987. It was reprinted in Maxwell E. Johnson, ed., *Living Water, Sealing Spirit: Readings on Christian Initiation*. Collegeville: Liturgical Press, a Pueblo Book, 1995.

theological discussion of infant baptism remains largely dominated by the inherited methodologies of historical study and deductive arguments from doctrinal first principles.

Yet infant initiation is deserving of more imaginative reconsideration. It remains an issue close to the experience of every believing family. But even from the theologian's perspective, if most of the issues of current theological interest come together in the sacraments,[1] most sacramental questions come together in a particularly concentrated way in the issue of the sacramental initiation of infants. Here converge such problems as how to speak of God, the relationship between the order of grace and the order of history, the relationship between grace and freedom, the nature and role of the Church as mediating the mystery of salvation, and the relationship between the language of faith and the basic experiences of human life. Conversely, of course, one's personal and denominational position on such issues as these will invariably color one's understanding of what, if anything, is transpiring when an infant is baptized.

The focus of this essay, however, will be considerably more modest. Less than a theology of infant initiation, this will be more of a prolegomenon for such a theology, looking at how the question of infant baptism has been raised in the past, how it poses itself today, and how it might be approached differently in order to break out of the stalemate to which traditional arguments have led.

Notes for a History of the Question

History shows for the most part that where the sacraments are concerned, practice is invariably a step or two ahead of theology. With the exception of the Reformation, the practice of baptism gives rise to theological reflection rather than being shaped by a priori theological principles. Thus it is necessary to distinguish between the practice of infant baptism and theological attempts either to justify it, to undermine it, or to influence the shape of its practice. Similarly there are two distinct if related histories: the history of the practice of infant baptism and the history of its theology. Here it is clearly impossible to give an adequate account of either history, so we shall be content to make some observations on each with a view to demonstrating the need for a fresh look at the whole matter.

On the History of Baptism. In most accounts of the history of infant initiation, too little consideration has been given to the relationship between infant baptism and clinical or deathbed baptism. The question of whether the early Church baptized has been debated to a standstill.[2] The evidence is insufficient to draw any firm conclusions either way, though in the final analysis what we know about familial unity and patriarchal authority in the ancient world makes it less than likely that the children of Christian parents would have been left to make a decision for themselves. The apparently fairly widespread practice of deferring baptism until rather late in life would seem to be a secondary development of the fourth century associated with the discipline of once-in-a-lifetime penance. What we do know with complete certitude, however, is that infants who were baptized (and the evidence becomes universal after the year 200) were initiated along with adult converts in the paschal sacraments of water, chrism, and altar.

The fact that infants and young children were wholly initiated needs to be underlined, because the subsequent breakup of Christian initiation into distinct celebrations of infant baptism, delayed confirmation, and separate "First Communion" was never something deliberately chosen or decided by the Church. It just happened. It happened despite the best efforts of Church authorities from late antiquity to the High Middle Ages to prevent it happening and to mitigate its effects. The ideal of unified sacramental initiation for infants and young children remains in place in the East and in some parts of Hispanic Catholicism. In most of the West, however, the postponement of episcopal confirmation lasted so long, despite efforts to avoid it, that it came to be accepted first as inevitable and eventually as desirable. Apparently resigning themselves to the disintegration of the rites of initiation, the Churches of the West came increasingly to endorse the separation of confirmation and First Communion from baptism, though it only became a universal policy after the Council of Trent.[3]

The root causes of this drift towards separation are to be found as far back as the third century in provisions made for the baptizing of catechumens in danger of death. The fourth-century Church historian Eusebius cites the comments of Pope Cornelius († 253) on the sad history of the heretic Novatian. The Pope ascribed Novatian's defection from the unity of the Church of Rome to the fact that he had been baptized in an emergency when he had fallen seriously ill and was thought to be near death. When subsequently he recovered, he allegedly never went to the bishop for the completion of the rites of initiation: "Without receiving these, how could he receive the Holy Spirit?"[4]

Whatever the facts of Novatian's case, the practice of baptizing catechumens thought to be on the point of death and the subsequent completion of their initiation by the bishop if they recovered are clearly attested in the following period. Thus the Council of Elvira, Spain, in 305 ordained as follows:

Canon 38: *That in cases of necessity even laypersons* [fideles] *may baptize.*

> It was agreed that a faithful man who has held fast to his baptism and is not bigamous may baptize a sick catechumen at sea, or wherever there is no church at hand, provided that if he survives he shall bring him to a bishop so that he may be confirmed [*perfici*] through the laying-on of a hand.[5]

Presumably the same held true for infants who were born sickly and considered unlikely to survive. Normally children would be kept for baptism at Easter, to be initiated along with the rest of the catechumens, but if their life was in danger they would, like any other catechumen in danger of death, be baptized without delay and would have their initiation completed by the bishop if and when they recovered.

But what had at first been the exceptional case eventually became commonplace as an increasing percentage of the candidates for baptism came in fact to be children in a period where infancy was itself so precarious a condition that to be newborn was ipso facto to be in a life-threatening situation. Even without the additional encouragement of the Augustinian doctrine of the damnation of unbaptized infants, it is hard to imagine that emergency baptisms would not have been more common in the fifth and sixth centuries simply because baptismal candidates were predominantly children and because of the high incidence of infant mortality. Surviving documentary evidence would seem to support this hypothesis. Although the eighth-century supplement to the *Hadrianum* contained a form of catechumenate and initiation liturgy suitably abbreviated for infants, it is significant that this did not apparently catch on. Instead, infant baptism was increasingly celebrated using the much older Gelasian *Order for the Making of a Catechumen or for Baptizing.* But this rite was nothing other than a rite for baptizing the dying! So common did its use become in the Middle Ages that it eventually came to serve as the basis for the rite of infant baptism in the Roman Ritual of 1614.[6]

Thus is seems obvious that *quamprimum* infant baptism was simply a form of clinical baptism. Much later on, the Council of Florence implicitly admitted as much in its decree of 1442:

> Concerning children: because of the danger of death, which occurs fre-
> quently enough, since nothing else can be done for them except to bap-
> tize them, whereby they are snatched from the power of the devil and
> adopted as children of God, the Council admonishes that holy baptism
> is not to be delayed for 40 or 80 days or for some other period of time, as
> some are wont to do, but they should be baptized as soon as conve-
> niently possible [*quamprimum commode fieri potest*]. Therefore, in immi-
> nent danger of death, let them be baptized in the form of the Church
> even by a layman or woman, if no priest is at hand, quickly and without
> delay.[7]

What came to differentiate the situation of infants from that of unbaptized adults who fell gravely ill was that in the course of time, beginning in the late thirteenth century, the subsequent completion of
their initiation came deliberately to be postponed until they had
reached the "age of discretion," if indeed they lived that long.[8] Slowly
and imperceptibly the Church had completed a volte-face, gradually
abandoning its insistence that surviving children be brought to the
bishop as soon as possible after baptism and suggesting instead that
confirmation be "prudently" delayed until the children were old
enough to need the sacrament.

The facts of the story are well enough known. What is not always recognized is that with this unwitting change of policy, the Western Church
gave up trying to initiate infants. Once infant baptism is recognized as a
form of clinical baptism—an emergency measure—it has to be acknowledged that, with the move to defer confirmation and First Communion,
Christian initiation was in fact deferred until the child was old enough
to be catechized. Instead of initiating infants, as had been the universal
policy of the first millennium or more, the Church now put them on
hold—baptizing them as a precautionary measure—until they came of
age. The Catechism of the Council of Trent endorsed this deferred initiation for the Roman Church when it described the administration of confirmation to children under seven as "inexpedient" and went on to say:
"Wherefore, if not to be postponed to the age of twelve, it is most proper
to defer this sacrament at least to that of seven."[9]

What made this change of direction thinkable, of course, was the
new theology of confirmation as a distinct sacrament, which the early
medieval theologians had elaborated in an effort to persuade parents
to bring their children to the bishop for the completion of their initiation. As it happens, the rationale for receiving the sacrament, eventually became a rationale for delaying it until the age of seven, the age at

which for many purposes a child ceased to be regarded as a child and was numbered among the company of adults.[10] The net result is that, beginning in the late thirteenth century and universally from the sixteenth, the Roman Catholic Church has really only initiated "adults," even though it continued to baptize the newborn as a precautionary measure within a few hours or days of birth. There is an irony here not often remarked upon: Roman Catholics and Anabaptists were actually closer together in their positions on infant baptism than they thought. Recognizing the precautionary and emergency character of infant baptism in the Roman Church does go a long way towards accounting for the largely remedial attitude towards baptism in post-Tridentine theology, as well as for the emphasis on catechesis as a necessary precondition for being confirmed and for making one's first confession and First Communion.

Since it is only in the twentieth century that the full history of the practice of initiation in the West has become available, such developments as we have described occurred without much sense of anyone introducing radical change. With that history now available, however, the Church is for the first time in a position to ask the question of whether the "accidental" reversal of her original policy with regard to the initiation of children is something she still wants to endorse. But since there is no virtue in returning to an earlier practice simply because it was earlier, such a decision will require serious reflection on the place of the child in the economy of grace.

On the History of Baptismal Theology. Here again we shall confine ourselves to some remarks about the way the question of infant baptism has been posed at certain key moments in its history, with a particular eye to seeing whether the child as such was ever taken into account.

The New Testament and the Subapostolic Church. There is little or no evidence that infant baptism was ever posed as a question, unless Luke 18:15-17 be read that way.[11] Though some, such as Kurt Aland,[12] would take the silence of the first two centuries as indicating that the Church did not baptize infants, it is more likely, for the reason mentioned above, that the inclusion of infants and small children among the ranks of the baptizands was simply taken for granted. Moreover it should also be noted that children are among the beneficiaries of Jesus' miraculous cures in the Gospels, and that when they are mentioned at all in the teaching of Jesus it is to hold them up as paradigms of those who receive or are received into the kingdom of God (see Mark 10:14-15; Luke 9:47-48; 18:15-17; Matt 18:1-5; 19:13-15). Thus while there is nothing directly excluding the baptism of children, children are put in a very positive light where the appropriation of salvation is concerned, a fact all the more remarkable in view of the predominantly negative view of children which subsequently came to prevail in the West.

Tertullian (North Africa, ca. 150–220). Tertullian is the first writer known to have challenged the practice of baptizing infants and children.[13] It is notable that he neither challenges the validity of such baptisms nor questions the authenticity of the practice as an apostolic tradition. Instead he is content merely to argue that it is unnecessary and unwise. It is unnecessary, he says, because children have committed no sins—"why should innocent infancy come with haste to the remission of sins?" Yet elsewhere Tertullian seems firmly convinced that every child born into this world is born as a child of Adam and subject to Satan's dominion.[14] The baptism of children is also unwise, for it involves a double jeopardy: jeopardy for the baptized themselves, if they grow up unfaithful to their baptism, and jeopardy for their sponsors, who may be prevented by death from fulfilling their commitment or may be thwarted by the child growing up with "an evil disposition." It is far wiser, Tertullian argues, to "let them be made Christians when they have become competent to know Christ." That competence means more than attaining catechizable age is clear from his advice in the same context that the unmarried should also defer baptism until such time as they have settled down either to marriage or to a life of continence.

What seems to be operative behind these suggestions is Tertullian's view of the *sacramentum* as a sacred oath of commitment and of the Church as a community of the vowed.[15] "All who understand what a burden baptism is will have more fear of obtaining it than of its postponement."[16] Thus for Tertullian baptism is a covenantal relationship in which both God and the baptized have reciprocal responsibilities, responsibilities which a child should not assume (apart presumably from imminent danger of death), because the risk of postbaptismal sin is too great. While Tertullian is the only author on record to have stated this position so clearly, the tendency to defer baptism, which becomes widespread in the fourth century, indicates that his views came to be widely shared.

Augustine (North Africa, 354–430). The major contributor to a theology of sacraments in the West was Augustine, and nowhere was his influence more keenly felt than in the area of infant baptism. At a time when Christian parents frequently enrolled their children as catechumens but postponed their baptism indefinitely while their children were healthy, Augustine provided a major impetus toward *quamprimum* baptism.[17] Against the Pelagian emphasis on human responsibility in the work of salvation, Augustine stressed the absolute necessity of the grace of Christ. What was at issue was not the baptism of infants as such but the significance of the redemptive work of Christ in human history and in the life of each individual. Infants became a test case, and Augustine was able to point to the Church's traditional practice of baptizing even newborn children with the "one baptism for the forgiveness of sins" as evidence that they, too, were in sin and in need of Christ's saving grace.

Yet Augustine's autobiographical *Confessions* reveal a profound ambivalence in his attitude towards children and childhood.[18] On the one hand there is his extraordinary journey back into his own childhood, where he finds the roots of his later sins in the anxious grasping of the child, which he identifies as concupiscence. On the other hand, when he begins to speak of his conversion, it is to childhood that he again returns for images of the truly converted experience. Margaret Miles summarizes Augustine as follows:

> The imagery with which he introduces the conversion experience is that of the child just learning to walk: "Throw yourself on him. Do not fear. He will not pull away and let you fall. Throw yourself without fear and he will receive you and heal you" (*Confessions*, VIII:1). This strong imagery suggests, as do several other elements in the account, that what is necessary is a return to the earliest psychic condition of anxiety, a stripping of the cumulative object-orientation which, in adulthood, has become ingrained behavior.[19]

The ambivalence of Augustine's imagery is reflective of the ambivalence of the child. On the one hand childhood is the primordial experience of the dialectic between dependence and autonomy, grasping and letting go, to which true conversion must return and which it must redeem through reliving this dialectic under the influence of grace. In that sense childhood is an ideal state to be recovered, not just a past to be left behind. On the other hand, since the child unconsciously seeks to resolve its anxiety by reaching and grasping and demanding, the root of all sin, concupiscence, is vividly displayed in its crying and its orality. As such, the child represents all that is wrong with fallen humanity: "Who would not tremble and wish rather to die than to be an infant again if the choice were put before him?"[20]

In subsequent Western theology it was the darker side of the child, accentuated in Augustine's anti-Pelagian writings, which seems to have come to dominate. In the ninth century Walafrid Strabo reversed Augustine's argument: "Since all who are not delivered by God's grace will perish in original sin, including those who have not added to it by their own personal sin, it is necessary to baptize infants."[21] Thereafter the practice of infant baptism will be justified on the basis of the doctrine of original sin, not vice versa, and the negative view of childhood will prevail until modern times.

The High Middle Ages: The Eleventh to the Thirteenth Centuries. This period witnessed a resurgence of Manichean dualism, which saw the world of material creation as diametrically opposed to the world of the spirit and as the creation of the Evil One. This resurgence, occurring in the context of demands for Church reform and a return to the simplicity and purity of the Gospel, was often marked by a literal interpretation of the Scriptures. One such instance was the repudiation of infant baptism by the Cathars. As part of their argument they cited Mark 16:16: "Whosoever believes and is baptized shall be saved and whosoever refuses belief shall be condemned." This challenged orthodox theologians to find ways of justifying the traditional doctrine that infants were saved by baptism even though they were clearly incapable of believing.

One answer was to distinguish between faith as an act of belief and faith as the habitual capacity for making such acts. "The infant," wrote Peter of Poitiers, "can neither believe, nor hope, nor love; yet it has faith, hope and love, just as it is endowed with reason even though it cannot yet reason and has the capacity for laughter even though it cannot yet laugh."[22] St. Thomas Aquinas would make the same point, while adopting Plato's dubious analogy with the sleeping adult: "The inability of the child to act results not from the lack of the *habitus*, but from bodily incapacity, just as people who are asleep are prevented by sleep from exercising the virtues even though they do have the *habitus* of the virtues."[23] So infants are suitable subjects for baptism, the sacrament of faith, because despite their natural incapacity they receive the infused virtue of faith—together with hope and love—through the sacrament itself. Here, clearly, the Augustinian view of the child as equipped with an active if perverted will is temporarily eclipsed by a view of childhood centered on its dormant rationality. The child is the passive recipient of the ministrations of the Church as it is the passive recipient of the ministrations of its own parents, at least until its latent rational powers begin to stir.

The Sixteenth-Century Reformation. Since the key issue of the Reformation was justification, and since the Reformers generally accentuated the role of faith in the Christian life, it was hardly surprising that infant baptism became an issue. For Martin Luther the sacraments were quite secondary to faith in the divine promises, of whose reality they were tangible evidence, but it was a relatively small faction of the Reformers who took this doctrine to its logical conclusion. The Anabaptists, who derived their nickname from their refusal to recognize the validity of infant baptism and their insistence on rebaptizing those baptized in infancy, held that God's grace came through his Word and that baptism only had value for someone who submitted to baptism as an act of submission to the Gospel.

While the Anabaptists represented a number of divergent views, they were generally of one mind in seeing baptism as a personal response to the Word of God, whereby a person covenants with other converted Christians to become the Church, the witnessing community. Since children are inherently incapable of such response or responsibility, they are incapable of baptism. The problem of original sin was resolved largely by ignoring it, since it was not clearly taught in Scripture.

Behind this Anabaptist approach to baptism, as behind much of the reforming program of both the Protestant Reformation and the Catholic Reformation, was the emerging modern concept of the person as an autonomous individual.[24] Whereas earlier and non-Western concepts of the person tended to identify the person in terms of his or her place in the community, the modern concept of the autonomous individual makes the individual self the source of its values and its own identity. Hence we have the emphasis on individual conversion and commitment and on the education that would shape each individual to take his place in the Church or in society. Through diligent training of intellect and will, Catholics and Protestants alike believed, a new generation of committed individuals could be formed. The Anabaptists in a sense set the pace for the other Churches in the sixteenth century by taking the logical step of deferring baptism until the child's education—the training of intellect, will, and conscience—had been completed, and a full, conscious, and deliberate act of obedience to the Gospel could be made. "This emphasis on personal, individually-sought baptism, exclusive of the religious community into which one entered at birth, earmarked Swiss, Dutch and German Anabaptists alike."[25]

Both Martin Luther and John Calvin rejected the Anabaptist position and retained the practice of baptizing infants, each of them for reasons that had little to do with baptism as such and still less to do with any sympathetic understanding of childhood.[26] Yet the same trend, symptomatic of the new humanism of the age, manifested itself in these other Churches as well, even though for various reasons its complete logical expression, denial of baptism to children, was inhibited. In a direct response to the dilemma raised by the Anabaptists, the other Protestant Churches reinterpreted confirmation—which they regarded not as a sacrament but as an ecclesiastical institution—as a rite of personal profession (confirmation) of faith which concluded the catechizing of those baptized in infancy.

The conservative defensiveness of the Roman Church towards everything suggested or promoted by the Reformers strongly mitigated the influence of this focus on the individual, but one symptom of it that does appear is the definitive move to postpone confirmation and First Communion, if not until the age of twelve, then at least until the child reached the age of intellectual and moral discretion. The child might continue to be baptized in the faith of the Church, but the fullness of sacramental initiation would have to wait until the child was old enough to profess its own faith.

Implicit in this position is the identification of Christian life with adult life and with *individual* adult life. Until such time as they develop such adult capacities as intellect, will, and conscience, children can have no real place in the Church; they are barred from the sacraments. Childhood is seen merely as a period between birth and personhood. Not much more can be said for it than that it will pass.

The Twentieth Century. Modern discussions of infant baptism have been largely stimulated by a growing sense of the fragility of Christianity in the modern Western world and by the perceived need for a more credible witness to the Gospel in contemporary society. At first the discussion tended to focus among Protestants on whether the New Testament and the historical tradition offered any legitimation for the practice of infant baptism, but soon the argument shifted to more explicitly doctrinal positions.[27] What was ultimately at stake was less the salvation of infants (for the doctrine of original sin in its Augustinian formulation had been considerably diluted in the course of the nineteenth century) than the salvation of the Church as a witnessing community. The indiscriminate practice of baptizing any child presented at the font was agreed by all to be detrimental. What was at issue was whether infant baptism as such was an apostolic practice compatible with the Gospel or whether it was a later practice symptomatic of a loss of evangelical consciousness.

Among Roman Catholics the legitimacy and validity of infant baptism was never called into question, but in the de-Christianized conditions of postwar Europe, the Catholic Church faced the problems of a vast nominal membership and few deeply committed Catholics. Moves to curtail indiscriminate baptism were accompanied on the one hand by a recovery of the rich patristic teachings on sacramental initiation, and on the other hand by the first steps towards a restoration of the ancient catechumenate.[28] In America these issues were taken up after the Second Vatican Council and especially in the wake of the promulgation of the *Rite for the Christian Initiation of Adults*.[29] As the name indicates, this was not exactly a full restoration of the baptismal discipline of the patristic Church, since it was now reserved for adults and for children of catechizable age. Younger children, who had taken their place alongside their elders in the original catechumenate, were henceforth excluded. For them a separate rite was provided, the *Ordo Baptizandi Parvulos* (1969).

This twofold economy of sacramental initiation has not taken care of the issue of infant baptism, however. In fact it has served to raise new theological problems about what we are doing in baptizing small children.[30] Nor are these problems confined to discussions among academic theologians, for the contrast between the extensiveness and symbolic richness of the adult rite and the relatively perfunctory character of the children's rite, both witnessed in the same parishes, has raised questions for pastors and faithful as well. Since this is where matters currently stand, it is worth identifying some of the challenges posed to infant baptism by the RCIA more closely.

Infant Baptism in the Shadow of the RCIA. There has been a tendency since the elaboration of the Scholastic synthesis of sacramental theology in the thirteenth century to focus on the individual minister and recipient at the expense of the ecclesial context, on the sacramental moment at the expense of the initiatory process, on the efficacy of the sacramental act at the expense of the role of faith, and on the remedial value of baptism at the expense of the rich symbolism of the unified rites of baptism, confirmation, and Eucharist. On all these counts the RCIA brings welcome redress, but in doing so it calls into question the strategy of infant baptism whose ritual remains comparatively impoverished. The newly restored practice of adult initiation serves to highlight precisely those aspects of baptismal theology which the new rite of infant baptism continues to obscure. We shall identify four such elements, four elements with which any rethinking of infant baptism will require us to come to terms.

The Faith of the Candidate. In contrast to the passivity of the infant, the adult coming to baptism is capable of faith and of all that faith implies. He or she can play a full, conscious, and active role in responding to the call of God's Word and submitting to the power of God's grace.

This powerful event of adult conversion has traditionally been envisaged in America in one of two ways. First, there is the early Anabaptist tradition, maintained by present-day Mennonites and some Baptists, for which this coming to faith is essentially cognitive and the product of conviction: a submission to the judgment of God's Word upon one's life and upon the world. It issues in a lifestyle which takes the Gospel seriously and glories in its countercultural challenge. Such conversion is radical, evangelical, and ethical. But there is another more widespread and certainly more recent tradition among American Protestant fundamentalists, in which conversion is less a matter of conviction than of experience. Here baptism itself is subordinated to the "amazing grace" of discovering Jesus as one's personal savior.

These two traditions of adult conversion—the one issuing in a common life of evangelical discipleship, the other in a more individualistic, feeling experience of "being saved"—have both had some influence on American Roman Catholics as they adopt the RCIA. The effect of both is to render infant baptism an anomaly, and if Roman Catholics have shown themselves hesitant to rule out infant baptism altogether, they have certainly begun to raise questions about its value. These two native American conceptions of conversion come together with a traditional Catholic emphasis on faith as belief, to make conversion a highly personal decision and the celebration of baptism the occasion of a maturely considered faith commitment. It thereby achieves successfully what Catholics have been trying to do with confirmation with far less effect. The problem of "what to do with confirmation" is itself a trailing symptom, some would argue, of the problem created by infant baptism: membership in the Church without any guarantee that those so baptized will ever come to own their baptismal faith.

The Ecclesiological Factor. As in the past, so, too, in the present, a preference for adult over infant baptism is closely tied to a particular ecclesiology. This connection is sometimes explicit, as with the Anabaptists and Mennonites, but it often lurks behind the screen of other arguments, as was the case with Tertullian. Today in the Roman Catholic Church, as in previous eras of reform, there is something of a reaction against the Church's perceived cultural compromises and the dream of a more faithful if smaller Church. Instead of the security and blandness of the *Volkskirche*, some hope for a believers' Church: a Church of small base communities whose members are committed to working in the world with uncompromising fidelity to Gospel values. Since Karl Rahner, Catholics have been accustomed to refer to this as the "diaspora Church." It envisages a fully active membership, gathered in small congregations, which will be fully participatory in their polity and marked by an evangelical lifestyle. Priority will be given to local congregations and to their self-discipline within the larger communion of the Church as a whole, rather than to the large, amorphous entities represented by national and international religious denominations. The dream of many contemporary Catholics could be summed up as "solidarity without legalism and pastoral responsibility without clericalism."

Among Avery Dulles' five models of the Church,[31] this one obviously corresponds most closely to the "Herald" model, with strong overtones of the "Servant" model, but it is interesting to note that Catholics often appeal in support of such a vision to conciliar texts such as *Sacrosanctum Concilium* 41 and *Lumen Gentium* 26. Here the Church is said to manifest itself most adequately and visibly in the local assembly, where the faithful gather under the presidency of the bishop for the celebration of the liturgy. In appealing to these texts, it is not always recognized that two quite different models of Church are being fused. While this is of itself quite legitimate, the debate over infant baptism is muddied by the failure to acknowledge the new hybrid ecclesiology and to work out the implications of clinging to the sacramental model of Church while opting to develop a form of Church organization on the herald model. The Anabaptists in adopting the herald model rejected sacramentalism. Catholics appear as yet unwilling to face the issue: can a congregational model of Church with its emphasis upon the Word of God and on the need for adult decision be reconciled with the Catholic sacramental tradition, with its faith in the power of grace to work below the level of consciousness, even in the baptism of a child?

New Understanding of Sacramentality. One of the major contributions of the RCIA to Catholic life and to sacramental theology is the way in which it has forced us to break with an almost magical understanding of the sacraments as discrete moments of divine intervention, and to adopt a more flexible understanding of sacramentality as a process admitting of degrees. In this latter perspective the temporal duration of the catechumenal process, the various stages in the journey of faith undertaken by the candidates, the various ritual celebrations that mark the way culminating in the solemn Easter rites of baptism, confirmation, and Eucharist are all sacramental in varying degrees. The liturgy of Easter night is less the setting for three discrete sacramental "moments" than it is the climax of a process which is sacramental in its entirety.

The concept of a gradual growth in faith, marked by a succession of rites and stages which are themselves sacramental in a broad sense, offers an obviously attractive solution to the problem of infant baptism.[32] By enrolling infants in the catechumenate, we can give them something, whether their parents are committed Christians or not, while still withholding baptism until the children are old enough to ask for it themselves and to make a lasting commitment. There is obviously a precedent for such an arrangement in the Church of the fourth and fifth centuries.

What is remarkable in most of the discussion of the proposed infant catechumenate, however, is that two points are rarely, if ever, addressed. First, the rite of enrollment in the catechumenate requires of candidates that they already have manifested some initial conversion and that they be prepared to make their intentions known to the Church.[33] Second, the issue of when a child would be old enough to be elected for baptism is rarely indicated. Would it be at the age of three, as Gregory Nazianzen suggested in the fourth century, when the child is old enough to remember its baptism? Would it be a year or two after the child is old enough to be catechized? Or would baptism be withheld until the child is old enough to make a mature personal decision? Any solution but the latter—which would perhaps delay baptism until the child was of marriageable age—is vulnerable to at least some of the objections raised against infant baptism and would thus constitute only a partial solution.

In actual fact, while enrolling the child in the catechumenate is often promoted on the grounds that the rite of enrollment is itself a kind of sacrament, the desire to delay the baptism of children until they are old enough to take part actively in their own initiation is itself associated with a "low" view of sacraments. The deferment of the sacrament makes sense because sacraments are seen more in terms of their nature as human actions than in terms of their nature as acts of God. There is, in other words, a possible inconsistency in subjecting the helpless infant to the "sacramentality" of enrollment in the catechumenate but refusing to submit it to the "sacramentality" of the complete rite of initiation.

The Meaning of Baptism. For centuries, as we saw, popular Catholic understanding of baptism was dominated by Augustine's teaching that children dying in original sin would be excluded forever from the vision of God. Conciliar teaching on the Christian life and the renewed rites of Christian initiation have shifted attention to the more positive aspects of baptism and especially to the paschal character of the Christian life as a sharing in the death and resurrection of Christ. This is an immense gain, but the paschal character of baptism is sometimes propounded in such a way as to seem to preclude the baptism of infants. When Aidan Kavanagh, for example, describes baptism as "a transitus from shame to celebration, from the conviction of sin to the appropriation of one's complete forgiveness in Christ"[34] little room appears left for the baptizing of preconscious infants.

With respect to this emphasis on the radical discontinuity between the "before" and "after" of baptism, two points need to be made. The first is that studies on the meaning of *pascha* in Christian usage have shown that it was used in three distinct if related senses and that the translation *pascha = transitus* (transition, journey) is relatively late and only became widespread with Augustine.[35] The popularity of the *transitus* meaning and its eclipse of the earlier meanings (which interpreted the term as referring either to God passing over the children of Israel and sparing their lives or to the lamb—Christ—by whose Blood they were spared) was largely due to the association of adult baptism (passage through the waters) with the Easter Vigil. Thus it is somewhat tautologous to argue that the paschal character of baptism requires the kind of break with the past which characterizes adult conversion, when it was precisely that sort of conversion that led to *pascha* being identified with the people's passage through the Red Sea rather than with God's merciful sparing of his children.

Secondly, research on the early history of Christian baptism, especially in East Syria, has made it abundantly clear that not everything in Christian life can be reduced to the death/resurrection motif and that this was not quite the root metaphor for baptism either in the New Testament or in early Christianity that some have supposed it to be. In fact, for reasons no one has yet been able to explain, the Pauline doctrine on baptism as a participation in the death and resurrection of Christ was totally without influence in the first three centuries of the Church.[36] Instead, the dominant image, especially in Syria, was not Calvary but the Jordan, not the death of Jesus, but his baptism and manifestation as Son.[37] Around the image of the baptism of Jesus and his messianic anointing being shared by those being baptized, there clustered a whole range of images much more congenial to the baptism of infants: adoption, divinization, sanctification, gift of the Spirit, indwelling, glory, power, wisdom, rebirth, restoration, mission, and so forth. These, it should be noted, are as much a part of the traditional meaning of baptism as the death and resurrection imagery. But this is not to suggest that we retain one set of meanings for adult initiation and another set for infant initiation. On the contrary, both sets of images are properly activated in any baptism, which means that adult initiation needs to be thought of in terms of rebirth and return to infancy, while infants, if they are to be baptized, must be capable in some way of dying and rising with Christ.

Conclusion. Having selectively reviewed some aspects of the history of baptismal practice and baptismal theology and looked at some of the challenges to infant initiation posed by the restored adult rite, it is now time to try to pull together what we have learned from this review which might suggest that a rethinking of infant initiation is both timely and necessary. Traditional ways of thinking appear inadequate for the following four reasons.

First, it is striking that past and present discussions about infant baptism are rarely about baptism alone or about infants at all. Usually the subject of infant baptism is raised in the context of another argument, whether it be about the nature of the Church as a community of witness or about the relationship of God's grace to human works. John

Calvin's position on the baptism of the children of believers, for example, is entirely derived from his conviction concerning the essential unity of the Old and New Covenants, so that what was said of circumcision for the Jews may be said of baptism for Christian children. The traditional arguments for or against infant baptism, then, are characteristically deductive arguments from a priori doctrinal principles in which the nature of childhood itself is rarely made the subject of theological reflection.

Second, the necessity, legitimacy, and advisability of infant baptism have been addressed from many different angles. The question has been posed in historical terms (did the primitive Church baptize infants?), in pastoral terms (is baptizing people in infancy the best way to socialize them?), in ecclesiological terms (is the Church intended by Christ one that requires adult commitment?), and in sacramental terms (are the sacraments such that they can be effective without the free and knowing cooperation of the recipient?). But the question has rarely if ever been posed theologically (is there any place in the divine economy for the child as child?) or christologically (what soteriological value is to be ascribed to the infancy and childhood of Jesus?).

Third, infant baptism tends to be favored by those who see the sacraments primarily in terms of the work of God and to be opposed by those who see the sacraments primarily as divinely instituted ways of responding to God's Word. Thus pedobaptists characteristically justify infant initiation on the grounds that it is prime evidence of God's initiative in human salvation; antipedobaptists see God's merciful initiative as located in his intelligible Word, to which only a conscious and informed mind can offer adequate submission. Thus the arguments for or against infant baptism at a doctrinal level appear to be *au fond* arguments about the relative value of Word and sacrament. Does the Word merely prepare for the sacrament? Does the sacrament merely seal our acceptance of the Word in faith? Is baptism the beginning and precondition of further Christian socialization, or is it its crowning moment? Once again, though, the problem with posing the question in this way is that it still neglects to pay any serious attention to the condition of the child as child. Neither the view of the child as not-yet-adult, nor the view that baptism "infuses" a supernatural habitus of faith, hope, and love into the infant, takes seriously the possibility that the infant might live a life of faith, hope, and love precisely as a child and precisely as a child-in-relationship within the context of its own *ecclesia*, the Christian family.

Fourth, the history of the theology of baptism would seem to corroborate the thesis first put forward by Philippe Ariès, namely, that the characteristic attitude of adults towards children until modern times was one of indifference. In his classic work *Centuries of Childhood*, published in 1962, Ariès sets out to refute those pundits who idealize the family life of previous generations while decrying the degeneration of family life in the contemporary world. In this mission Ariès admirably succeeds, painting what must seem to us a shocking portrait of neglect and abuse in the raising of children in the medieval and early modern periods. He concludes that adults, including mothers, were generally ignorant of the inner life of the child and, what is more, indifferent to it. Children under the age of six or seven were not really considered as persons but as subrational and thus subhuman. Ariès, of course, is talking about cultural attitudes and about a culture in which the concepts of childhood and family as we understand them had not yet emerged. This cultural mindset does not preclude genuine instances of love for children, of course, any more than our culture's high valuing of children is able to prevent the continuing abuse and exploitation of children in our own society.

Ariès' study on the medieval and early modern periods finds an echo in Robert Pattison's survey of the place of the child in the literature of classical and late antiquity. He writes:

> Certainly the most striking feature of classical literature's attitude towards children is the thunderous silence that envelopes the idea of childhood, especially when compared to the outpouring of concern and attention recent centuries have produced on the same subject.

"The classical silence does not necessarily indicate indifference," he argues; yet he admits that "Roman infants were largely neglected before they came to a reasonable age. . . . Childhood raised a few questions and evoked only the slenderest train of associations. The child may have contained the possibility of perfection, but until the possibility actually bore fruit, he remained subrational and therefore subliterary."[38]

It is really only in the seventeenth and eighteenth centuries that Pattison begins to find the child coming to play a role in English literature, a finding which matches Ariès' claim that it was only at this period that the concept of childhood began to emerge. Before that time and to a very large extent for a long while afterwards, children were usually regarded as defective adults. Infancy and young childhood represented a precarious and insignificant introduction to life which properly began somewhere between the ages of four and seven, when the child—now able to speak, understand, and act—was given more or less complete admission to adult life.

In a more recent study of childrearing in seventeenth-century France, David Hunt has introduced an important qualification to Ariès' thesis. He writes:

> Far from viewing the unfolding of infantile potentials with benign indifference, grownups in that period were deeply disturbed by some aspects of the orality, the obstinacy, and the sexuality of their offspring and made determined efforts to mold or thwart altogether such inclinations.[39]

What this correction to Ariès seems to suggest is what the history of the doctrine of original sin would also seem to indicate: children have either been dismissed as subhuman because subrational and thus ignored, or their wilfulness has been recognized and has come to serve as a hook for the projection of adult fears and fantasies. As we remarked before, it is the latter attitude which seems largely to have prevailed in the West until relatively recent times, making children bear the brunt of adult anxieties about sin and salvation.[40] It is only in the twentieth century that serious studies of childhood have come into their own, but even so, serious theological reflection on the matter has hardly begun.[41]

A New Approach to Infant Initiation

There are at least three different angles from which a fresh evaluation of the practice of initiating infants to the Christian life might be approached.

From the perspective of the Church itself, which has to be concerned with the effective socialization of each new generation if it is to survive, the whole issue of what constitutes an effective way of socializing needs to be looked at and the place of sacramental celebrations within such a process needs to be considered.[42] It remains the case that because such socialization is presumed to be parish-based, it is only undertaken with preschoolers at the earliest. The Church apparently has nothing to say to or about young children from the time they are baptized shortly after birth until the time when they are old enough to be enrolled in preschool religious education programs. Thus pastoral practice is at odds with the rhetoric of the Second Vatican Council and of the baptismal liturgy, which speaks of the parents and the family as "the first and foremost educators of their children."[43] Any worthwhile rethinking of the Christian formation of the children of believers will therefore have to take both the children and the family more seriously as active participants in the life of the Church.

This would mean, in turn, that the perspective of the family itself needs to be considered and its experience taken into account. More specifically the Christian family is called to understand the events of its life—especially something as significant as pregnancy and childbirth—in the light of faith, and to recognize the birth of each new child not only as a gift of God in some generic sense but as a specific word-event of God addressed to them.

Finally the event of baptism needs to be reflected upon from the child's point of view, once it is admitted that there is such a thing as a child's point of view. This would mean exploring how it can be said that the child as *child* can be said to be delivered from sin, adopted by God, incorporated into Christ, and made a dwelling-place of the Holy Spirit.

Here we shall leave the ecclesiastical angle aside to focus more closely on the family and the child. We shall first explore the implications of a theology of the family as a "domestic church" and then look at the possibility of regarding the child as an active participant in the sacramental process.

The Family as Church. The key to a new understanding of infant baptism is the vision of the family as a domestic church, *ecclesiola in ecclesia*, in virtue both of baptism and of the sacrament of marriage.[44] This means that the family, a communion of life in Christ within the larger communion of the local and universal Church, participates in the mystery of the one Church as a sacrament of Christ and in the threefold operation of the Church's priestly, prophetic, and royal mission. Indeed, whatever can be said of the Church as a whole can be said, *mutatis mutandis*, of the Christian family. Where the arrival of a new child and the decision for baptism are concerned, this ecclesial identity of the family suggests the following observations.

a. The family, exercising its prophetic function, has to discern the meaning of pregnancy, childbirth, and parenting, not in general but in terms of the birth of this particular child at this particular time. As Herbert Anderson points out, this is not a cue for mindless romanticizing.[45] Very often feelings about the child are ambivalent, while the emotional and physical costs involved in pregnancy, birth, and childrearing are high, the future prospects may appear daunting. It is, in any case, from the specifics of the event and the actual history of its occurrence that faith will seek to read the merciful will of God, so that the event becomes itself a moment of revelation, a Word of God expressed in the contingencies of family life.

b. The events of conception, pregnancy, birth, and parenthood, read in faith, evoke in turn the priestly function of the domestic church: a priesthood exercised in thanksgiving and intercession certainly, but also in the rituals and "sacraments" of family life which include everything from prenatal diet and exercise to the most mundane aspects of caring for the newborn.

c. The word and sacrament encountered and lived in the domestic setting find their fulfillment and their touchstone in the liturgical proclamation and celebration of the local church, especially in the sacraments of the bath, the oil, and the table. Here the old axiom *sacramenta propter homines* (sacraments are for people) needs to be complemented with the corresponding axiom *sacramenta propter ecclesiam* (sacraments are for the Church). In contrast to the scholastic identification of the purpose of the sacraments as twofold—forgiveness and sanctification—the Second Vatican Council teaches that the sacraments have a triple purpose: to sanctify, to build up the Church, to glorify God (SC 59). Thus baptism is to be understood as celebrated not only for the recipient but for the benefit of the whole community of faith. Realistically this means that baptism is celebrated not only for the infant but for the parents and siblings and for the parish. This is not to suggest, as sometimes seems to be suggested, that the baptism is *really* for the parents or that infant baptism justifies itself as a "teachable moment" in the life of the parents. In a more profound sense the liturgy of baptism depends for its ability to "translate" the child from outside to inside the Church upon the reconstituting of that Church in the liturgical assembly and particularly upon the reconstituting of the family in its organic unity as an *ecclesiola in ecclesia*. If the child is baptized in the faith of the Church, then the identity of the family as constituted by faith, as itself a sacrament of faith, must be "confected" anew in the process and event of sacramental initiation. In short, the family is part of the sacramental sign of baptism and will be confirmed as such by taking its part in the enactment of the rites themselves.[46]

d. The family-as-Church is probably the best context, too, in which to address the issue of what it means to say that baptism is for the forgiveness of sins, or that baptism "washes away" original sin. A major problem with much discussion of the doctrine of original sin is that it is not always sufficiently acknowledged that the concept of original sin is derived by way of contrast to the prior concept of the new life of Christ made available in baptism, and is thus to be understood in contrast to the life of the Spirit lived in the communion of the Church. If St. Augustine led us to think of this contrast in terms of natural generation versus sacramental regeneration, a way of resolving the embarrassments provoked by some of the formulations deriving from this contrast (for example, on the inherent sinfulness of sexual activity even within a sacramental marriage) would be to highlight the mystery of the Church—and thus of the Christian family—as the embodied mystery of grace. Such an embodiment of God's eschatologically victorious grace in Jesus Christ is never totally unambiguous: we see now only as in a glass darkly. But the ambivalence of marriage and of the family is matched by the ambivalence of the Church itself as a social and historical institution, pointing beyond itself only more or less adequately, both being natural institutions as well as sacraments of life in Christ.

Just as the Church has consistently to remind herself and others of her otherworldly inner nature, so, too, must the family. This being so, the celebration of baptism for the forgiveness of sins, for the overcoming of alienation from God, would serve to reinforce the intentionality of the family in its specific role as a community of Christ's holiness and grace in the world. The dual nature of the Christian family requires a "double birth" for each new child: the one in the delivery room and the one in the baptistery.

Were the child of Christian parents not baptized, the opportunity of re-presenting its vocation to holiness would be passed up and the ambivalence of the family would be rendered all the more ambiguous. Correspondingly if a family merely "goes through the motions" of having its child baptized without at the same time taking stock of its own vocation to be a sacrament of grace and holiness, the child would be validly baptized as a member of the institutional Church, but the reality signified by membership of the Church—participation in the very life of God, which is forgiveness of sin—would be unlikely to be realized, and the shadow of original sin would still linger over the child precisely because that shadow would be cast by members of the family. The overcoming of original sin by the grace of Christ is not magic. It happens sacramentally, that is, through signs. It happens because the rite is a sacrament of the faith of the Church which, where a small child is concerned, is in effect the faith of the family. Where the family does not consciously live the life of faith and grace, it is hard to see how baptism can then and there be fruitful for the forgiveness of sin. The child will have to await the effective intervention of some other representative of the faithful Church for its baptism to "revive" and to become fruitful in the life of grace and faith.[47]

The Child as Subject of Sacramental Initiation. For the historical reasons suggested above, children, especially the newborn, have traditionally been regarded as passive recipients of adult ministrations: clean tablets to be written on, clay to be molded by parental hands. Or else they were seen as active only in manifesting the signs of concupiscence, the fallen will. As Robert Pattison observes: "In the Augustinian view, the child is perhaps subrational, but this is of no importance and properly the business of philosophy, not religion. More important, the child is a creature of will, a sinner *ab ovo* and in this no different from adults."[48]

Such primitive psychotheologizing can no longer be entertained in the wake of the immense amount of research done in this century into the world of the child. Andrew Thompson has brought together an impressive array of insights into the child's experience of the world, especially in terms of the child's relationship to its parents and siblings.[49] We shall be content here to highlight some aspects of this recovery of childhood which relate to the capacity of the child for sacramental initiation.

Before that can be done, however, there is a preliminary step to be taken. Unless there are good reasons for thinking that the child *as child* has some part in the economy of grace and may be called, precisely as a small child, to witness as part of the sacramentality of the whole Church which is "a sacrament or sign of intimate union with God and of the unity of all mankind" (LG 1), there is a danger of romanticizing childhood and of reading into the life of the child salvific realities in fact suspended until such time as the child gradually acquires those adult characteristics of intellect and will, and which are the preconditions for their realization. But, as Karl Rahner has demonstrated, there is every reason to believe that childhood not only falls within the compass of God's grace, but that

> childhood itself has a direct relationship with God. It touches upon the absolute divinity of God not only as maturity, adulthood and the later phases of life touch upon this, but rather in a special way of its own. . . . The fact that it contributes to the later stages of life is not the sole criterion of its own intrinsic rightness.[50]

Not the least of our grounds for believing that this is the case is to be found in the Incarnation itself. "What was not assumed is not redeemed," is the old patristic axiom, but childhood was assumed. Irenaeus put this best:

> Christ came to save all [human beings] by himself: all, I say, who through him are reborn in God: infants and children, youths and adults, and the elderly. For this it was that he lived through every age [of life]: made an infant for the sake of infants; a child for the children, sanctifying those of that age and setting them an example of devotion, fairness and obedience; a youth for the sake of young people, becoming an example for them and sanctifying them for God. . . .[51]

Thus infants and young children are sanctified in principle insofar as the Son of God became a child and lived through childhood's experiences in total union with the will of the Father, thereby redeeming infancy and childhood. Thereafter, childhood lived in the Spirit of Christ—albeit necessarily in a preconscious and prereflective way—is sanctified and may be seen as a sign of the glory of God and of the unity of the redeemed human family.

Let us briefly spell out the implications of this with reference particularly to those aspects of the baptismal event which infant baptism might be supposed to obscure.

Faith and the Sacrament of Faith. While all the sacraments of the Church are sacraments of faith, the term applies particularly to baptism, which, from the New Testament onwards, has always included the candidate's profession of faith. It was for this reason that the Anabaptists and their successors have denied the validity of infant baptism, and that some modern Catholics have been led to question its value. There is no denying that the practice of having parents or godparents answer the faith interrogation on behalf of the child was inappropriate at best and a subterfuge at worst.[52] It was simply a way of getting around the fact that the candidate was *in statu infantis*. What helped compound the problem was the increasing tendency to consider faith primarily in cognitive terms.

It is not clear that St. Augustine had a conceptual understanding of faith in mind when he spoke of the child being baptized in the faith of the Church,[53] but this understanding was certainly operative in the twelfth and thirteenth centuries when the issue arose again.[54] Recognizing that a child cannot "believe" in the sense of making an active submission of the intellect, St. Thomas Aquinas taught that in baptism

faith was infused as a habitus, which he defined as "a quality not easily removed, whereby one may act easily and pleasantly."[55] It is hard to
see what sense can be made of the idea of "infusing" a child with the
capacity for acts of faith, especially when the analogy is drawn, for the
purposes of distinguishing between the virtue of faith and its exercise,
between a child and a sleeping adult.

Instead of redefining faith to fit in with one's preconceived notions of
infancy, however, it might be more fruitful to reconsider the child and its
capacity for some kind of life of faith even in its status as an infant.
Clearly an infant is prerational. If faith is conceived of simply as an act of
grace-enlightened reason, then the child has nothing to do but wait until
its rational capacities are sufficiently developed as to be able to cooperate with grace. Its Christian life, like its adult life, remains a thing of the
future. But the Second Vatican Council moved to counter an excessively
cognitive view of faith with a return to the Pauline concept of faith as an
"obedience of faith," which it went on to define as that obedience
"whereby a person entrusts his whole self freely to God."[56] For an older
child or an adult this will surely mean, as the council says, "offering full
submission of intellect and will to God who reveals, and freely assenting
to the truth revealed by him."[57] But this second part of the definition is a
specification of what it means to entrust one's whole self freely to God, a
specification which undoubtedly applies to all who have attained the
use of reason, but which does not preclude the possibility that those
such as infants and retarded adults might not also live a life of total dependence upon God. Indeed, it is the infant and the "youngest child"
who constantly bring the subversive message of the Gospel as salvation
by obedience of faith to a Church constantly prone to place too much
confidence in its intellectual respectability.[58]

James Fowler has proposed a view of faith which corresponds
closely to the conciliar understanding of theological faith. In Fowler's
view, faith need not be necessarily thought of as an exclusively religious phenomenon. "Rather," he suggests, "faith becomes the designa-
tion for a way of leaning into life. It points to a way of making sense of
one's existence. It denotes a way of giving order and coherence to the
force-field of life. It speaks of the investment of life-grounding trust
and life-orienting commitment."[59]

As he goes on to point out, this understanding of faith "means to
imply that is it a human universal." He traces its development through
infancy and early childhood and argues that the development of faith
of some kind, some sort of making sense of the world, some sense of

what one may base one's trust on and what makes life worthwhile, is an inevitable development in every child. Even before it becomes articulate—if indeed it ever becomes articulate about its faith, for this "leaning into life" is rarely brought to full consciousness—the child comes to faith. The question then is less one of whether a child can "have" faith than it is a question of the kind of faith it comes in fact to exercise in the first weeks and months of life. There is no need to have recourse to St. Thomas Aquinas's distinction between *habitus* and *actus*, tailored as it is to a cognitive understanding of faith. With a pre-cognitive understanding of faith, the child is seen, from the moment of its birth, to be enacting its developing faith as it encounters its human environment, experiences dependency and separation, shared meanings and ritual patterns, provision for its bodily needs, and a sense of its own social and sexual identity.[60] Faith is a holistic, prerational sense of who we are and of the kind of world we live in, an integrated vision of how things are and what it all means. From a theological perspective, then, what is at issue in the celebration of the sacraments is not so much whether the candidates have faith, but of whether their faith is faith in the God who raised Jesus from the dead. For adults this means that evangelizing is a matter of uprooting false faith as well as a matter of communicating true faith, a realization that has enormous implications for the catechumenate. For the children of the Church, it means forming them in right faith from infancy. To wait until they attain the use of reason is already to wait too long and to leave their faith to chance.

For Christians right faith is baptismal faith and baptismal faith is paschal faith. But how can infants be said to be baptized into such faith?

Paschal faith is the faith which was Christ's, the faith whereby he was made perfect through suffering and consistently surrendered his life into the hands of the God who alone could save him out of death (see Heb 5:7-8). Such a pattern, as something lived out by the community of the baptized, is what constitutes the faith of the Church. By baptism we have been fitted into a pattern of surrender and exaltation, of self-abandonment and deliverance, of dying and being raised. But such a pattern, far from being alien to the life of the child, is intrinsic to it. Having experienced the trauma of separation from the womb, the child is confronted with the task of learning to live as both autonomous and yet dependent, caught between the desire for communion and the need to accept separation, instinctively struggling to satisfy its own immediate needs yet learning to wait in trust for what it really needs. "The nerve to separate," says Fowler of the many experiences of separation and nonfulfillment in the infant's life, "depends upon the assured return to communion."[61]

Now this is clearly not the same as adult conversion (though it would seem to be something that would condition the very possibility of genuine adult conversion), but neither is it merely an illustration of some aspect of the paschal mystery. Is it not rather the paschal mystery as lived by every child that is born into this world? Or perhaps we should turn that around and say that Christ, in assuming our human condition, assumed the pattern which constitutes one of the most basic tasks of every human life and redeemed it. Unless we wish to withhold the life of the small child altogether from the drama of redemption, must we not see here, *in statu infantis*, the primordial and universal pattern of human life Christ assumed and redeemed? Is it not because of false faith, trust in false gods and false values, that sin has such an obvious hold upon the world? Sin cannot be reduced simply to individual, conscious, wilful acts. Similarly the redemptive gift of paschal faith, the Christlike way of "leaning into life," is not necessarily anything which has to await our conscious decision or deliberate choice. It is rather something we discover to be already operative in us by the grace of God by the time we become aware of it.

This grace, this gift of faith, comes through hearing, through the Word of God addressed to the child. But the Word here is not the written Word, as yet unavailable to the infant, so much as the biblical *dabar*, mediated in this instance by the community of faith and especially the believing family. Thus it is not so much that baptism infuses faith into a child as that baptism is the deliberate and conscious insertion of the child into the environment of faith, which faith is the faith of the Church, which in turn is the faith of Christ himself. If the Church did not continue to live by the pattern of Christ's own faith in its dying and being raised to life, it would cease to be Church. Such existential faith constitutes the identity of the Church and the identity of the family as domestic church. It is into this faith that the child is baptized when it is baptized in the faith of the Church.

Integration into the Church. A major stumbling block to Anabaptist recognition of the validity of infant baptism is the view of the Church as a participative community of faith and mutual correction. Though situated at the opposite end of the baptismal spectrum, Roman Catholics seem to share the view that infants, being purely passive, are incapable of actively engaging in the life of the faith community. Believers' Churches apparently consider that the child has nothing to contribute to the faith life and witness of the local congregation, while Catholics, by neglecting small children between *quamprimum* baptism and the age of reason, seem to regard the child as unfit for active participation in community life. Why else should children, alone of all the baptized, be barred from confirmation and Eucharist?

In fact, however, as Andrew Thompson amply demonstrates, a newborn infant alters the configuration of family relationships from the day of its birth, if not sooner, having a major impact on the lives of its parents and siblings. Nor should this impact be seen as merely financial or psychological. The Second Vatican Council spoke perhaps more truly than it knew when it said: "As living members of the family, children contribute in their own way to making their parents holy" (GS 48). Stanley Hauerwas puts the point more strongly when he writes that

> a good deal of sentimental drivel is written about children. Sentimentality not only belies the hard reality of caring for children, but worse, it avoids the challenge with which they confront us. Generally our children challenge the kind of self-image that finds its most intense expression in the expectations we have for them. If we are lucky, these expectations are modified by our children's refusal to be what we want them to be. . . . Children train us not only to be parents, but sometimes even better parents.[62]

Translating this into the terms of Christian theology, we might say that children bring both joy and the Cross. Children will test the sacrificial self-commitment, the self-delusions, and the spurious faith of those with whom they come in contact for any length of time. They summon parents particularly to a deeper understanding of the mystery of grace and of the limitations of human abilities. They probe the ambivalences of their "way of leaning into life." But they also evoke a spirit of wonder and benediction and become messengers of unsolicited consolation. All this is merely to suggest that in their own way children in fact play an extremely active, even prophetic, role in the household of faith. The obstacle lies not in the child but in the faithlessness of the adult believers. If there is any reason for not admitting an infant to faith and baptismal life in the communion of the Church, it may only be that the child's own God-given household is not faithful.

Theology of Baptism. We have already noted that one of the most significant effects of the introduction of the adult catechumenate and a unified rite of sacramental initiation for adults has been the recovery of a fuller and richer understanding of baptism. In comparison with the rich heritage of patristic teaching on baptism, most modern Christians have inherited a drastically impoverished understanding of the wealth and wonder of the baptismal life. As we also noted, there is sometimes a tendency to blame this impoverishment on infant baptism, though it would probably be more accurate to say that it is the result of the institutionalization of *emergency* baptism. Conversely, the recovery of the paschal dimensions of baptism is sometimes promoted in such a way as to challenge, if not to preclude altogether, the practice of infant initiation. We attempted to suggest that this conclusion need not necessarily follow, since while some aspects of a positive theology of baptism (for example, adoption) are very much congruent with the baptizing of small children, other aspects (for example, dying and rising) can be seen to be viable even for infants, provided the state of infancy is carefully considered. But besides the questions of faith and participation in the paschal mystery already touched on, there are other important dimensions of sacramental initiation which are actually highlighted by the baptism of a small child.

A newly baptized infant is not merely one who is delivered from sin and from the threat of damnation, but one claimed by the irrescindable Word of God to be an adopted child of God, a living member of Christ, a temple of the Holy Spirit. The child in baptism enters into a new set of relationships with God, with the Church, and—we have argued—with its own family. In this instance, at least, water is thicker than blood! From early in our tradition comes the story of the father of the great Alexandrian theologian, Origen. This historian Eusebius reports: "It is said that often when the boy was asleep, he would bend over him and bare his breast and, as if it were the temple of the Spirit of God, would kiss it reverently and count himself blessed in his promising child."[63]

St. John Chrysostom reflects the same sort of sentiment in an Easter sermon:

> Those who were prisoners yesterday are free men and citizens of the Church. Those who so recently were in sin and shame now enjoy righteousness and security. They are not only free, but holy; not only holy, but righteous; not only righteous, but children; not only children, but heirs; not only heirs, but brothers and sisters of Christ; not only brothers and

sisters of Christ, but co-heirs with him; not only co-heirs with Christ, but members of him; not only members of Christ, but temples; not only temples, but instruments of the Holy Spirit.

Blessed be God, for he has done wonders! (Ps 72:18) Do you realize how manifold are the blessings of baptism? While many believe that the remission of sins is the sole benefit of baptism, we have counted ten. That is why we baptize even tiny children, even though they have no sins, that they might gain righteousness, filiation, inheritance, and the grace of being brothers and sisters and members of Christ and the grace of being the dwelling-place of the Holy Spirit.[64]

Furthermore one must agree with Karl Barth that "too little attention has been paid to baptism as a glorifying of God, that is, as a moment of his self-revelation. . . . While baptism does its cognitive work . . . the far greater and primary thing occurs: God receives glory in that he himself, as man recognizes him in truth, once more secures his just due here on earth."[65]

Admittedly Barth is thinking here of believers' baptism, but his words apply equally well, it would seem, to infant baptism as an act of thanksgiving and glorification of God. But it is important to draw a clear distinction between infant baptism and various forms that exist for giving thanks for the birth of a child. While childbirth is itself a striking moment of religious disclosure—one sufficiently powerful to have lent itself and its terminology as a metaphor even for adult initiation—and while it is properly a moment for the blessing of God, baptism cannot be reduced to a celebration of birth. A service of thanksgiving for the safe delivery of a child should be an option for those whose faith extends so far, but who are uncertain as to the meaning of the order of redemption and of Christian baptism, and whose allegiance to the community of faith is consequently less than firm. But it should be clear to believers and unbelievers alike that baptism is more than a celebration of birth. It is, as we have already stressed, a celebration and sacrament of rebirth: it is incorporation into the Body of Christ and into the pattern of his death and exaltation; it is a divine act of adoption, whereby a child is claimed by God for his own kind purposes; it is a consecration and sanctification effected by the outpouring of the Holy Spirit of Christ; it is an anointing with the Spirit of holiness for life and mission in this world and for the sanctification of the divine Name, in this world and in the world to come.

All this belongs to a child in principle, as surely and as undeservedly as the kingdom belongs to the heir apparent. Like many an heir apparent, the Christian child may be defrauded of its birthright, may even grow up knowing nothing of it. But, for all that, baptism remains a performative act with certain ineluctable entailments which, even though they may be frustrated by the faithlessness of the family or parish, remain nevertheless eternally valid.

Since the practice of infant baptism predates the Augustinian doctrine of original sin, and since that doctrine has not played the major role in the East that it has in the West, one must assume that it is these positive benefits of baptism which have long underlain the Church's instinct to admit infants and small children to the font and the altar. In any case the practice of baptizing infants does not depend for its legitimacy upon the belief that without baptism infants are excluded forever from the vision of God. But it does suppose that possibility that infants *as infants* might be called to share the divine life in the Body of Christ, a possibility which, as we have argued, derives substantial support both from the fact that the Church has always baptized infants and from the insights into the nature of childhood gained from the research of the human sciences.

But while every human being is called to share the life of God, it is obvious that not every human being is called to live as a member of the Church. In the case of an infant born into a believing family, however, there is an a priori assumption that the fact of its being born into an ecclesial community constitutes a reasonable indication that this child is called by God to grace and to glory within the communion of the visible Church. This has nothing to do with John Calvin's assertion that the Old Testament precept concerning circumcision continues to operate under the new covenant. On the contrary, the distinctions we have made between first birth and second birth, between baptism and a celebration of thanksgiving, clearly indicate that Christian identity is precisely not inherited from Christian parents, but that the "accident" of being born into a practicing Christian household is rather an indication of the child's vocation, which it is the duty of the Church to affirm, ratify, and nurture. Consequently whenever a child is presented for baptism, it will be the responsibility of the local community to discern whether this child is certainly called to the life of faith by looking at the faith life of the family. More positively, those with pastoral responsibilities will take seriously the ecclesial character of the family as a household of faith and seek to raise the community's awareness of the sacramentality of the family.

Infant Baptism as a Sacrament for the Church. There was a time when the definition of a sacrament tended to focus on the matter and form of each sacrament, thus tending to depersonalize the sacraments.

The twentieth-century renewal of sacramental theology has overcome this narrow and static understanding by seeing the sacraments more dynamically as an interaction between the recipient and the minister who, representing the Church, represents Christ. More recently the public and ecclesial dimension of the sacraments has been recovered, enabling us to recognize that sacraments, when properly celebrated, are meant to redound to the benefit not only of the recipient but of the whole ecclesial community. Such an understanding finds authoritative expression, for example, in the General Introduction to the Order of Penance which goes so far as to say that "the faithful Christian, as he experiences and proclaims the mercy of God in his life, celebrates with the priest *the liturgy with which the Church continually renews itself*" (par. 11, emphasis added).

The truth of this axiom is, of course, even more apparent in the experience of the RCIA, which is teaching us that the initiation of new members not only affects their own lives, but calls for new configurations of relationships within the host community itself.

In infant baptism, we have argued, the ecclesial ramifications of the rite have immediate importance for the family, which is reconstituted by the liturgy of baptism in its God-given identity as a household of faith, a domestic church. Thus the importance of the renewal of baptismal promises (for the parents no longer speak in the name of the child, but in their own name) consists in the fact that the making of the promises is a sacramental act as well as a moral commitment: it is the family actualizing itself as a domestic household of faith within the communion of the local assembly. The formulae of renunciation and profession of faith are, as it were, words of consecration whereby the local church confects itself as a living sacrament of faith. This perspective on the family-as-ecclesial-sacrament enables us then to grasp more profoundly what is meant by speaking of the parents in particular as the child's "first teachers of the faith." Stanley Hauerwas makes this point more broadly applicable when he says that the Church does not *do* religious education, but *is* a form of education that is religious.

> Religious education is not . . . something that is done to make us Christians, or something that is done after we have become Christians; rather it is the ongoing training in those skills necessary for us to live faithful to God's Kingdom that has been initiated in Jesus. For that Kingdom is constituted by a story that one never possesses, but rather constantly challenges us to be what we have not yet become.[66]

Consequently, parents do not so much promise at their children's baptism to teach them merely what they know. Instead, they commit themselves anew to learning the story by living it, and it is chiefly by the parents living the Christian story that their children will come to pick it up and to develop the skills necessary to be faithful to it. The story and the skills are only partially conveyed in explicit lessons. Christianity, it has been said, is more caught than taught, and the model for learning it is close to that of an apprenticeship than that of a classroom. In this apprenticeship the accent is on doing the things that Christians do, which makes the practice of withholding from small children the anointing of the Spirit and regular participation at the eucharistic table all the more unfortunate.[67] It suggest that these sacraments are rewards for lessons learned or markers in the child's growth to maturity, instead of being what they are, namely, the means of our continuing formation in Christian fidelity.

But besides the immediate liturgical sacramental dimensions of infant baptism for the family and the local church, there is also the question of whether, when the sacraments of initiation are made accessible to small children, something important is not gained for the Church's own self-understanding. This is not the place to discuss whether and in what sense adult initiation might be said to be "normative," but even if this were to be admitted, it could not be used to disparage the practice of infant initiation as such, except at the cost of departing from the Catholic tradition or at least sacrificing significant elements of that tradition. N. P. Williams in *The Ideas of the Fall and Original Sin*[68] identifies two sets of conflicting ideas in the theology of redemption: those associated with what he calls the image of the "once born" and those associated with the image of being "twice born." The former gives rise to a theology which stresses continuity and growth in human life, the latter to a theology which highlights conversion and discontinuity. While we would resist, for reasons given earlier, any attempt to describe infants who are baptized as "once born," the contrast between a theology of continuity and a theology of discontinuity accurately summarizes the differences between those who support infant baptism and those who see it as difficult to reconcile with the evangelical values manifest in adult conversion and adult initiation.

Adult baptism, the economy of the "twice born," tends to draw to itself the vocabulary of regeneration as opposed to generation; of brothers and sisters rather than sons and daughters; of voluntary decision rather than divine vocation; of change rather than faithfulness; of breaking with the past rather than growth towards the future; of death and resurrection rather than adoption and filiation. The language of infant initiation, on the other hand, is inclined to speak in terms of the womb rather than the tomb, of election rather than choice, of loyalty rather than commitment, of the preconscious operations of grace rather than of personal convictions, of nurturing the life of faith rather than of passing from unbelief to belief. In Jungian terms, a regime which attaches importance to infant initiation gives a larger role to the "feminine" aspects of Christianity, while adult initiation displays the more "masculine" elements of Christian imagery.

While there are many other and stronger reasons for upholding the baptism of infants, this would seem a further argument for retaining it. At a time when the Church is so intent on rescuing the humane values of Christianity and is concerned to do greater justice to the role of the family and to the Christian vision of sexuality, and at a time when the role of the nonrational and prerational dimensions of the life of faith is being recovered,[69] perhaps infant initiation ought to be seen less as a problem to be grappled with than as an opportunity to be grasped. Far from barring children from the font, the chrism, and the altar, the Church should welcome their participation in these sacraments as a reminder both of the catholicity of the Church and of the fact that, no matter how informed or committed we might be as adults, when we take part in the sacramental liturgies of the Church we are taking part in more than we know.

Conclusion

Historically speaking, the practice of infant baptism always seems to have preceded and in some way eluded attempts to justify it theologically. It seems to have been more a matter of the Church's instinct than the putting into effect of a clearly thought out strategy, while attempts to make sense of it have always fallen short of success. Similarly with this essay. It would be foolish to claim that the argument is now settled, but it may legitimately be claimed, if the arguments advanced here hold water, that the grounds of the discussion need to be changed. This in turn will influence practice, since a fresh grasp of what is involved in baptizing an infant will suggest ways of assessing when baptism may properly be celebrated for infants, how it may be prepared for, and most importantly how it may be lived in a process of ongoing initiation to the life of faith in the context of family and parish.

Central to this reconsideration of baptism, however, will be theological reflection on the data of the human sciences concerning the child-in-relationship.

---

[1] Stephen W. Sykes, "The Sacraments," in *Christian Theology*, eds. Peter C. Hodgson and Robert H. King, rev. ed. (Philadelphia, 1985) 274–301.

[2] Among a very extensive literature, the following must be accounted the most significant works: Oscar Cullmann, *Baptism in the New Testament* (London, 1950); Karl Barth, *The Teaching of the Church Concerning Baptism* (London, 1948); Karl Barth, *Church Dogmatics* IV:4 (Edinburgh, 1969); Markus Barth, *Die Taufe ein Sakrament?* (Zollikon-Zurich, 1951); Kurt Aland, *Did the Early Church Baptize Infants?* (Philadelphia, 1960); Joachim Jeremias, *Infant Baptism in the First Four Centuries* (Philadelphia, 1960). More recently see Paul Jewett, *Infant Baptism and the Covenant of Grace* (Grand Rapids, 1978) and Geoffrey W. Bromiley, *Children of Promise* (Grand Rapids, 1979).

[3] J.D.C. Fisher, *Christian Initiation. Baptism in the Medieval West. A Study in the Disintegration of the Primitive Rite of Initiation*, Alcuin Club, n. 47 (London, 1965). See *Catechism of the Council of Trent* II, iii, 17 (Dublin, 1829) 183.

[4] Eusebius, *The History of the Church* VI, 43:20, trans. G. A. Williamson (Minneapolis, 1975) 283.

[5] E. C. Whitaker, *Documents of the Baptismal Liturgy*, Alcuin Club, n. 42 (London, 1970) 222–3.

[6] Cfr. M. Righetti, *Storia liturgica*, IV (Milan, 1953) 82–3; P. de Puniet, *Le sacrementaire romain de Gellone*. Bibliotheca Ephemerides Liturgicae IV (Rome, 1938) 90–1.

[7] DS 1349.

[8] P.-M. Gy, "*Quamprimum*. Note sur le baptême des enfants," *La Maison Dieu* 32 (1952) 124–9.

[9] See note 3 above.

[10] Interest in the history of childhood is relatively recent, largely inaugurated by Philippe Ariès' benchmark study, *Centuries of Childhood* (New York, 1962). For a reassessment of Ariès' claims, see *The History of Childhood*, Lloyd de Mausse, ed. (New York, 1974) and David Hunt, *Parents and Children in History. The Psychology of Family Life in Early Modern France* (New York, 1970). It is now clear that the "age of reason" or "age of discretion," typically identified in Roman Catholic sources as around the age of seven to ten years, is less a determinate stage of psychological maturity than a juridical-social convention. Thus under Anglo-Saxon law a child who reached the age of seven could no longer be sold into slavery, while under Roman Law a child of that age became liable for criminal acts. In general it was the age at about which children began to mix with adults in medieval life and work.

[11] So Cullmann, *Baptism in the New Testament*, 72–8, and Joachim Jeremias, *Infant Baptism*, 48–55. For an opposing viewpoint see G. R. Beasley-Murray, *Baptism in the New Testament* (Grand Rapids, 1973) 320–9.

[12] Kurt Aland, *Did the Early Church Baptize Infants?*

[13] *de baptismo*, 18. (ET: *Tertullian's Homily on Baptism*, trans. E. Evans [London, 1964] 36–8.)

[14] *de animata*, 39–40, C.S.L., II, 842-843.

[15] D. Michaélides, *Sacramentum chez Tertullien* (Paris, 1970).

[16] *de baptismo*, 19.

[17] The most celebrated instance of the deferment of baptism is St. Augustine himself. See *The Confessions of St. Augustine*, Bk. I, ch. 11, trans. John K. Ryan (Garden City, N.Y., 1960) 53–4.

[18] See Margaret Miles, "Infancy, Parenting and Nourishment in St. Augustine's Confessions," *Journal of the American Academy of Religion* 50 (1982) 3, 349–64.

[19] Ibid., 355.

[20] St. Augustine, *The City of God*, XXI, 4.

[21] *De ecclesiasticarum rerum exordiis et incrementis*, c. 27, text in J.-Ch. Didier, *Faut-il baptiser les enfants? La réponse de la tradition* (Paris) 239–40.

[22] *Sentences* V:6, text in Didier, *Faut-il baptiser les enfants?* 256.

[23] *Summa Theologiae*, Pars III, q. 69, art. 6.

[24] See Louis Dumont, "A Modified View of Our Origins: The Christian Beginnings of Modern Individualism," *Religion* 12 (1982) 1–27.

[25] H. Schwartz, "Early Anabaptist Ideas about the Nature of Children," *The Mennonite Quarterly Review* 47 (1973) 2, 104. See also James McClendon, "Why Baptists Do Not Baptize Children," *Concilium* 24 (1967) 7–14.

[26] For a summary of Luther's and Calvin's views on infant baptism, see E. Schlink, *The Doctrine of Baptism*, trans. H.J.A. Bouman (St. Louis, 1972) 130–70.

[27] For the main literature see note 2 above.

[28] Henri Bourgeois, "The Catechumenate in France Today," in *Becoming a Catholic Christian*, ed. W. J. Reedy (New York, 1979) 10–21.

[29] *Ordo initiationis christianae adultorum*, 1972 (ET: 1974, 1985).

[30] Aidan Kavanagh, *The Shape of Baptism* (New York, 1978) 109–14, 196–7. For an overview of Roman Catholic discussions of infant baptism, see Paul F. X. Covino, "The Postconciliar Infant Baptism Debate in the American Catholic Church," *Worship* 56 (1982) 240–60.

[31] Avery Dulles, *Models of the Church* (New York, 1974).

[32] R.-M. Roberge, "Un tournant dans la pastorale du baptême," *Laval Theologique et Philosophique* 31 (1975) 227–38 and 33 (1977) 3–22.

[33] *Rite for the Christian Initiation of Adults* (Washington, 1985) n. 41. See also Congregation for the Doctrine of the Faith, *Instruction on Infant Baptism* (Oct. 20, 1980) nn. 30–31. English text in *Origins* 10:30 (January 8, 1981) 479.

[34] Kavanagh, *The Shape of Baptism*, 199. For a trenchant review of Kavanagh's position, see T. A. Droege, "The Formation of Faith in Christian Initiation," *The Cresset* 66 (1983) 6, 16–23.

[35] Antonius Scheer, "Is the Easter Vigil a Rite of Passage?" in *Liturgy and Human Passage*, eds. David N. Power and Luis Maldonado (Concilium, 112) (New York, 1979) 50–61.

[36] André Benoit, *Le baptême chrétien au second siècle: la théologie des pères* (Paris, 1952).

[37] On the Syrian baptismal tradition see S. Brock, "Studies in the Early History of the Syrian Orthodox Baptismal Liturgy," *Journal of Theological Studies* n.s. 23 (1972) 16–64; Gabriele Winkler, "The Original Meaning of the Prebaptismal Anointing and Its Implications," *Worship* 42 (1978) 24–45; S. J. Beggiani, *Early Syriac Theology* (Lanham, Md., 1983) 101–24.

[38] Robert Pattison, *The Child Figure in English Literature* (Athens, Ga., 1978) 5–6.

[39] David Hunt, *Parents and Children in History*, 190.

[40] Nineteenth-century changes in cultural attitudes towards children and in corresponding approaches to childrearing appear to have been reflected in a gradual abandonment of the classical Augustinian teaching on original sin. See Bernard Wishy, *The Child and the Republic. The Dawn of Modern American Child Nurture* (Philadelphia, 1968); H. Sheldon Smith, *Changing Conceptions of Original Sin. A Study in American Theology since 1750* (New York, 1955).

[41] Karl Rahner, "Ideas for a Theology of Childhood," *Theological Investigations*, vol. VIII (New York, 1971) 33–50; Randolph C. Miller, "Theology and the Understanding of Children," *The Nature of Man in Theological and Psychological Perspective*, ed. Simon

Doniger (New York, 1962) 142–50; Nathan Mitchell, "The Parable of Childhood," *Liturgy* 1 (1981) 3, 7–12; Guy Bédouelle, "Reflections on the Place of the Child in the Church," *Communio* 12 (1985) 4, 349–67.

[42] See P. M. Zulehner, "Religionssoziologie und Kindertaufe" in *Christsein Ohne Entscheidung, oder Soll die Kirche Kinder Taufen?* ed., Walter Kasper (Mainz, 1970) 188–206.

[43] See *Rite for the Baptism of Children*, n. 70. See also nn. 5, 39, 56, 64.

[44] Second Vatican Council Dogmatic Constitution on the Church, n. 11; Pastoral Constitution on the Church in the Modern World, n. 48; Decree on the Apostolate of the Laity, n. 11; Decree on Christian Education, n. 3. The reference to the sacrament of marriage is not intended to preclude the possibility that single parent families or irregular marriages might not de facto be microchurches in virtue of the quality of the faith life and public witness of such families, but merely to underline the sacramental and ecclesial dimension formally established by a marriage witnessed by the Church.

[45] Herbert Anderson, "Pastoral Care in the Process of Initiation," in Mark Searle, ed., *Alternative Futures for Worship*, vol. 2: *Baptism and Confirmation* (Collegeville, 1987) 103–36.

[46] The willingness of the Church in the past to baptize dying infants without even consulting the parents is simply one aspect of the diminished sign value of emergency baptism. Other aspects would include the absence of an ecclesial community, the celebration of baptism outside the Easter season, the lack of a full ritual setting, and the omission of confirmation and Eucharist. Unfortunately Scholastic theology of the sacraments took such extreme cases as the starting point for a theology of baptism. The Second Vatican Council repudiated this approach by making the fullness of the sacramental sign, in all its communitarian and ritual dimensions, normative. See Constitution on the Liturgy, nn. 26, 27, 67.

[47] This view is consistent with that of Augustine (*Ep.* 98, 10) that the child unlike the adult cannot place an obstacle to the grace of the sacraments. Recognizing the mediation of the family in the sacramental process also necessitates recognizing that the family itself may constitute an obstacle to the child's life of grace.

[48] Pattison, *The Child Figure*, 18.

[49] Andrew D. Thompson, "Infant Baptism in the Light of the Human Sciences," in Mark Searle, ed., *Alternative Futures for Worship*, vol. 2: *Baptism and Confirmation* (Collegeville, 1987) 55–102.

[50] Rahner, "Ideas for a Theology of Childhood," 36–37.

[51] *Adversus haereses* II, 22.4. Text in Didier, *Faul-il baptiser les enfants?* 95.

[52] It is to be noted that in the Roman Catholic *Rite for the Baptism of Children*, the parents and godparents profess their own faith and do not presume to speak for the child. See nn. 2 (Latin text) and 56.

[53] St. Augustine uses *fides* and *credere* in several different ways. On the meaning of faith for Augustine, see among others: J. M. Egan, "'I believe in God': I. The Doctrine of St. Augustine," *Irish Ecclesiastical Record* 53 (1939) 630–6; R. Aubert, *Le problème de l'acte de la foi* (Louvain, 1945) 21–30; M. Loehrer, *Der Glaubensbegriff des hl. Augustinus* (Einsiedeln, 1955); Chr. Mohrmann, "Credere deo, credere deum, credere in deum," in *Mélanges J. de Ghellink*. Gembloux: Eds. J. Duculot, 1951, vol. I, 277–85.

[54] See note 10 above.

[55] *Summa Theologiae*, Pars III, q. 69, art. 4. See also III, q. 68, art. 9 and q. 69, art. 3. On the meaning of "faith" for St. Thomas, see Wilfrid Cantwell Smith, *Faith and Belief* (Princeton 1979) 78-91. See also Ibid., 70–8, on faith/*credo* in relation to baptism.

[56] Dogmatic Constitution on Divine Revelation, n. 5.

[57] Ibid.

[58] See R. Haughton, *Tales from Eternity* (New York, 1973) 19–49.

[59] James Fowler, "Perspectives on the Family from the Standpoint of Faith Development Theory," *Perkins Journal* (Fall 1979) 7.

[60] Erik Erikson. *Toys and Reasons. Stages in the Ritualization of Experience* (New York, 1977) esp. 85–92.

[61] Fowler, "Perspectives on the Family," 3.

[62] Stanley Hauerwas, "Learning Morality from Handicapped Children," *The Hastings Center Report* (October 1980) 45.

[63] Eusebius, *History of the Church* VI, 2:15, trans. G. A. Williamson (Minneapolis, 1975) 241.

[64] St John Chrysostom, *Baptismal Homily III*, 5–6, text in Didier, *Faut-il baptiser les enfants?* 111–2.

[65] Karl Barth, *The Teaching of the Church Concerning Baptism*, 31.

[66] Stanley Hauerwas, "The Gesture of a Truthful Story: The Church and Religious Education," *Encounter* 43 (1982) 319–29.

[67] While the Churches have begun to give more consideration to the presence of preschool children at the liturgy (see, for example, R.C.D. Jasper [ed.] *Worship and the Child*. Essays by the Joint Liturgical Group [London, 1975]), serious attention to the issue of infant Communion is mainly confined to the Anglican churches. See, *Communion Before Confirmation?* Church Information Office (London, 1985) and *Nurturing Children in Communion*, Grove Liturgical Studies, n. 44 (Bramcote, Notts, 1985). See also, David Holeton, *Infant Communion Then and Now*. Grove Liturgical Studies, n. 27 (Bramcote Notts, 1981).

[68] N. P. Williams, *The Ideas of the Fall and Original Sin* (London and New York, 1927).

[69] Vatican II retains the definition of faith given at Vatican I ("the full submission of intellect and will to God who reveals") but subordinates it to the broader concept of an "obedience of faith," thus making submission of intellect and will the form that such obedience will take for those already endowed with intellect and will, but leaving open the possibility that those not so endowed—infants, young children, and the retarded—might still be said to be capable of faith. In any case, intellective and voluntary capacities vary enormously from person to person and of themselves do not adequately describe the full scope of personal life that is being claimed by the grace of God.

Mark R. Francis, c.s.v.

Introduction to "Private Religion, Individualistic Society, and Common Worship"

Since the 1963 promulgation of the first document of the Second Vatican Council, the Constitution on the Sacred Liturgy, much ink has been spilled over discussions on the relationship between Christian worship and its cultural context. Articles thirty-seven through forty of this document dealing with cultural adaptation radically changed the relationship of the liturgy of the Catholic Church to its cultural context. For the first time since the approval of the rubrically rigid liturgical books issued in the sixteenth and seventeenth centuries in the wake of the Council of Trent—especially the Missal of Pius V in 1570—the Constitution on the Sacred Liturgy opened Catholic worship to a dialogue with human cultures. By permitting the translation of the liturgical books into living languages and for a simplification of much of the liturgical tradition inherited from medieval Western Europe, the council intended that the official prayer of the Church become once again the prayer of the people.

Much of this postconciliar discussion of how to accomplish this task often centered on the term "inculturation"—a neologism that has become a watchword in the fields of missiology and liturgy. In the liturgical context, the term is often used to describe the process by which the received liturgical tradition is modified or transformed in order to help the words and the other symbols of worship communicate in a more effective and meaningful way to a given culture.

In the heady days of liturgical reform of the 1960s and 1970s, and with the subsequent publication of the new liturgical books, popular and even more scholarly literature understandably presented liturgical "inculturation" as an activity that was consciously done. It was to be carried out in accordance with the options presented in the *editiones typicae* of the liturgical books themselves, by following the directives of national bishops' conferences and at the discretion of presiders and the

181

creativity of liturgical committees. This "activist" understanding of inculturation, though nuanced by writers such as Anscar Chupungco,
proved largely congenial to many liturgists, especially in the United
States. This understanding of inculturation immediately appeals to the
practical side of the U.S. character. North Americans tend to confront
problems head on and seek pragmatic solutions, often eschewing more
theoretical debates that tend to take time and often prove to be "ineffi-
cient." Therefore, many parish liturgists, in a sincere effort to make
liturgy "more meaningful," invoke inculturation in defending their
modifications of the Roman *editiones typicae*.

The contribution of Mark Searle's article, "Private Religion, Individualistic Society, and Common Worship," is to draw our attention to the
fact that once the liturgy has been opened to a relationship with local
cultures, the worship of the Church will be changed—not necessarily
by Roman dicasteries, national bishops conferences, liturgical experts
or committees—but inevitably and often inadvertently by the cultural
patterns or *Zeitgeist* of the human context in which it is celebrated.
The received liturgical tradition may indeed be formally altered by
liturgical authorities in the interests of making it more intelligible, but
experience teaches that much of ritual change usually comes about unconsciously and over time, initiated by the people at worship. While
Church authorities and liturgical ministers may change texts and other
ritual details, the way the liturgy is prepared and how it is experienced
has more to do with the often unintended inculturation that comes
about as a result of contact with the cultural context itself. As Searle
succinctly puts it, "It may not be too much of an exaggeration to say
that the major transformations occurring in our liturgical practice have
occurred not as a result of deliberate decision, but by casual contagion
and incorporation."

Mark Searle's observation that liturgical inculturation is not always
an unequivocally positive phenomenon is amply demonstrated by history. The formation of the Roman Rite itself[1] as well as its subsequent
transformation at the hands of the Germanic peoples gives ample
proof that Western Catholic worship reflected the cultural context in
which it developed.[2] In another article on the relationship of liturgy to
culture, Searle himself wrote about pre-Vatican II attempts at "inculturation" proposed by the National Liturgical Commission of Germany in June of 1942.[3] In a letter addressed to Pope Pius XII of that
same year, two bishops of the commission argued for approval of the
then common practice in Nazi Germany of dropping Jewish names

from the Scriptures which appear in the Nuptial Blessing and other places in the liturgy. The Pope quickly responded in July, denying this request and affirming that the writings of the Old and New Testaments were part of the same divine revelation, "no matter what ever events occur or tendencies arise."[4] Inculturation, when seen as more than top-down changes in the order of worship, can cut both ways. Searle was quite aware that Christians ignore this truth at their own peril. He was also quite aware that the Church in the U.S. was not an exception to the "dark side" of liturgical inculturation.

This sensitivity to the unintended effects of culture on worship led Searle to comment on the contemporary liturgical scene in U.S. parishes, with its emphasis on liturgy as celebrations of "community." Like the nineteenth-century French cultural observer Alexis de Tocqueville, who was able to intuit U.S. cultural patterns more easily, being an outsider, Mark Searle, although a longtime resident in the U.S., was an Englishman. He was able to point out cultural tendencies that were largely taken for granted and uncommented on by U.S. liturgists. He quite clearly states his thesis: "[W]ith the liturgical reforms, we have moved from the private Mass to the shared celebration, but we have not yet, by and large, recovered the meaning of public worship."

Truly "public worship"—worship that involves a broad social-economic cross-section of society in the same liturgical event—has become a challenge in the postconciliar U.S. Church. As Searle points out, in opening the doors to cultural dialogue, the council also introduced the Church into a relationship with modernity with its emphasis on the individual subject and private meaning, especially in matters of religion. This challenge is compounded by U.S. civil religion which presents God in the "lowest common denominator," that is, a God who is there mainly to shore up the status quo. Our worship is further crippled by the social alienation caused by an increasingly technically oriented society where people no longer feel in control of their lives or their futures. While many yearn for community and connectedness in a world that offers little stability, in many cases what is often achieved in middle-class U.S. parishes is a "lifestyle enclave" where like-minded and economically homogeneous groups of people come together out of choice to be with people like themselves. This reality masquerades as "community," and it is often reduced to a sentimentalized affirmation of the assembly and is oblivious to the wider world.

Mark Searle's attention to truly interdisciplinary dialogue with the sociologist of religion Robert Bellah,[5] and ecumenical theologian Martin

Marty, as well as his interpretation of the Notre Dame Study of Parish Life that had just issued at the beginning of the 1990s, help the reader appreciate the U.S. social context that so influences the experience of liturgy in the average middle-class, Euro-American parish. It needs to be noted that Searle's article needs to be read in just this context. Other liturgical scholars and social critics such as M. Francis Mannion, Richard Gaillardetz, and Gordon Lathrop[6] will have also noted the often unintentional influence of U.S. culture on Catholic worship and developed the theme that is so clearly expressed in the article. It is Mark Searle's principal contribution in much of his later writings and as exemplified in this essay, that in maintaining a fruitful dialogue with other disciplines such as cultural anthropology, semiotics, and sociology, he never lost sight of the theological/liturgical dimension of his subject. Because of this grounding in the theological tradition, his work is invariably insightful and will remain pastorally relevant for years to come.

Mark R. Francis, c.s.v., is superior general of the Clerics of St. Viator. He resides in Rome and teaches part-time at the Pontificio Instituto Liturgico di Sant' Anselmo.

---

[1] See Anscar Chupungco, "Greco-Roman Culture and Liturgical Adaptation," *Notitiae* 15 (1979) 202–18, as well as Marcel Metzger, *History of the Liturgy: The Major Stages. (Histoire de la liturgie: Les grandes étapes)* (Collegeville: Liturgical Press, 1997) and Burkhard Neunheuser, *Storia della liturgia attraverso le epoche culturale* (Rome: Edizioni Liturgiche, 1983).

[2] See Mary Collins, "Evangelization, Catechesis and the Beginnings of Western Eucharistic Theology," *Louvain Studies* 23 (1998) 124–42; James Russell, *The Germanization of Early Medieval Christianity: A Sociohistorical Approach to Religious Transformation* (New York: Oxford University Press, 1994).

[3] Mark Searle, "Culture" in *Liturgy: Active Participation in the Divine Life* (Collegeville: Liturgical Press, 1990) 27–5.

[4] *Denkschrift der Bischöfe Stohr und Landerdorfer an Papst Pius XII von 2. Juni 1942*, 529.

[5] Bellah, Robert et al. *Habits of the Heart: Individualism and Commitment in American Life* (New York: Harper and Row, 1985).

[6] M. Francis Mannion, "Liturgy and the Present Crisis of Culture," *Worship* 62 (1988) 98–123; Richard Gaillardetz, "North American Culture and the Liturgical Life of the Church: The Separation of the Quests for Transcendence and Community," *Worship* 68 (1994) 403–16; and Gordon Lathrop, "New Pentecost or Joseph's Britches? Reflections on the History and Meaning of the Worship Ordo in the Megachurches," *Worship* 72 (1998) 521–38.

Private Religion, Individualistic Society, and Common Worship[*]

Introduction

It is, on the face of it, rather odd that twenty-five years after the promulgation of the Liturgy Constitution we should still be worrying about how to form worshipping communities. The reformed rites and concomitant "programs of instruction" (SC 14) were supposed to cultivate the kind of active participation that would of itself engender a sense of the Church at prayer. However, as we now see more clearly, the worship community is formed not only by liturgy and catechesis, but by the larger culture in which its members live and work. In a sense, this makes talk about adapting the liturgy to our culture somewhat otiose: while we have been talking, adaptation has been happening anyway. It might not be too much of an exaggeration to say that the major transformations occurring in our liturgical practice have occurred not as a result of deliberate decision, but by casual contagion and incorporation.[1]

We tend to think too much of what the Church might bring to society and too little of what society is already bringing to the Church. We enthuse about what new prayers and new liturgical music might do to shape the liturgical assembly, overlooking the fact that culture has gotten there before us, unconsciously shaping the attitudes and language of both the experts and the participants. While this paper cannot claim to offer anything very original, it will have served its purpose if it brings to the attention of those responsible for liturgy some of the findings of those whose task in life it is to study our culture. We shall begin by identifying some of the chief characteristics of our culture, particularly as they affect religiosity in our society; then we shall

* This article first appeared in *Liturgy and Spirituality in Context. Perspectives on Prayer and Culture*, ed. Eleanor Bernstein (Collegeville: Liturgical Press, 1990) 27–46.

look for indications of the influence of these cultural traits in our liturgical practice. Finally, I will offer some tentative suggestions about the possibility of genuinely public worship in America.

I. Culture

As I have already suggested, one of the problems faced by those of us whose preoccupations center on the parish and its liturgy is the tendency to become narrowly parochial in outlook. All too rarely do we consider the wider world in which the parish is situated or become actively engaged in issues affecting the broader life of the community. We have, many of us, little sense of what the liturgy looks like to parishioners who come from that larger world or of how limited a role religion can play in their larger lives. This same innocence of the society in which Christians actually live characterizes much writing on liturgy, not least the Liturgy Constitution itself. Paragraphs 41 and 42 of the constitution, in describing the life of the diocese as centered around the bishop presiding in his cathedral—and in only acknowledging as an afterthought that the bishop cannot be everywhere, so that we have to have parishes led by priests—seem to hearken back to the simpler days of late antiquity when, though the reality rarely matched the ideal, one bishop presided over one Eucharist celebrated by an undivided community in a small Mediterranean town.

There is more than a hint of nostalgia here which feeds into our modern hunger for community. British sociologist Bryan Wilson, with a foreigner's critical eye, picks up the way American churches attempt to bring a sense of old-fashioned community to modern life:

> The Church . . . represents the values of the agrarian or communal preindustrial society: its forms are moulded from that stage of social development and it participates in the warmth, stability and fundamental mutual involvements of a type of community life. That this community is, in the nature of American society, not so much a fossil as a reproduction piece, is less damaging in the eyes of those who have little experience of community life than in the eyes of visiting Europeans. The synthetic nature of the community-orientation of many American churches is evident to those from more traditional cultures; the personalized gestures of the impersonal society acquire an almost macabre quality for those who have experienced the natural, spontaneous operation of rural community life. . . . And yet it seems evident, whether the Church does fulfil functions of this kind or not, men obviously get some, perhaps purely sentimental, satisfactions from presuming that it does.[2]

If Wilson is right, much of our talk about the worship community is really self-delusion. We yearn for the homely togetherness and directness of an earlier and simpler age, but our attempts to restore it merely parody it. Behind the cheery informality of our celebrations and our "ministers of hospitality," the profoundly impersonal quality of our interactions remains untouched. To get some idea of why this might be the case, we need to look at some of the distinguishing characteristics of modern American life. Here I have to reproduce in broad strokes the more nuanced findings of a number of sociologists and to risk the appearance of describing a universal state of affairs when I am only trying to single out some particular tendencies selected for the corrosive effect they can have on communal religious identity.

1. *Religious Privatism.* For over 1500 years, European Christianity experienced a form of social life in which Church and state were united and in which religious uniformity was the safeguard of social coherence. But the United States has never known this experience. It was founded by dissenters, recusants, and nonconformists looking for precisely the space to live out their religious convictions that they could not find in Europe. Deliberately repudiating the establishment of a single state Church, America self-consciously nurtured religious tolerance which meant accepting religious pluralism—not one Church binding the nation together in a single religious community but a growing multiplicity of Churches and sects offering every citizen the freedom to worship in accordance with his or her conscience.

The benefits of such an arrangement we have long since learned to take for granted, but it has also had consequences for religion which we often overlook. It has essentially privatized religion in this country, and in two senses.

In the first place, religion is privatized for the individual. Freedom to practice religion in accordance with one's conscience also implies freedom to choose which religion, if any, one will practice. It devolves into a matter of purely personal preference. "My religious beliefs are my own business and nobody else's."

Second, privatization affects the denominations themselves since they have no public role to play and no official standing. They are demoted to secondary institutions caring for the needs of private individuals. In the eyes of the state, all religions are equally good and equally useful, and all are equally banned both from direct intervention in affairs of state and from access to the state educational system.

Their place is in the domestic and private sphere where they may seek to motivate and guide individual citizens, but there the line is drawn.

Because religion is relegated to the private sphere and because religious affliction is purely a matter of personal choice, the Churches find themselves in competition with one another for members. Having lost the power to compel a following, their moral authority undermined by the very variety of religious brands on the market, they are reduced to peddling religion as something that meets people's personal needs. The image of religion as a market is one that recurs in writings about religion in America. So David Martin writes:

> The clergy are assimilated to the role of rival entrepreneurs running varied religious services on a mixed laissez-faire and oligopolistic basis. . . . Religious styles constantly adapt and accept vulgarization in accordance with the stylistic tendencies of their varied markets. . . .[3]

Martin Marty, an astute observer of American religion, confirms this point: "The drift of religion today is, if anything, moving towards an utterly free market in which little trace of fate, election, or predestination remains."[4] The result is a tendency for Americans to belong to churches, but on their own terms. They come, not to submit to historical tradition and religious discipline in response to God's call, but for their own personal reasons and to meet their own personal needs.

This drift towards privatism and subjectivism in religion is not merely the result of religious pluralism. It is a religious symptom of a larger upheaval in social life which we might call "massification."

2. *Massification.* The term "massification" is intended to identify a stage in the evolution of a society where the different social institutions have become so specialized and the ordering of society so complex that the democratic process can no longer work effectively. Instead, basic decisions affecting the life of the people are made by technocrats, and most of the population, losing perspective and control, are "maneuvered by the mass media to the point where they believe nothing they have not heard on the radio, seen on television, or read in the newspapers."[5] As the fate of our lives rests in the hands of fewer and fewer people further and further away, we are rendered powerless in our own society, incapable of engaging effectively in the direction of its processes. We are, as Karl Marx would say, "alienated."

Marx, of course, analyzed the problems of alienation in the wake of the nineteenth-century industrial revolution in which the advent of machinery dramatically altered the patterns of labor and made mass production possible. Society suffered the mass displacement of workers from the rural areas into the new towns, people uprooted from their traditional communities and reduced to the status of units of production. Yet, as sociologist David Martin has pointed out, this first industrial revolution left intact many of the characteristic features of the preindustrial world: the small business, the family farm, personal contact between masters and servants, a "respectable" working class. Many of the traditional forms of social relations continued to exist, and where they did, religion held its own.

It was the advent of the second industrial revolution, that of the twentieth century, argues Martin, that led to the further and almost complete disintegration of social bonds. Ironically, this second revolution was essentially a revolution in the means of communication: the development of the telephone, of radio and television; the replacement of the railroads by the interstate highways, of ships by air transportation. The new communications media have finally swept away the remnants of the older forms of community.

> The institutions congruent with modern industry, with bureaucracy and technical rationality, are large, impersonal, and mechanical in their operation. The intimate bonds of horizontal community, working-class or otherwise, are broken up; the ecology of the city encourages fragmentation; the small shop gives way to the supermarket; the family firm enters the international consortium; the small farm is rationalized into larger units run by scientific agriculture; the moderate-sized office is swallowed up in large-scale bureaucracy; the community of school is wrecked by education factories operated by mobile teachers.[6]

Not every American, of course, is affected by these changes to the same degree, but these new developments set a style of life, establish expectations, and engender attitudes and values very different from those of the world we have now lost. Most generally and most importantly, the premium placed on cost-efficiency and profitability, on functional specialization and expertise creates a society where the dominant values are functional values and where matters of "ultimate concern" are relegated to the private realm. Since religion is about matters of "ultimate concern," it finds no place in public life, being left for each individual to decide for himself.

The effect, then, of massification is to reinforce the effects of pluralism, making the individual the sole arbiter of ultimate values and thereby undermining the bonds that create genuine community. What holds us together as a society is not, as in most societies, a common world view, a "sacred cosmos,"[7] but the patterns of production and consumption into which we are socialized by secular education and the seductions of the mass media.

3. *Individualism.* The wondrous capacity of human beings to adapt to their environment is strikingly displayed in the manner in which modern people have come to terms with the split between public and private selves and with the removal of questions of ultimate concern from the public to the private forum. Radical individualism is an outlook on life which results from making a virtue of necessity and turning the loss of community into a gain for the self. Radical individualism celebrates the freedom that is now ours to select our own values and priorities without reference to any wider framework of common purpose or beliefs. In the words of Robert Bellah: "We believe in the dignity, indeed the sacredness, of the individual. Anything that would violate our right to think for ourselves, make our own decisions, live our lives as we see fit, is not only morally wrong, it is sacrilegious."[8] With the supports, the constraints, and the commitment required by genuine community removed, we are free to pursue the good as we see it. Bellah says:

> What is good is what one finds rewarding. If one's preferences change, so does the nature of the good. Even the deepest ethical values are justified as matters of personal preference. Indeed, the ultimate ethical rule is that individuals should be able to pursue whatever they find rewarding, constrained only by the requirement that that not interfere with the "value systems" of others.[9]

So much do we take the autonomy of the individual for granted that it is difficult to get a clear perspective on this radical individualism. It is hard to observe when it is itself the lens through which we observe all else. Nonetheless, its characteristics would include the following:

- a proclivity for seeing the individual as prior to society and thus for seeing society—and the Church—as a conglomeration of autonomous individuals rather than seeing them as products of a historical community;
- a tendency to prefer one's own judgment over the judgment of tradition or authority, a tendency which, paradoxically, also tends to make for uncritical conformism since one tends to look to others to confirm one's own opinion and to seek out the company of like-minded people;
- a preference for "gut feelings" and emotional spontaneity over the arduous task of rational argument, for following one's feelings rather than

thinking things through; thus public debate declines into sloganeering and elections into popular contests and public decision-making into a contest between pressure groups;

- the intrinsic value of work and service is overlooked and replaced by a quest for self-realization or, where that fails, by the pursuit of greater income;
- the freedom to make personal decisions is gained at the expense of turning over public decisions to managers and technocrats: in other words, the expanded opportunities for personal freedom occur at the expense of our involvement in the public life of our society.[10]

All this flows from the nature of modern individualism: the assertion of self-interest at the expense of public interest, the claim of the self to be the final arbiter of ultimate values, the abdication of responsibility for one another and for society in the belief that each of us is finally only answerable to ourselves.

The effect of such radical individualism, where it prevails, is a radical incapacity for community. In an older understanding of society, Philip Rieff points out, "The sense of well-being of the individual was dependent upon his full, participant membership in a community." This is still the vision upheld by the Church and her liturgy, we might note. But to the degree that communitarian values are subordinated to the ultimate conviction that people "must free themselves from binding attachments to communal purposes in order to express more freely their individualities,"[11] our attempts at fostering a sense of community in our liturgies will remain exercises in self-delusion. For clearly we have not given up on community altogether: indeed, some parishes talk of little else. But to the extent that we seek community as a means of self-fulfillment, looking to it to meet our needs but reluctant to submit ourselves to its constraints, we merely succeed in turning our parish liturgies into "life-style enclaves," as Bellah calls them,[12] the coming-together of people who enjoy the same things. Since such a coming-together is predicated only on the overlapping of particular tastes and interests, it can never engage the whole person and will only continue to be frequented as long as those tastes continue to be satisfied and those interests met.

4. *Civil Religion.* Despite all that has been said, it would be a mistake to suppose that, because religion has been rendered a matter of personal predilection and because the Churches no longer have a public role, there is no place for religion in public life. On the contrary, what

Robert Bellah, following Rousseau, has called "civil religion" has a significant role in our national life.[13] The Pledge of Allegiance speaks of our being "one nation under God," while the name of God is quite regularly invoked in public discourse. But this American God is not to be confused with the God of the Jews and Christians and is never trinitarian. Martin Marty calls it "the God of Religion-in-General, a harmless little divinity who has nothing in common with the God of Christianity."[14] While Bellah argues the positive value of civil religion—its subordination of the will of the people to a transcendent sacred, its ability to build up national solidarity or to evoke personal motivation for national goals—it is also important to recognize that it constitutes a sort of national pan-religiosity which coopts and assimilates to itself the specific beliefs and value systems of historical Christian Churches. To the degree that it succeeds, church-going Americans fail to discriminate between the religion of nationalism and the Christianity they profess. All become jumbled up together, thereby depriving Christian communities of the distance they need to distinguish between historical Christianity and contemporary American culture. They lose their critical and prophetic voice, serving only to affirm the cultural values we have been discussing. Instead of being resources for the recovery of genuine community, the Churches and their liturgies end up peddling "synthetic" community, designed to accommodate people's longing for community but finally incapable of actually engendering community.

Religious privatism and massification, radical individualism and civil religion are the divisive forces with which liturgy and catechesis must contend if a genuine community of worship is to be built up. They are all the more powerful and pervasive because they are not the subject of conscious reflection in most parishes. We go with these forces because we know no other way, so that even the communitarian language and practices of our tradition are reinterpreted, quite unconsciously, to conform to our cultural expectations.

II. Cult

We need hardly wait, then, for some national commission to undertake the work of cultural adaptation of the liturgy in this country since it is already well under way. Our parishes and our parish liturgies reflect our times as much as they harbor memories of time past and proclaim a vision of time to come. David Martin, an English sociologist of religion, reflecting on the pressures of modernity, gives some clues about where to look for symptoms of acculturation:

> The Church itself must reflect these varied pressures: the bureaucratiza-
> tion and impersonality, and the reaction in the form either of a familistic
> suburban religion or else in radical celebrations of personal authenticity
> or community. The rationalization of church organizations and liturgy
> proceeds *pari passu* with cults of encounter, authenticity and religious ex-
> citement, all of which leap over the constricting limits of the contempo-
> rary organization of role.[15]

Martin is suggesting that Church life in general and liturgy in particular will vacillate between, on the one hand, reflecting the anonymity
and bureaucratization of society and, on the other, manifesting signs of
reaction against the conditions of contemporary life either in the
pseudo-family atmosphere cultivated by suburban fellowshipping or
in the more intensive emotional atmosphere of renewal groups.

The first pole is familiar enough: the large, anonymous parishes
where one can go for years without knowing more than a handful of
people by name; the congregation where, week by week, most people
seem to be from out of town; the Saturday evening Masses in half-
empty churches where elderly Catholics accompany the hurried mut-
ter of the Mass with the flutter of missalettes and the reluctant singing
of an opening and closing hymn before hurrying home to lock their
doors and settle down to an evening of television. In short, those liturgies we commonly assert to be "dead" merely reflect the life of our
times: anonymous, private, functional, and individualistic.

The second pole, on the other hand, is represented by what usually
passes for "good liturgy": the smoothly orchestrated celebrations of
suburbia with their choirs and folk-groups, their "easy-listening"
music, their firm handshakes, and their abundance of lay ministers in
bright dresses and sharp suits. But for more radical reactions against
the anonymity and impersonalism of our society, we should probably
look outside the usual parish setting to Masses celebrated on the liv-
ing-room floor in religious houses where "Father Mike" wears a stole
and all join hands as he improves on the eucharistic traditions of centuries with a sizeable dose of earnest informality; or we might look to
youth Masses where the Gospel is reduced to God wanting us to be
ourselves, and the last vestiges of ritual formality yield before a burning desire for authenticity. Better still, look to the culminating liturgy at
experiences of encounter and renewal where deep and extensive sharing

over twenty-four hours reaches climax and consummation in a "meaningful worship experience" oblivious both to history and to the future, celebrating the "now."

Robert Bocock, in his *Ritual in Industrial Society*, argues that ritual survives into the modern era but with quite a different role from that which it exercised in earlier times. In societies simpler and more homogeneous than our own, fixed rituals give expression to a collective consciousness shared by all members of society, thereby enabling individuals to find themselves in a communitarian context. In industrial society, however, what collective consciousness there *is* is the product of the processes of production and consumption. Some ritual actions, like the rites of civil religion—including going to church—still serve to foster a shared world view and catch us up and identify us with the larger society, but, says Bocock:

> at the level of total society this is rarely the case. Rituals can be used in modern society for coming to know ourselves as individuals, as our own center of action. "The individual feels himself less acted upon; he becomes more a source of spontaneous activity. . . . It is still from society that [ritual] takes all its forces, but it is not to society that it attaches us; it is to ourselves."[16]

In other words, what we often adjudge "good liturgy" or "meaningful liturgy" does not usually take us beyond the stalemate represented by dull, impersonal celebrations. We take part because we choose to do so, and we choose to do so because we like it, or it makes us feel good about ourselves, or because we enjoy praying and singing with others. It gives an evanescent experience of togetherness, a passing *frisson* of religious excitement, but it doesn't impose the constraints of discipline and commitment. It merely satisfies some obscurely felt need for the time being but will have to be fresh and different and exciting every time if it is to keep drawing us back.

I have a thesis, and it is this: that, with the liturgical reforms, we have moved from the private Mass to the shared celebration, but we have not yet, by and large, recovered the meaning of public worship.

The *private Mass* was the model adopted by the Missal of Pius V. A priest and server were all that were needed: the congregation was dispensable. Even when the congregation was present, it made little or no difference to the rite; the faithful, for their part, remained private individuals at prayer. Whether they listened to the choir, followed the Mass in their missals, or said the rosary, their religious privacy and anonymity were never breached.

With Vatican II all this was transformed. Communal celebrations were explicitly preferred over private or quasi-private celebrations. The full, active, and conscious participation of the assembled faithful was required; hence the vernacular, the prayers of the faithful, congregational singing, lay ministries, and the rest. All this was permitted, indeed demanded, but no legislation or instruction could cure us overnight of our ingrained individualism and privatism. To the degree that liturgical celebrations have been suffused with individualism, they remain *shared celebrations* rather than common prayer. To the degree that we are there for our own private reasons, whether to express our faith or to enjoy singing and praying together, the liturgy is not yet that of a community, but merely an assembly of people all "doing their own thing." However impressive or exhilarating it might be, it remains shared therapy; it is not yet public domain.

The Liturgy Constitution, following the definition of the liturgy given by Pius XII, spoke of it as "the full *public worship* . . . performed by the Mystical Body of Jesus Christ, that is, by Head and members."[17] Liturgy is meant to be public worship, then, and its full public character is manifest when the following conditions prevail:

1. It is understood and undertaken as "an action of Christ the priest and of his Body the Church" rather than as something we do on our own terms, "an exercise of the priestly office of Jesus Christ" in which it is our bounden duty, in virtue of our baptismal calling, to participate.

2. Like the redemptive work of Christ which it memorializes and represents, the liturgy is celebrated for the life of the world, not for the personal convenience and consolation of the participants.

3. The sacred duty, *divinum officium*, of celebrating the liturgy is a participation in the unceasing prayer of Christ before God for the salvation of the world and is undertaken with a profound and lively awareness of the larger society which we represent and on whose behalf we offer thanksgiving and intercession to the Father through Christ in the unity of the Holy Spirit.

4. The motivation and direction guiding and shaping the liturgy derives not from our private biographies, but from the larger historical tradition to which we belong and from the eschatological hopes for all humanity which it embodies and projects.

By its nature, then, liturgy is more than shared celebration meeting private needs: it is an act of civic responsibility, of public duty. An anonymous early Christian apologist in his *Epistle to Diognetus* described the relation of the Christian community to the larger society as that of the soul to the body, the source and expression of society's relatedness to God. "Such is the important post to which God has assigned them, and it is not lawful for them to desert it."[18] The local church, then, has public responsibilities, among which not the least important is the offering of public worship.

III. Toward a Public Worship

The effects of modernity, and especially of the radical individualism that is its hallmark, have reduced American society to a state of internal incoherence. Such are the conclusions of Robert Bellah and his colleagues, following their study of individualism and commitment in American life.[19] It is not only our natural ecology that is being ravaged by technocracy, they point out, but the human ecology, society itself.

> Human beings have treated one another badly for as long as we have any historical evidence, but modernity has given us a capacity for destructiveness on a scale incomparably greater than in previous centuries. And social ecology is damaged not only by war, genocide, and political repression. It is also damaged by the destruction of the subtle ties that bind human beings to one another, leaving them frightened and alone.[20]

In place of current ideologies of pure undetermined choice—free of tradition, obligation, and commitment—we need to recover, Bellah argues, a sense of community, "a 'community of memory' that does not forget its past."

> In order not to forget that past, a community is involved in retelling its story, its constitutive narrative, and in so doing, it offers examples of the men and women who have embodied and exemplified the meanings of the community. . . .
>
> The stories that make up a tradition contain conceptions of character, of what a good person is like, and of the virtues that define such character. But the stories are not all exemplary, not all about successes and achievements. A genuine community of memory will also tell painful stories of shared suffering that sometimes creates deeper identities than success. . . . And if the community is completely honest, it will remember stories not only of suffering received but of suffering inflicted—dangerous memories, for they call the community to alter ancient evils. The communities of memory that tie us to the past also turn us towards the future as communities of hope. They carry a context of meaning that can allow us to connect our aspirations for ourselves and those closest to us

with the aspirations of a larger whole and see our own efforts as being, in part, contributions to a common good.[21]

Can our parishes become such "communities of memory" and "communities of hope"? Can our parish liturgies carry a context of meaning that would connect us with the aspirations of the rest of humanity instead of cutting us off from them?

Translated into traditional Catholic vocabulary, such questions become questions of vocation. Can we recover a sense of baptismal vocation, personal and collective, to live as prophets, priests, and servants in the society where we have been placed? In our theological tradition, there have always been two dimensions to vocation: the personal and the ecclesial, the inner journey and the public call, neither being complete without the other. This is because, in our tradition, personal vocation is never a purely personal and private matter but finds its definition and scope—whether it be a vocation to a specific kind of ministry or to a particular form of life—within the context of the mission and vocation of the whole Church, which is to serve the kingdom of God in the world. Even a vocation as seemingly personal as a vocation to the contemplative life has always been tested and guided by the Church and justified in terms of the fullness of the Church's own witness. Ordinations and religious professions serve to ritualize this ecclesial call.

Moreover, a vocation is not given and answered once and for all; it is to be received and taken up anew each day. This, in turn, requires communities—capable of reflecting on the world of which they are a part—to discern their vocation in the light of our tradition. In our lifetime, we have witnessed the whole Church engaged in this process at the Second Vatican Council and have seen national synods, pastoral councils, and general congregations of religious orders continuing the process for their own constituencies. At diocesan and parish levels such thoroughgoing efforts to discern our common vocation to be the Church in a specific social context have been less common, but the *communidades de base* in Central and Latin America have offered an influential model. At their best, these and other forms of so-called "intentional community" consist of relatively small groupings of people mutually committed to one another, sharing a critical awareness of and commitment to the cultural, political, and economic systems of their society, in continuous and lively contact with other similar communities, and faithfully attentive to the Christian character of their common life.[22]

The recovery of truly public worship is not something that can be achieved by liturgy-planning committees alone. It requires of us all a

conversion of outlook and of language, a re-conceiving of the role of
the parish and of the Christian community, and a reformulation by
each of us of our Christian identity in terms of public vocation rather
than private choice.

Karl Rahner describes such a reformulated identity precisely in reference to liturgy in a little essay entitled "Secular Life and the Sacraments." After describing how God's grace permeates the whole of
human existence and how it was most visibly manifested in Jesus, "in
a life made up of everyday things—birth and toil, bravery and hope,
failure and death," Rahner argues that the liturgy of the Church is simply the place where we become most profoundly aware of and committed to this "liturgy of the world":

> The world and its history is the terrible and sublime liturgy, breathing
> death and sacrifice, that God celebrates for himself and allows to be held
> throughout the free history of men, a history which he himself sustains
> through the sovereign disposition of his grace. Throughout the whole
> length and breadth of this colossal history of birth and death, a history
> on the one hand full of superficiality, folly, inadequacy and hate—and all
> these "crucify"—a history on the other hand, composed of silent sub-
> mission, responsibility unto death, mortality and joy, heights and sud-
> den falls: throughout all this there takes place the *liturgy of the world*.

The liturgy of Christ's life and death is the culmination of that liturgy,
and it is that liturgy and its redemptive culmination that we celebrate
in the liturgy of the Church. The Church is a community of memory,
then, because it is called to remember and celebrate not only the memory of Christ but the whole "colossal history of birth and death" which
Christ assumed and redeemed when he became one of us.

Such an awareness would profoundly alter the frame of mind with
which we entered into a liturgical celebration. Rahner, in his vivid and
inimitable way, describes how such a person might go to Mass:

> He is profoundly aware of the drama into which his life is unceasingly
> drawn, the drama of the world, the divine Tragedy and the divine Com-
> edy. He thinks of the dying, those facing their end glassy eyed and with
> the death rattle in their throat, and he knows that this fate has taken up
> lodging in his own being. He feels in himself the groaning of the creature
> and the world, their demand for a more hopeful future. He grasps some-
> thing of the burden born by statesmen, their responsibility for decisions
> demanding all their courage and yet whose effects will be extending into
> an unknown future. He bears within himself something of the laughter
> of children in their unshadowed, future-laden joy: within him resounds

also the weeping of the starving children, the agony of the sick, the bit-
terness caused by betrayed love. The dispassionate seriousness of the
scientist in his laboratory, the hard determination of those struggling to
liberate mankind—all these find their echo in him.[23]

Rahner has much more to say along these lines, and it all deserves
our careful and prayerful consideration. While it would certainly be
true that someone taking part in the liturgy with such an attitude
would be celebrating a public liturgy, it is equally true that such an attitude is not likely to become a hallmark of Catholic worship until our
celebrations themselves begin to move beyond the level of "shared
celebrations" at which they are currently stuck. To overcome the cultural momentum towards religious individualism, we would need
forms of worship which actually cultivated such awareness of the
"liturgy of the world." What such forms of worship might look like is
not easy to predict, but my own hunch would be that, since the basic
elements of our tradition derive from an era in which liturgy was acknowledged as public worship, these new forms would, paradoxically,
be rather more traditional than we are currently used to. Perhaps it
would be more a matter of style than of form. If so, what would a more
public style of worship look like?

Liturgies celebrated as public worship will not be celebrated for the
sake of togetherness nor for private intentions. They would be characterized by a certain fixity and solemnity, an objectivity which would
constitute an invitation to us to enter in and be shaped by the ritual
process. Congregations will not be whisked in and out in forty-five
minutes, and missalettes will probably be less in evidence. The proclamation of the scriptural Word would be taken more seriously than it
presently is, being heard as a Word addressed more to the community
for the sake of the world than to the individuals for their private consolation. In the homily, monologue will yield to dialogue as the Word
of God establishes an agenda for the examination of social issues not
only during but before and after the liturgy itself. Inspired by the
Word, the congregation will become once again a "community of
memory," remembering especially the things that our culture forgets:
the radical equality of all human beings before God and the centrality
in the Christian economy of those—like women and children, the un-
employed, the handicapped, the sick, the dying, and the unsuccessful—whom society relegates to its margins.

Because it is a "community of memory," the local church will call to
mind not only the sins of the world and the failings of individuals but

its own collective collusion in those sins so that the celebration of penance will be a genuinely communitarian exercise in prayer, fasting, and examination of community conscience. Marriage will be celebrated not as a personal troth between a man and woman alone but as an ecclesial vocation sanctioned and blessed by the community to bear witness to God's faithful love in the Church and in society. Liturgical ministries will be more closely associated than they now are with community service: ministers of the Word with study and teaching of our tradition and with prophetic analysis of contemporary situations; eucharistic ministry with care of the sick and with provision for the hungry at home and abroad; the ministry of hospitality with caring for the homeless, visiting the imprisoned, and welcoming the alien and the stranger.

Daily prayer will assume renewed importance in the lives of individuals and communities as an exercise of the priesthood of Jesus Christ on behalf of the world. As in Judaism and early Christianity, fixed forms and times of prayer will be widely known and observed, tying the rhythms of society's day into the economy of our salvation. Psalmody and hymnody will continue to exist side by side, but the hymnody will be marked by the objectivity of the mysteries it celebrates. Its musical forms will be less sentimental and less closely derived from current popular music than is now the fashion. The Church will once again evolve her own musical idiom, reflecting the distinctness of her own identity in the world.

There will be a more profound awareness than we now have of the historic symbols of our community, especially of the symbol of the Body which is the community in Christ. The bread and the cup will weigh heavily as symbols of common destiny, embracing not only the community of the baptized but all who labor for bread and whose sufferings and joys make them participants in the "liturgy of the world." Precisely that awareness that we, as Church, are for the world will make boundaries once again important, defining the community over against a culture it must repudiate. But the boundaries are likely to be drawn somewhat differently from the way in which they are now drawn to include all those who live by their baptism. Water and oil, exorcism and blessing will mark those boundaries more sharply, not because we are withdrawing from the world but because, as a community, we are more clear sighted about who we are. Conversely, within the community, awareness of and concern for the larger society will result in common prayer that is not afraid to be specific and does not hide its lack of commitment behind pious generalities. Above all, the weekly celebration of the Eucharist will serve as a weekly renewal of the community's baptismal covenant for the service of God's kingdom in the world, while the observance of the Lord's Day will be itself a celebration of our freedom from the impersonal and depersonalizing forces that dominate our postindustrial culture. It will be a day for meeting and remembering, for celebrating and hope: in short, a day for community.[24]

Does this seem so far-fetched? Recent pastorals from the American Roman Catholic bishops suggest, both in the topics chosen and in the consultative methodologies employed, that the Church is in process of becoming a public Church once again. Moreover, because language and reality never exactly coincide, we are often less individualistic than our ways of talking suggest. The Notre Dame Study of Catholic Parish Life which focused on the kind of average American Catholic parishioners most of us work with found that American Catholics drop easily into the individualistic language of our culture yet still retain considerable community commitment.

The study found, for example, that the single most important reason given by parishioners for their attachment to their parish was not the quality of liturgy or preaching, their family ties, or their love of the church building, but the opportunities their parish offered for community service. Furthermore, it found that the parishioners who claimed the strongest sense of attachment to their parish were those who took advantage of these opportunities to serve and who most regularly interacted with other parish members. As Report No. 10 notes, "Opportunities for participation and service, coupled especially with caring pastors and parishioners, are the hallmarks of parish attraction and parishioner attachment."[25]

Moreover, the study found that, contrary to what one might expect, the sense of community in the thirty-six parishes surveyed was not necessarily stronger in smaller parishes. Three of the five parishes with the strongest sense of community were large, nonethnic, city and suburban parishes. This finding is probably connected with what was discovered about people's sense of attachment—the presence of opportunities for service. "Parishes . . . are not straight-jacketed by the social characteristics of their members. Parishes that recognize the great variations among their members but who find ways to develop interdependence among them, will be rewarded by a greater sense of community than parishes who serve very homogeneous populations."[26]

Where such a sense of commitment and service prevails, public communities of memory and hope are possible. If these committed energies can be harnessed to the service of the wider society instead of merely being turned back into the maintenance of the parish itself, we have the possibility of there emerging what Martin Marty calls "the public Church," a Church which is in the world but is critically reflective about the problems of our society and culture and is committed to working in the public forum for the common good. The emergence of such a public Church is the precondition for public worship and our only antidote to the debilitating effects for privatism, individualism, and massification.

Whether or not that will transform the face of religion in America and so contribute to the transformation of America itself is not for us to know. As Martin Marty says, "It is not for Christians to weigh the odds, but only to be faithful."

---

[1] See David Martin, *A General Theory of Secularization* (New York: Harper and Row, 1978) 31.

[2] Bryan Wilson, *Religion in Secular Society* (London: Watts, 1966) 91.

[3] Martin, *A General Theory of Secularization*, 28.

[4] Martin Marty, *The Public Church* (New York: Crossroad, 1981) 25.

[5] Paulo Freire, *Education for Critical Consciousness* (New York: Continuum, 1973) 34. See also Freire, *Cultural Action for Freedom* (Harmonsworth: Penguin, 1972) 79–82.

[6] *A General Theory of Secularization*, 87.

[7] Thomas Luckmann. *The Invisible Religion. The Problem of Religion in Modern Society* (New York: Macmillan, 1967) esp. 50–68.

[8] Robert Bellah et al., *Habits of the Heart. Individualism and Commitment in American Life* (Berkeley: University of California Press, 1984) 142.

[9] Ibid., 6.

[10] Here following *Habits of the Heart*, passim.

[11] Philip Rieff, *The Triumph of the Therapeutic. The Uses of Faith after Freud* (Chicago: University of Chicago Press, 1987) 71.

[12] Bellah et al., *Habits of the Heart*, 72ff.

[13] Robert Bellah, "Civil Religion in America," in Wm. G. McLaughlin and Robert Bellah, eds., *Religion in America* (Boston: Beacon Press, 1968) 3–23.

[14] Martin Marty, *The New Shape of American Religion* (New York: Harper, 1959) 37.

[15] *A General Theory of Secularization*, 89.

[16] Robert Bocock, *Ritual in Industrial Society* (London: George Allen and Unwin, 1974) 56, citing Emile Durkheim, *The Division of Labour in Society*.

[17] Liturgy Constitution 7. See Pius XII, *Mediator Dei* (New York: Paulist, 1948) par. 29.

[18] *Epistle to Diognetus*. Trans. H. G. Meecham (Manchester: Manchester University Press, 1949) 80.

[19] Bellah et al., *Habits of the Heart*, 275–96.

[20] Ibid., 284.

[21] Ibid., 153.

[22] Bernard Lee and Michael Cowan. *Dangerous Memories. House Churches and Our American Story* (New York: Sheed and Ward, 1986) 91–3.

[23] Karl Rahner, "Secular Life and the Sacraments," *The Tablet* (6 March 1971) 236–8; (13 March 1971) 267–8.

[24] For more specific and imaginative suggestions, see Bernard Lee (general editor), *Alternative Futures for Worship.* 7 vols. (Collegeville: Liturgical Press, 1987).

[25] David C. Leege, *The Parish as Community*. Notre Dame Study of Catholic Parish Life, Report No. 10 (March 1987) 9.

[26] Ibid., 5–6.

Jan Michael Joncas

Introduction to *"Fons Vitae*: A Case Study in the Use of Liturgy as a Theological Source"

There are scholars whose contributions to a field are lauded during their lifetimes, but whose thought proves to be a dead-end fairly soon after their productive lives end. One thinks of Franz Joseph Gall, whose "phrenological science" (a method of determining human character by the external shape of the skull) was all the rage in Victorian Britain and the United States but is now relegated to the annals of voodoo science. There are other scholars who labor in obscurity during their lifetimes, but whose thought, retrieved by later thinkers, proves to be fruitful in a later era. One thinks of Gregor Mendel, whose contributions to genetics only became apparent in the decades after his death. Then there are scholars like Bernard Lonergan, whose thought is recognized by the scholarly community during their lifetimes, but whose groundbreaking insights set a trajectory and an agenda for those who come after them. For the field of liturgical studies, Mark Searle is best understood as a scholar in this third category. The reprinted articles and appreciative introductions gathered for this collection may be the best argument for so considering him.

I had the privilege of studying with Searle at the University of Notre Dame in the 1970s where he introduced me to the historical development and recently promulgated contemporary revisions of the structures of Christian Initiation for Roman Rite Catholics. I was impressed with his command of the sources, his ability to derive theological insights from the worship practices of the Church, his passion for celebrations marked not only by faithfulness to the reformed rites but animated by a spirit of recollection and awe before the mystery of the Living God. I was even more impressed by his generosity to his students, patiently answering our often naïve questions, gently critiquing our research, but most of all encouraging us to devote ourselves to serve the praying Church in the local communities where we found ourselves. Like Ralph

Keifer, another Notre Dame liturgical studies professor of that era whose life was tragically cut short at the height of his productive scholarship, Searle demonstrated both historical and theological mastery of liturgical data but resisted becoming an antiquarian or pedant. Although Mark Searle's personality was almost completely opposite to Keifer's, both found that the traditional approaches to liturgical studies needed to be supplemented by examination of the lived experience of communally praying communities. Keifer's method was evocative and poetic: he would tease out the implications of worship practices affecting him as a "man in the pew"; his insights were often brilliant, but they were not grounded in any clearly articulated method. By contrast Mark Searle focused on methodological questions, offering in his vice-presidential address to the North American Academy of Liturgy an extraordinary challenge to rethink the contours of the field in his call for the development of "pastoral liturgical studies."

If historical liturgical studies found its primary conversational partner in the disciplines of history (cataloguing manuscripts, creating critical editions of texts, unearthing archeological remains, categorizing worship implements, and tracing their transformations over time) and theological liturgical studies found its primary conversational partner in the disciplines of philosophy and systematics (exploring the truth-claims made by worship language, clarifying the epistemological status of symbolic communication, examining how theological concepts such as revelation, Scripture, tradition, doctrine of God, Christology, soteriology, pneumatology, sacramentality, eschatology, etc., relate to Christian worship), Searle called for a pastoral liturgical studies whose primary conversational partners would be the social or human sciences: psychology (especially social psychology), sociology, and anthropology. While it was perfectly legitimate in Searle's view to learn how human beings had worshiped in the past (historical liturgical studies) and to move beyond description of past events to their putative normative character for present worshipers (theological liturgical studies), his scholarly interest increasingly became the actual behavior of contemporary worshipers, examined not anecdotally but with academic rigor (pastoral liturgical studies). This engagement with the human sciences bore fruit in a research project Searle codirected in the 1980s examining the worship behavior of United States Roman Catholic parishes, involving him in the creation of various instruments to gather data, the training of dozens of parish liturgists as participant observers, and the writing of a series of reports interpreting the data collected.

Having gained some insight into the value the human sciences could bring to liturgical studies, Mark Searle turned to yet another academic discipline—semiotics—as a possible conversation partner with pastoral liturgical studies. He spent a year studying with some of the foremost Dutch liturgical scholars who were pioneers in the application of semiotic theory to liturgical studies. His article, "*Fons Vitae*: A Case Study in the Use of Liturgy as a Theological Source," hints at the contribution his immersion in semiotics might have made to pastoral liturgical studies if only he had lived longer.

Semiotics is usually defined as a "science of signs," with the proviso that the discipline studies *how* signs mean, not *what* they mean. Extrapolating from insights proposed by the Swiss linguist Ferdinand de Sassure and the American philosopher Charles Saunders Pierce, two fundamental streams of semiotic theory were developed in the latter half of the twentieth century. In one the fundamental sign system is taken to be language, with other sign systems assimilated to a linguistic paradigm; I would place the Paris school associated with A. J. Greimas (and thus Searle's adaptation of this framework for pastoral liturgical studies) in this category. In the other, the linguistic sign system is not privileged, and semiotics instead attempts to account any sign system in terms of its production of artifacts (poietics), the co-creation of meaning by those receiving and interpreting the artifacts (esthesics), and a "neutral level" account of the significant elements of the system (its codes) bracketing the processes of creating and decoding the artifacts. This approach, articulated by Jean Molino, has been well developed for musical sign-systems by Jean-Jacques Nattiez (and I have been involved in applying it to the analysis of liturgical music). Most interestingly, Willem Speelmann has recently attempted to apply Greimasian theory to the conjunction of text and music in liturgical music.

What is prophetic about Mark Searle's article is his recognition that taking liturgical worship as humanly significant behavior demands accounting for a vast number of codes interacting in a variety of ways to produce meaning. He recognized that earlier forms of liturgical studies had concentrated almost totally on the texts of worship (their historical development and theological content) without recognizing that the meaning of these texts can be reinforced, interacted with, or subverted by other codes operating in the same event (e.g., the ritual performance of a eucharistic prayer in which alternation of speech and singing may highlight certain texts and downplay others, ritual gestures during the Institution Narrative may dramatize the actions of the Last Supper thus removing the text from a prayer addressed to God the Father to a drama performed for the congregation-as-audience, or having the clergy stand while the laity kneel during most of the recitation of the prayer constrains the meaning of "We thank you for counting us worthy to stand at your altar and serve you.") While many liturgical scholars instinctively attended to some of these text/nontext yokings (gendered roles, posture, gesture, locomotion, color, time, spatial deployment, etc.), Searle called for a rigorous accounting for all the coded interactions, even though he himself seemed most comfortable doing textual and gestural analysis. For example, in the "Fons Vitae" article he brackets the directive that the congregational acclamation prescribed in the "Blessing of the Water" he analyzes is meant to be sung; that different melodies will highlight or downplay different aspects of the text; that the contrast between presidential texts spoken or chanted and congregational acclamations sung in unison or harmony, with or without instrumental accompaniment, will all contribute to the enacted meaning of the text.

In the years since Mark Searle's death, the category of pastoral liturgical studies has increasingly taken its place alongside historical and theological liturgical studies in the academy. However, scholars have not followed Searle's lead in steeping themselves in semiotic theory as a tool for examining the sign-systems operating in a liturgical act. I suspect there are many reasons for this: a scholarly movement from a "closed" structuralist theory (of which semiotics is a late development) exploring fixed levels of meaning manifest in cultural artifacts to an "open" post-modernist deconstructing of the notion of fixed meaning(s) inhering in any sign-system; the esoteric vocabulary and difficult thought-forms employed by semioticians; the difficulty of bringing the semiotic analysis of multiple interacting codes into a global analysis; and the lack of clear pastoral impact from such studies. But just as I dream that the epistemology articulated in Bernard Lonergan's *Method in Theology* could provide a framework not only for theologians to collaborate in their tasks but also a way to further conversation among all thinking people, so I dream that semiotic theory as articulated by Mark Searle may yet provide a framework not only for discussion among academic liturgists, but also a way to further conversation among all those concerned with the worship of the Living God.

Rev. Jan Michael Joncas is associate professor in the Department of Catholic Studies and the Department of Theology, University of St. Thomas, St. Paul, Minnesota.

Fons Vitae: A Case Study in the Use of Liturgy as a Theological Source[*]

While the complaint is common that theologians rarely use liturgy as a theological source, it is equally true that many liturgical scholars—and Niels Rasmussen was an outstanding example—are often quite sceptical concerning what passes for "liturgical theology" or "theology of liturgy." Liturgists, especially those who are historians, are inclined to distrust theological approaches to worship and sacraments grounded more in general ideas of the liturgy than in actual liturgical tradition and practice. Theologians, for their part, while accepting the *lex orandi* in principle, mostly seem to look at the liturgy as a townsman might look at a milk cow, uncertain at which end to begin to exploit its potential.

A refreshingly honest statement of some of the unease felt by the dogmatician about the use of liturgy as a theological source is to be found in Herbert Vorgrimler's 1986 article, "Die Liturgie als Thema der Dogmatik."[1] While welcoming and encouraging collaboration between liturgists and theologians, Vorgrimler confesses to a series of misgivings about how liturgy has been used historically, about the theological positions seemingly implied in certain liturgical practices, and about certain commonplaces of liturgical and sacramental theology. In partial response to his call for dialogue, it seems worthwhile to take up just one of his misgivings—concerning claims made for the efficacy of the sacraments—and attempt to test its validity by taking one liturgical practice as a case study.

* This article first appeared in *Fountain of Life*. Ed. Gerard Austin, 217–42. Washington, D.C.: The Pastoral Press, 1991 and is reprinted with permission of Pastoral Press, a division of OCP Publications, Portland, Oregon.

The Problem

It is commonly said that the liturgy consists of a double movement, from God to the gathered Church (descending or *katabatic*) and from the gathered Church to God (ascending or *anabatic*) and both these dimensions are usually rooted in the mediatorship of Christ as the outreach of God to us and humanity's response to God. The problem, as Vorgrimler sees it, lies in the claim that the liturgy possesses an efficacy beyond any other kind of divine-human transaction, and that the movement of God to humankind is in some sense more particularly reliable in the liturgy than elsewhere.

> The dogmatic theologian has problems with the kind of talk about the katabatic dimension of the liturgy as act of God which seems to suggest that there is something automatic about it, as if it were the liturgy that somehow 'gets God going' and ensures that God performs some specific activity. This, of course, means that God's sovereignty is no longer respected.[2]

While not using the phrase *ex opere operato*, this is clearly what he has in mind as he goes on to point to the use of the indicative formula,[3] the tendency to focus on the words of institution at the expense of the epiclesis, and the theory of character as an indelible mark printed on the soul by baptism, confirmation, and holy orders.[4]

Against this, Vorgrimler asserts—presumably on broader theological grounds—that sacramental efficacy cannot be thought of except in the framework of faith.

> All Christian existence, even prayer, even the sacraments (*sacramenta fidei!*), even the liturgy—all are grasped and sustained through faith; and the only thing of which faith can be certain is that it is itself the product of God's unattainable grace.[5]

Does the liturgy in fact give grounds for thinking that there is an anabatic and a katabatic dimension, and that the latter is somewhat automatic? What place do the rites make for faith, and what is its role in the sacramental liturgies themselves? How are institution narrative and epiclesis related? Instead of exploring these questions in the abstract, I propose to take, as a test case, a classic text of the Roman liturgy: the blessing of baptismal water at the Easter Vigil. To this text we shall pose the more general question of what is actually going on in the ritual performance in the hope that a closer look at what is said and done might offer new ways of posing these tradition theological questions.[6]

A Note on Method

The only way in which a genuine dialogue between liturgists and theologians can take place is on the basis of a close study of the liturgy itself. Here we immediately run into problems, since one of the characteristics of liturgy which poses difficulties for using it as a theological source is that it uses a number of codes—verbal, iconic, proxemic, visual, and the like—simultaneously and cannot be reduced to liturgical texts. One of the advantages of semiotics, as a general theory of signification, is that it applies in principle to all signifying systems and should provide a way of taking seriously the multidimensionality of ritual behavior. For the purposes of this exercise, however, we shall restrict ourselves to the examination of the text and rubrics of the blessing of water, since it is the normative meaning projected by the script that engages us here, rather than the specific meanings that may be operative in a particular blessing of a particular font at a particular time and place.

Semiotics is the study of how meaning is produced. It developed out of linguistics and carries over from linguistics two convictions that undergird the whole enterprise: first, that meaning is produced by difference and, second, that differences are found on different levels. The import of the first axiom is that a significant whole can be broken down into contrastive units whose meaning-value derives from their opposition to each other: a classic example is that of the pieces on a chessboard. The significance of the second axiom is that it is essential to compare things on the same level. It is not only the chessboard that is a sign-set: the room in which the game is being played, the clothes the players and onlookers are wearing, and so on, also consist of sign-units in contrast with each other: chair vs. table, spotlight vs. subdued lighting, uniforms vs. civil clothing, and the like. But it would be a mistake to contrast the pawn to the light fixture: they operate on different levels of signification.

Within a text, too, there are different levels at which contrasts and oppositions are operative. In the method we will use here—that of the Paris School, associated with A. J. Greimas[7]—it is customary to distinguish the form of the signifier from the form of the signified and to focus on the latter. (In other words, we shall not examine the presentation and layout of the blessing, but the form of its semantic content). Within the form of the content, there are three levels: that of the discourse (the images employed by the text), that of the narrative which underlies the images and organizes them to reflect a certain logical sequence, and that of the "deep structures" or underlying values that account for the fact that this text says what it says.

The study that follows does not attempt to provide a complete analysis of the text of the blessing. Instead, trying to respond to Vorgrimler's misgivings, we shall operate mainly at the narrative level, drawing on the imagery of the discursive level only as much as may be necessary. This is somewhat less than satisfactory from an analytical point of view, but it will allow us to focus on the question that most interests us: what is going on in the text?

The Text[8]

Blessing of Water[9]

(A) R1. *The priest then blesses the baptismal water. With hands joined, he says or sings the following prayer:*

1. Father, you give us grace through sacramental signs, which tell us of the
wonders of your unseen power.
2. In baptism, we use your gift of water,
which you have made a rich symbol
of the grace you give us in this sacrament.
(B) 3. At the very dawn of creation
your Spirit breathed on the waters,
making them the well-spring of holiness.
4. The waters of the great flood
you made a sign of the waters of baptism,
that make an end to sin and a new beginning of
goodness.
5. Through the waters of the Red Sea
you led Israel out of slavery,
to be an image of God's holy people,
set free from sin by baptism.
(C) 6. In the waters of the Jordan
your Son was baptized by John
and anointed with the Spirit.
7. Your Son willed that water and blood
should flow from his side
as he hung upon the cross.

8. After his resurrection he told his disciples:
   "Go out and teach all nations,
   baptizing them in the name of the Father
   and of the Son and of the Holy Spirit."

(D) 9. Father, look now with love upon your Church,
   and unseal for her the fountain of baptism.

10. By the power of the Holy Spirit
   give to the water of this font
   the grace of your Son.

11. You created man in your own likeness:
   cleanse him from sin in a new birth of innocence
   by water and the Spirit.

(E) R2. *The priest may lower the Easter candle into the water*
   either once or three times, as he continues:

12. We ask you, Father, with your Son,
   to send your Holy Spirit upon the waters of this
   font.

R3. *He holds the candle in the water:*

13. May all who are buried with Christ
   in the death of baptism
   rise also with him to newness of life.

14. We ask this through Christ our Lord.

(F) 15. R. Amen.

(G) R4. *Then the candle is taken out of the water as the people*
   sing the acclamation:

16. Springs of water, bless the Lord.
   Give him glory and praise for ever.

R5. *Any other appropriate acclamation may be sung.*

Semiotic Analysis

The text under study exists in the pages of the Rite for the Christian Initiation of Adults as the script for an act of prayer. Two levels must therefore be distinguished: that of the *script* which prescribes an event of communication, and that of the *performance* of the communication. Here we are studying the script rather than the performance, but as a script it has to be studied precisely as something to be enacted.

Moreover, thinking of the performance itself, we must also distinguish the act of saying (in semiotic terms, the enunciation) from what it is that is said (the utterance). The "saying" is a verbal act of communication that transpires in the doing of the rite between a Speaker (the priest speaking in the first person plural in the name of the community) and a Hearer addressed as "Father." The "utterance," on the other hand, is what is said: an implicit narrative[10] referring to events of the past and to further events hoped for in the immediate future. The "saying" (enunciation) is thus an event that occurs between the past which is remembered and the future which is prayed for, both of which are figured more or less concretely in the utterance (what is said).

A prayer is clearly not a narrative, a recounting of events. Yet it seems almost inevitable that any prayer beyond the shortest ejaculation contains narrative elements. And not just random elements, but elements belonging to an implicit narrative sequence or syntax. In Greimassian semiotics, this syntax consists in part of what is called the "canonical narrative schema." What this means is that the temporal clues given in the surface discourse (verb tenses, temporal adverbs like "yesterday," "meanwhile," "henceforth") suppose an underlying logical and temporal structuring or schema. This schema, common to all narratives, and without which narratives would lapse into absurdity, consists of four phases, each one of which logically supposes the others: mandate—competence—performance—sanction.[11] Any performance logically supposes a Subject of the performance who is mandated or motivated for it and who has the necessary resources and know-how ("competence") to carry it out. After the performance is completed, the sanction phase consists of the recognition of the Subject's performance and of the new state of affairs it brings about.

In the text we are studying, we have to distinguish different levels of narrativity. At a first level, the enunciation, or act of saying the prayer, corresponds to the "mandate" phase (phase 1) of an unfolding timeline in which the praying community is itself a participant: the community tries to "motivate" God to undertake a proposed performance (phase 3) for which he is recognized to be already competent (phase 2). This recognition of God's competence, an integral factor in the persuasive force of the prayer, is at the same time a very positive sanction on God's previous performances and on God himself (phase 4 of a prior timeline). These past performances, however, not only prove God's competence: they also constitute a mandate to the community to baptize (cfr. esp. v. 8). Finally, the praying community (PC) speaks for itself in sanctioning the performance of the priest ("Amen") and then itself mandating a new program (v. 16). There are thus three narrative levels operating here:

future act of God: mandate [>competence>performance>sanction]

↑

prayer offered: . . . >performance>sanction ("Amen")

↓

past acts of God: . . . >sanction

At each of the three levels, the same fourfold schema is logically supposed. The past acts of God were performances for which God was motivated and competent and which reach their final stage (sanction, or acknowledgment of what has transpired) in the liturgy itself. The future acts of God presume the same motivation and competence and will in turn be sanctioned. Between past and future narrative sequences (both of which, note, are only alluded to in fragmentary fashion in many prayers) there intervenes the ritual present and the unfolding timeline in which the praying community (PC) acts as a subject mandating a new performance or series of performances from God. The importance of all this is that it shows how the narrativity of the rite goes far beyond its allusions to stories past and future (the utterance, or *what* is said) to incorporate the community itself into a larger or higher level narrative line. By prayer, then, the praying community (PC) enters into salvation history.

Such, in very broad terms, is what is going on in the act of communication (or "blessing of the font") which takes place at this part of the baptismal liturgy. This account will have to be elaborated and refined in light of a closer study of the text and rubrics.

The priest then blesses the baptismal water. With hands
joined, he says or sings the following prayer:

1. Father, you give us grace through sacramental signs,
    which tell us of the wonder of your unseen power.
2. In baptism, we use your gift of water,
    which you have made a rich symbol of the grace
    you give us in this sacrament.

These first two verses are rather complicated, both in their syntax and in their allocation of roles, but if we ask what is going on here, the following can be identified as the main performances:

A. God gives grace to "us" in baptism.
B. "We" use water in baptism.

Now, when two performances occur together in a text like this, it is usually the case that one is subordinated to the other as means to end or that the two are in conflict. In this instance, however, they are presented as two performances related to one another in such a way that one (B) is the signifier and the other (A) the signified. The semiosis between the two is assured by two subordinate performances, one past and one present:

   a. God established water as a "rich symbol";
   b. sacramental signs "tell us" of God's power.

Two other things are worth noting about these opening verses. One is the use of "Father" as a vocative. The vocative always presumes *and enacts* some sort of relationship: in this case the particular kind of relationship which must be presumed already to exist between the Praying Community (PC) and God is one appropriately expressed by calling God "Father." We shall have to look for further clues in the prayer to what makes this particular appellation appropriate. The other thing worth noting is the absence of all temporal and spatial constraints on the various activities predicated of God and us. Apart from the use of the past tense with reference to the "institution" of baptism, the utterances are made in a sort of gnomic present, as if sanctioning an arrangement that is always and everywhere valid: namely, that sacramental activity is a joint program of such a kind that the performance of the praying community is always and everywhere the signifier of the performance of God in giving grace. Note that the sacrament is not the sign posited by the Church, but the signifier (ritual) conjoined with the signified (grace) and that these are not things, but performances.

   3. At the very dawn of creation
      your Spirit breathed upon the waters,
      making them the well-spring of holiness.
   4. The waters of the great flood
      you made a sign of the waters of baptism,
      that make an end to sin and a new beginning to
      goodness.
   5. Through the waters of the Red Sea
      you led Israel out of slavery,
      to be an image of God's holy people,
      set free from sin by baptism.

In contrast to the universally valid principle stated in the opening verses, the text now reverts to specific events of the past. Three successive utterances sanction three successive achievements with only a semantic, as opposed to a narrative, connection between them: not one story, but three stories involving "you" and "water." God establishes water as "the wellspring of all holiness"; God sets the flood up as a sign of baptism's role in making an end of sin and a new beginning of holiness; after its liberation by God, Israel becomes a sign of the community of the baptized, liberated from sin. Note that these are "anaphorizations"—cryptic references to stories presumed familiar to the PC—in which only those aspects of the original stories are retained that link them to baptism.

> 6. In the waters of the Jordan
>   your Son was baptized by John
>   and anointed with the Spirit.
> 7. Your Son willed that water and blood
>   should flow from his side
>   as he hung upon the cross.
> 8. After his resurrection, he told his disciples:
>   "Go out and teach all nations,
>   baptizing them in the name of the Father
>   and of the Son and of the Holy Spirit."

With this section a new character moves to center stage as "Father" yields to "your Son." Here again, we have three statements, each an anaphorization of a story presumed familiar and each relating a distinct performance. In this case, however, the three incidents are narratively linked and correspond to the "canonical syntax" of narrative grammar: competence, performance, and recognition or sanction.[12] This is confirmed by the fact that, whereas in verses 3–5 each incident resulted in some abiding value, in this instance the new state of affairs which is an abiding effect of the Son's performance is only manifest at the end: "after his resurrection."

Note, too, that traces of the subjects of the enunciation, or act of communication, while serving to maintain continuity in verses 6 and 7 ("*your*" Son), disappear entirely in verse 8. In verse 8, direct address cedes to impersonal narrative, creating the meaning-effect of "objectivity" characteristic of institution myths. (One thinks especially of the institution narrative in the eucharistic prayer.)

9. Father, look now with love upon your Church,
   and unseal for her the fountain of baptism.
10. By the power of the Holy Spirit,
   give to the water of this font
   the grace of your Son.
11. You created man in your own likeness:
   cleanse him from sin in a new birth of innocence
   by water and the Holy Spirit.

In contrast to the impression of "objectivity" given by verse 8, verse 9 immediately reverts to direct address—"Father" and "your Church" (i.e., the PC)—as the partners in the act of communication surface again in the text. There is also a temporal engagement of the enunciation in the use of "now," negating the "not-now" of the previous time frame ("after his resurrection"). This represents a major turning point in the trajectory of the discourse. Up to this point it was not clear where the prayer was going; now it appears that all the previous utterances were acts of sanction and veridiction[13] subordinate to the PC's larger program of "manipulation."[14] On the basis of what has been recalled and reaffirmed, the PC is now attempting to persuade God to do two things, one cognitive ("look . . . upon your Church") and one pragmatic ("unseal . . . the fountain of baptism"). The pragmatic performance is "for her," so that the community can carry out here and now the mandate given the disciples unrestrictedly.

It is characteristic of ritual in general and prayer in particular to be marked by "intentionality," by a tension between a virtual state (having to and wanting to baptize in accordance with the mandate) and a realized state (successful completion of the performance in the endowment of the candidates with the values intended by the Trinity as ultimate sender of the mandate). Such motivation and finality give the whole liturgy its semantic unity, unite all its parts into a single "line of action."[15] But among all those parts, the water-rite ("baptism") is the climax: it lends its name to the whole liturgy. By a similar synechdoche, "water" refers not just to the liquid, but stands for the ritual action in which it is used (much as "tea" may mean the meal and not just the drink). Hence it is referred to in verses 9ff. precisely as "the fountain of baptism" and "the water(s) of this font." The implication of this, as we shall see, is that the Spirit is invoked not to transform the waters, but to ensure the connection (semiosis) between the rite and what it signifies.

What is signified by the rite of baptism is spelled out in the very dense series of statements in verses 10–11. Here we see again how a whole series of narrative allusions tend to be compacted into a very small space in Christian prayer and they really require a rather more detailed analysis than is possible here.[16] Such analysis would attempt to identify the basic building blocks of narrative, namely, states of affairs and transformations of those states of affairs. In our own case, analysis reveals that two sets of transformations are envisaged, each consisting of the negation of one state of affairs and the affirmation of a new state of affairs.

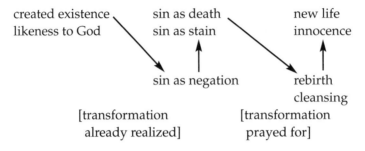

The story-line, in other words, is this. The unbaptized represent humanity which, having been made originally in God's likeness, has suffered a transformation in the form of a negation of that original life and likeness (act of sin), so that their state is one of "death" and "disfigurement" (state of sin). A second transformation is therefore sought, a negation of the first negation (rebirth from death, cleansing from sin), which will result in a new mode of existence, figurativized as "new life" and "innocence." The desired transformation from death to life, from stain to innocence, is to be achieved jointly by God and the PC by means of water (which the PC already has) and the Spirit. In the unpacking of verse 11, then, we can see how the logic of the "canonical schema" enables us to fill in what the text presumes when it jumps from creation in God's likeness to cleansing from sin.

R.2   *The priest may lower the Easter candle into the water*
       either once or three times, as he continues:

12.   We ask you, Father, with your Son,
            to send your Holy Spirit upon the waters of this
            font.

The gesture of "lowering the candle" seems on the face of it to be one of dramatizing the petition, "We ask you . . . to send the Holy Spirit upon the waters of this font." However, this creates a semantic problem, for the candle is figuratived in the rubrics (and would have been visually figurativized for those taking part in the opening of the Vigil) as "the Easter candle," an iconic metaphor of Christ. Out of this ambiguity we retain only the isomorphism between the /descent/ of "lowering the candle" and the /descent/ of "send the Holy Spirit upon the waters of this font."[17]

R.3   *He holds the candle in the water:*
13.   May all who are buried with Christ
      in the death of baptism
      rise also with him to newness of life.
14.   We ask this through Christ our Lord.

Here at last the (proposed) main performance appears to which all other (proposed) performances (opening the fonts, giving the water of grace of the Son, sending the Spirit) are merely ancillary. The candle is held *in* the water as the priest prays: "May all who are buried with Christ in the death of baptism rise also with him to newness of life." There are three things to note here: the candle is ceremoniously lowered and held in the water; the prayer uses the optative, "May . . . ", so that the addressee is not identified (though from the context it must be God); there is no explicit subject of the performance.

In actual fact, not one but two performances are envisaged here: "baptismal burial" and "rising to new life." The prayer is that those who undergo the (signifying) ritual performance of which the PC is the subject will all be beneficiaries of the other (signified) performance of which Christ is the operative subject. Praying for the descent of the Spirit upon the waters is a figurative way of expressing the hoped-for correlation between the two performances, so that those who participate in the rite may also participate in the paschal experience of Christ. The figure "Christ" is obviously a reference to something outside the text presumably known by all potential readers or hearers. If the hearers make the link between "Christ" and "your Son," then there is also internal referenciation, pointing back to verses 7 and 8 which speak precisely of *his* death and resurrection.[18]

But to return to the two performances, and specifically to that of the PC. The Church's prayer that God will effect what the ritual performance signifies—figurativized in the prayer that the Spirit be sent upon the waters of the font, etc.—seems to imply that "burial with Christ in the death of baptism" is as far as the Church can go. In terms of the diagram given above, the immersion-burial signifies on the part of the candidates and the Church a desire to negate the previous negation: the ritual act of washing and bringing to birth signifies a negating of the previous state of death and stain brought about by sin. But it cannot *achieve* it. It is a ritual mimesis of Christ's death and burial, but it cannot of itself achieve the rising with him to new life which is sought. The Church has the rite and the mandate, but remains radically powerless to achieve the values they are meant to realize because what the ritual performance signifies is precisely a performance of God.

The candle rubric, for all its ambiguity, is not without interest either. "Burial" carries the values of /below/, plus /conjunction/ and /duration/, precisely the semic values[19] of the candle held in the water. An isomorphism is thereby created between the baptized and Christ (the candle) *resting* in the water, as opposed to the earlier isomorphism between the *movement* of the Spirit and the *movement* of the candle. (This in turn corresponds to previous patterns of immersion: the baptism of Christ (v. 6) and his burial (implicit in vv. 7–8).) There is thus a certain "duplicity" in the meaning-effect created by the lowering of the candle into the water. On the one hand it accompanies (and is isomorphic to) the utterance of the virtual program of "sending (down) the Spirit" in verse 12, which repeats the "breathing" of the Spirit upon the waters in verse 3 and the "anointing" of Christ with the Spirit in verse 6. On the other hand, as symbol of Christ, the immersion of the candle figurativizes the descent of Christ into death and his *resting* in the tomb, a pattern which the baptizands will ritually enact in their immersion in the waters of the font.

In the last verse (v. 14) of the prayer, the PC invokes the name of the one who delivered the original mandate to baptize, thus providing a concluding (and conclusive?) move in this manipulative or persuasive discourse.

15.   R. Amen.

The "Amen" marks a shift at the level of the enunciation or communication. The PC no longer addresses God through the priest as its spokesman, but speaks directly to sanction both the performance undertaken by the priest in its name and the contents (values) of that prayer-performance.

R.4   *Then the candle is taken out of the water as the
people sing the acclamation:*

15.   Springs of water, bless the Lord.
        Give him glory and praise for ever.
R.5 *Any other appropriate acclamation may be sung.*

It is only at this point ("then") that the candle is removed, after the completion of the prayer and its sanctioning by the people. The use of the passive voice ("the candle is taken out of the water"), plus the fact that the move is made without any verbal accompaniment, being done under cover of the people's singing, indicates that it is purely a practical move, devoid of signification. Thus, in comparison with the /descent/, the /ascent/ is neutralized, perhaps because, while the Church can "baptize," it cannot "raise."

The acclamation raises a number of interesting problems, but only two of them are pertinent to our investigation of what is going on in the text.

First, the rubric mandates the PC to mandate the waters to bless "the Lord." In the context of the whole discourse, it seems that "the Lord" here is the "Father" to whom the prayer was addressed and who, "with your Son," was asked to send the Spirit upon the waters. The acclamation is an act of sanction or recognition which, in the canonical schema,[20] can only follow the completion of a mandated program by a subject of the performance. The question, therefore, is whether the sanction relates to past activities of "the Lord," or to the performance just completed in its name by the priest, or whether there is something more at stake. Certainly it is an assent to the prayer of the priest, both in its acknowledgment of God's past deeds and in its attempt to persuade God to act again now. What more could be going on?

Could the acclamation be an act of sanction on God's present performance? And which present performance? Is it the sending of the Spirit on the waters (an auxiliary program to the conjoint main performances of "baptizing as ritual death and burial" and "raising to life")? Or is God being sanctioned proleptically for his performance of "sanctification of the baptizands," even though the baptism of the candidates has not yet taken place, and God is not yet a realized Subject of this performance? In either case—but especially in the latter—the enunciation of this acclamation represents a remarkable act of *croire interprétatif* on the part of the enunciator (the Church). The proleptic "recognition" of God as realized Subject rests on an interpretation not only of the past acts of God but of the situation of the enunciation itself. In other words, God is acclaimed already for giving new life to the candidates in a sacramental performance which has still to take place—an acclamation which implies both confidence in God's saving activity and in the validity of the present ritual to signify it. Moreover, the fact that the subject of the performance of enunciation is here the community and not the priest alone seems to lend it additional weight.

The second problem concerns what sort of performance is indicated by the mandate to "bless the Lord." Since the issue touches on the nature of the prayer itself—identified as "The Blessing of the Water"—we will hold discussion of it over until the next section.

Summary

As we noted above, ritual is characterized by its intentionality, that is, by the fact that it represents a stage in the development of action between its conception (virtuality) and its realization, an intentionality that lends semantic unity to all its parts. In the overarching program of passing from outside the Church to inside the Church, from not sharing the new life of Christ to sharing it, the main phases are as follows:

Manipulation	Competence	Performance	Sanction
Christ's	acceptance	act of	Eucharist
mandate to	of mandate,	baptism	
baptize	tradition[21]		

But this program of baptizing undertaken by the Church is simply an instrumental program (signifier) in relation to the program of which God is the subject of performance (signified). In the blessing of the font, then, which takes place *immediately* before the act of ritual immersion, the PC asks God to ensure that what is signified by the ritual of baptism will, in fact, occur: that the baptized will experience an end to sin and a new beginning of goodness, will become part of a liberated people, will be raised to new life with Christ, and so on. This seems to reflect a rather clear understanding of the limitations of ritual even while expressing total confidence in the God who mandated baptism in the first place.

The Meaning of "Blessing"

The term "bless" occurs in two rather different contexts: first is the title and the first rubric, then in the acclamation. Can we identify the meaning of the term simply in the context of this text? The text of the "Blessing of Water" is essentially an act of manipulation or, rather, a hierarchical series of manipulations:

A. The text "manipulates" the community that uses it by laying down what is to be said and done and how it is to be said and done.

B. The Praying Community (through its priest) manipulates "Father" to a proposed course of action: to carry out the performance which is signified by the rite.

C. The Praying Community (directly) manipulates "springs of water" to another course of action:
sanctioning God.

According to R.1, "the priest blesses the baptismal water," but the text of the blessing turns out to be an act of manipulation, persuading God to act in regard to the water (or, metonymically, the water-rite). In the acclamation there is also an act of manipulation, in the form of the imperative, "bless." Here "blessing" is not the act of manipulation, but the "doing" proposed to the "springs of water," a "doing" which is synonymous with giving glory and praise, thus with an act of sanction in which God (and God's performance) is recognized.

The differences between the two can be set out as follows:

	Prayer	*Acclamation*
Level of Enunciation:		
Speaker/Hearer:	Priest/God	PC/springs of water
Performance:	manipulation	manipulation
Level of Utterance:		
Proposed subject:	God	springs of water
Proposed performance:		
auxiliary	-send Spirit, etc.	sanctioning (blessing)
main	-raise baptizands	God

In the case of the acclamation, the verb "to bless" denotes a benediction in the literal sense of the term: a speaking well of someone (positive sanction); in this instance, God. The prayer is more complex, since the text to be spoken is a communication in the form of a manipulation to action. If we situate both in the canonical narrative schema, this is how they appear:

cognitive level:	(1) PC manipulates God	(4) waters sanction God
	(mandate)	(sanction)
pragmatic level:	(2) God sends Spirit	(3) God raises candidates
	(competence)	(performance)

If we ask what the two cognitive/communicative performances have in common (so that they can both be said to be a "blessing"), we can say that the acclamation is a sanction, while the prayer-manipulation contains elements of sanction. We saw that the "argument" of the prayer consists in a recognition of God's competence as manifested in previous *mirabilia*. On these grounds, it might be suspected that the elements of benediction, while actually subordinate to the petitionary intentionality of the prayer, nonetheless give grounds for calling the prayer a "blessing."[22] An analogous situation seems to have occurred with the eucharistic prayer, in which *eucharistia* or acknowledgment of God by no means exhausts its content or intentionality. Nevertheless, as early as Justin Martyr, reference to "Eucharist" gave rise to calling the bread and wine over which it was spoken the "eucharistized gifts" or simply "the Eucharist." In similar fashion, the term "blessing" refers both to acknowledgment of God and to the whole petitionary prayer of which it is often part, and to the effects of such prayer when they are realized. In that sense, we may count our blessings.

While this accounts for certain features of the text, it does justice neither to the expression "blessing [of] water" in title and rubric, nor to the convention (expressed, *inter alia*, in the reverence accorded the "blessed" water) that the status of the water is altered as a result of the prayer pronounced over it. And, indeed, there is a semiotic distinction between blessed and unblessed water, expressed precisely in terms of the corresponding *uses* to which each is or is not put, which may account for what the term "bless" means. The question remains, however, whether the water is "blessed" (in the conventional sense of "transformed") *for* use in baptism, or "blessed" *by* its use in baptism.

The place of the blessing in the rite, coming as it does immediately before the central rite of immersion, does seem on the face of it like a preparation of the water, in the form of a dedication of the water to sacred use. In fact, however, the text of the prayer in its present form does not support this interpretation. We have already suggested that the ritual water referred to in verses 10–12 of the blessing functions, unlike the other water(s) referred to in verses 3–5 and 6–8, as a metonymic figure of the whole water-rite about to be undertaken by the PC (as "bread" is metonymic for all that one needs to survive). We have also seen that the main point of the prayer is to ask that the water-rite as signifier might be linked to the divine action which it signifies (the link being figurativized by "the Holy Spirit"). The focus of the petition, then, is not the water but the water-rite. The "Blessing of water" is a prayer for the fruitful celebration of the rite which is about to follow, a prayer whose main theme is precisely that the divine activity accompany the ritual activity which signifies it. In that sense, it might be more precise to speak of "a prayer for the blessing of the water-rite," where "blessing" is understood precisely as the "katabatic" dimension of the rite, as opposed to the "anabatic" dimension that is represented by the blessing of God by the PC.[23]

Conclusion

The purpose of studying the blessing of water at the baptismal vigil of Easter was not so much to harvest all its insights but to try to determine what is going on in a sacramental liturgy. The effort was prompted by the recognition that sacramental theology commonly discusses the katabatic dimension of the liturgy in such a way as to suggest that the divine action is somehow guaranteed once the ritual is performed. This, Vorgrimler objected, is an affront to God's sovereign freedom. The question is whether the view of sacramental efficacy to which Vorgrimler objects is really to be found in the texts of the liturgy, or whether he may not be jousting at windmills created by sacramental theologians dealing with the issue in abstraction from the liturgy itself. A text, of course, is not the whole liturgy, and one must be willing to concede the influence of sacramental theology on liturgical practice and sacramental discipline. The very way theologians have posed the question of how the sacraments "work" has contributed to a minimalizing of the sacramental signs in practice. Nonetheless, the faith of the patristic church is preserved in such older prayers as the one we have studied and must claim a larger authority than theological speculations over matter and form, efficient causality, instrumental causality, and so forth.

1. Liturgical prayer is an act of communication between a collective actant we have called the "praying community" and God, whom it confidently calls "Father." The intentionality of the prayer as a whole makes it an act of persuasive manipulation in which units commonly

identified as "anamnesis," "institution narrative," and "epiclesis" each have a subordinate and logical place. The performative character of the text, indicated by the "empty slots" ("we," "your Church," "now," "this font"), implies that relations between God, community, and baptizands are intended to be altered as a result of the ritual performance of baptism, for which the saying or singing of the "blessing of water" is a necessary presupposition.[24]

2. Semiotically speaking, all communication implies a "veridictory contract" between the partners concerning the truthfulness of what is said, that is, some degree of mutual trust. In the case of manipulation, the communication can only be successful in virtue of a "fiduciary contract" or some agreement between the parties concerning the values to be sought in the program proposed. In the case of prayer, this involves the necessary anthropomorphism of treating God as a partner who is to be persuaded. If this sounds theologically unacceptable, there is more to it than at first appears. For in fact, in the inevitable guise of persuading God to be present and to act—so that the signs are not rendered deceitful—the Praying Community is at the same time persuading *itself* that the signs are to be trusted, that the ritual stands to the divine operation as signifier to signified. The prayer is not merely a repetition of old "facts," but an exercise in auto-manipulation in view of the rite to follow.

3. The key issue for sacramental theology, as Vorgrimler indicates, is that of the semiosis—or signifying function—between ritual signifiers and the transformation they signify in relationships between God and the participants. Further analysis of the "deep structures" of this text reveals that this is precisely what the prayer of blessing is about: the relationship of signifier to signified, of "seeming" to "being." In the final analysis, (again, semiotically speaking), that is the point of recalling the past performances of God, the baptism, death, and resurrection of Jesus, and the mandate to baptize. Not only does the Praying Community affirm the truthfulness of the narratives it has inherited, and thus the truthfulness and competence of the God who features in them, but, on the basis of such conviction, persuades *itself* that the semiosis between the "rich symbol" and the grace of participation in Christ's paschal mystery can be relied upon. Far from manipulating God (in the usual sense of that term), the text shows by its "empty slots" (cfr. above) that the community gathered for the ritual is obediently submitting itself to the production of signifiers that incorporate it into the history it recalls and which should result in its

being conjoined with those values proposed by the Trinity in the divine mandate to baptize.

4. Greimassian semiotics brackets off all questions of extratextual referents and ontological truth, restricting itself instead to the study of referentialization as an intratextual process and to "truth-effects" produced in and by the text. This agnosticism is inherent in a discipline that sees everything in terms of signs, where the relation of signifier-signified is always a matter of belief rather than knowledge. Trust between persons establishes trust in their speech and, ultimately, trust in the things about which they speak.[25] In that sense, the prayers of the liturgy are not only expressions of faith, but rehearsals of faith, establishing a relationship of trust between the believers and God on the basis of which the sacramental signs may be taken seriously as effecting what they signify.

5. The problem with deception in ritual signs, then, lies less in the uncertainty about whether God can be relied upon to cooperate than in uncertainty about whether the human participants can be relied upon to enter into the relationship mediated by signs. This was recognized early on in the life of the Church, in the controversy over Donatism which gave rise to the distinction between valid and fruitful celebration of the rites. From a semiotic perspective, however, one is prompted to ask whether the distinction is not identical with that between the Church's program of sacramental ritualization and God's program of self-communication in grace. If this were so, then "character" need be nothing more mysterious than the ecclesio-social consequences of celebrating the rite, namely, that X is now a member of the Church, an ordained minister, and so forth, much in the same way that a ceremony of naturalization results in a person becoming a citizen, or inauguration makes someone an office-holder. The fact that the processes of baptism, confirmation, and ordination are not repeatable seems a matter of Church discipline[26] which could have been different, just as some nations practice irrescindible citizenship while other citizenships may be lost or withdrawn. In either case, "character" is the inherently public fact of having been made a Christian, or confirmed, or ordained, and thus assuming a wealth of rights and responsibilities within and without the community of the Church. It is a *res et sacramentum*: a *res* because it is the ecclesial meaning of the rites; a *sacramentum* because the ecclesial dimension of the rite is at the same time a signifier of a signified which is an interaction with God. This is true of both the ritual celebration and of its lasting effects. The ecclesial status

resulting from the rite is a sign of (and ought thus to be correlated with) an intersubjective relationship with God, just as the ritual celebration of the Church is a sign of (and ought therefore to be correlated with) the forging of that relationship with God.

The problem is simply that, while the issue of socio-ecclesial status can be resolved juridically, the relationship to God, like any interpersonal relationship, rests on its own inherent qualities and above all on faith. For semiotics, all relationships are based on a certain measure of trust (the "fiduciary contract"). A certain minimal level of mutual trust must exist between the community and the candidates, in the form of a willingness to baptize and a willingness to be baptized. Such minimal trust, at least a willingness to observe the convention and to abide by its social consequences, is expressed by the very fact of participation[27] and is usually sufficient to ground the new conventional relationship created between the participants and the Church in the rite. On the other hand, the relationship with God, while signified by the convention of becoming a member of the Church, is not identifiable with it any more than the Church is identifiable with the kingdom of God.

It is precisely this more-than-conventional quality of the relationship (expressed as "grace" or "participation in the divine life") which requires a faith that transcends simple belief in the conventional efficacy of the rite, a faith that opens the participants (community and candidates) to an intersubjective relationship with God. It is for this reason that the "blessing of baptismal water" comes where it does in the liturgy: preceded by the readings of the Word of God in the Vigil and followed by a collective renunciation of Satan and a personal profession of faith in the Father, the Son, and the Holy Spirit, in the holy Church, the communion of saints, the forgiveness of sins, the resurrection of the body, and life everlasting.

---

[1] Herbert Vorgrimler, "Die Liturgie als Thema der Dogmatik," in *Liturgie—eine vergessenes Thema der Theologie?* ed. Klemens Richter (Freiburg: Herder, 1986) 113–27.

[2] Ibid., 124.

[3] "Ego te baptize . . .", "Ego te absolvo . . .", "Conjungo vos . . ." Vorgrimler reports that one archbishop (now a cardinal) at the time of Vatican II wanted the words of consecration altered to something like "Ego dico tibi, pane, tu es corpus Christi" for the sake of being sure.

[4] Already it is worth noting that, of the three issues cited, the last is purely a theological view with no direct foundation in the liturgy as such, while the first and second became common in liturgical practice under the direct influence of theological and

canonical efforts to define precisely what a sacrament was at a time when the liturgy itself was not well understood.

[5] Vorgrimler, "Die Liturgie," 124–5.

[6] One of the characteristic features of liturgy which makes it difficult to use as a theological source is its syncretic character, namely, the fact that it uses several "codes"—verbal, visual, proxemic, iconic, etc.—simultaneously, and none of them, not even the verbal code, independently. It is the fact that Greimasian semiotic theory provides a general model for the production of meaning by both linguistic and nonlinguistic semiotic systems which makes its application to liturgy so promising. In this essay, however, we shall be content to analyze the text of the rite in terms of the codes of word and gesture alone.

[7] See J. C. Coquet, *Sémiotique: L'Ecole de Paris* (Paris: Hachette, 1980). The standard works of this school include: A. J. Greimas, *Sémiotique structurale* (Paris: Larousse, 1968) ET *Structural Semantics* (Lincoln and London: University of Nebraska Press, 1983); *Du Sens I* (Paris: Seuil, 1970); *Du Sens II* (Paris: Seuil, 1982); ET of selected essays from these two collections in *On Meaning: Selected Writings on Semiotic Theory* (Minneapolis: University of Minnesota Press, 1987). See also A. J. Greimas and J. Courtès, *Sémiotique: Dictionnaire raisonné de la théorie de langage, I* (Paris: Hachette, 1979) ET *Semiotics and Language: An Analytical Dictionary* (Bloomington: Indiana University Press, 1983); idem., *Sémiotique: Dictionnaire raisonné de la théorie de langage, II* (Paris: Hachette, 1986).

[8] The text as presented here includes the rubrics, the prayer, and the response and acclamation of the people, and is divided into seven segments. This segmentation is based on different "scenes" created in the text by changes of time (tense), place, and actors. It is less a case of strict disjunction between parts than a hypothesis as to how the text is organized, and may have to be rethought as analysis proceeds.

[9] The English text of the International Committee on English in the Liturgy is studied here since, unlike the Latin text, it is actually in use and is in that sense normative for a theology of the liturgy. Semiotically speaking, the English and Latin texts are two expressions of the same content. Thus while comparison of the two raises interesting questions of intersemioticity (i.e., how do the different versions differ in the way they represent the content), the English text is not considered a translation of the Latin, but a translation of the *content* of the Latin. In any case, the English text creates its own "meaning-effects" independently of any reference to the Latin.

[10] Implicit because it is in the form of a prayer.

[11] See A. J. Greimas, *Structural Semantics*, chapter 10, and Greimas and Courtès, *Semiotics and Language*, s.v. "narrative schema."

[12] The baptism and anointing of Jesus correspond to his becoming competent, his sacrificial death to the main performance, and the resurrection to the sanction phase. The contractual phase, the sending of Christ by God, while logically implied, does not appear in this version of the narrative, although it may be hinted at in "your Son."

[13] "Sanction" is an act of judgment upon the behavior and narrative program of a performing subject. See Greimas and Courtès, *Semiotics and Language*, 267. "Verdiction" is an act of judgment concerning what seems to be true or seems not to be true (ibid., 367–9).

[14] The term "manipulation," while having dysphoric connotations in ordinary language, is used here in the technical sense of a "making to do or not to do," which may be either positive (persuasion) or negative (coercion). See Greimas and Courtès, *Semiotics and Language*, 184–6.

[15] The concept of "line of action" is borrowed from symbolic interactionism. See Herbert Blumer, *Symbolic Interactionism: Perspective and Method* [1969], 1986, 1–60.

[16] In particular, only very careful semantic analysis can untangle the apparent inconsistencies between verse 10 ("By the power of the Holy Spirit give to the water of this font the grace of your Son") and verse 12 ("We ask you, Father, with your Son, to send the Holy Spirit upon the waters of this font").

[17] The use of slashes / . . . / is to indicate a seme, or minimal unit of meaning. In this instance, the one seme /descent/ is figurativized in two different ways, in words ("send . . . upon") and in gesture.

[18] This presents a quandary at the level of discoursive syntax. On the one hand, the death and resurrection of Christ were reported in verses 7 and 8 as past events relating to an individual subject. As such they are marked by the semic values /punctual/, /complete/, and /individual/. Now, however, the text reconfigures the events so that they become /durative/ and /collective/. In other words, Christ's death and resurrection are somehow rendered contemporary with the baptizands, so that "all who are buried with Christ in the death of baptism [might] rise with him to newness of life."

[19] A seme is a minimum unit of meaning; its contribution to the semantics of the whole text is its semic value.

[20] See what I have written under "Semiotic Analysis" above and note 12.

[21] Acceptance of any mandate logically presumes faith in the mandator and in the values of the program proposed. Consequently, "competence" in the broad sense includes the whole life of faith; in the narrow sense it refers to the will and know-how required for baptizing.

[22] It is presumably this understanding of the liturgical act in question which led to its being re-titled *Benedictio et invocatio Dei super aquam* in the *Ordo Baptismi Parvulorum* (Rome: Typis Polyglottis Vaticanis, 1978), although the General Instruction accompanying the same document still speaks of the celebrant "blessing the water of baptism" (no. 18).

[23] This seems to hold true even when baptism does not immediately follow, or when the water is used in connection with the renewal of baptismal promises. In the latter case, the sprinkling symbolizes baptism, again by metonymy.

[24] "Necessary" in the sense that the logic of performance in the canonical schema requires previous motivation ("manipulation") and competence.

[25] See the important article of A. J. Greimas, "Knowing and Believing: A Single Cognitive Universe," in *On Meaning*, 1987, 165–79.

[26] The discipline itself may be a further signifier, denoting the faithfulness of the Church to its own as an appropriate reflection of the fidelity of God to the Church.

[27] See Roy Rappaport, "The Obvious Aspects of Ritual," in *Liturgy, Ecology and Meaning* (Richmond, Calif.: North Atlantic Books, 1979) 173–222.

Paul Covino

Introduction to "Marriage Rites as Documents of Faith: Notes for a Theology of Marriage"

Most of the graduate students in the windowless classroom in the basement of Notre Dame's Hesburgh Library, including me, had studied Christian initiation with Mark Searle the previous semester. His presentation of the history and theology of the initiation sacraments had been so impressive that after his final words in the last class, the students spontaneously applauded. Now, we took delight to see our esteemed teacher so clearly excited by our simple gift of a stroller in anticipation of the birth of his first child. As he immersed himself in the intricacies of unfolding the clever feat of engineering that is a modern baby stroller, more than one of us commented on how appropriate it was that one who knew so much about the baptism of infants would soon be experiencing, with his wife Barbara, the reality of life with a baptized infant!

This story of my former teacher and thesis director points, I believe, to one of the strengths and contributions of Mark Searle's scholarship, one that is reflected in this concluding essay from the 1992 book *Documents of the Marriage Liturgy* that he edited with Kenneth Stevenson. Not content with knowledge about liturgical rites both historic and contemporary, Searle was concerned with what these rites said about the lived reality of Christian faith in particular places at particular times. The easy access that *Documents of the Marriage Liturgy* provided to twenty-eight marriage rites spanning almost twenty-two centuries, along with the brief introductions by the two coeditors, was in itself a contribution to the field of liturgical studies. In the concluding essay, though, Mark Searle's deeper interest in the collection became apparent as he invited the reader to see in these texts how marriage was understood and lived by people of faith in various times and places. Noting that most of the texts were "not the work of theologians or canonists, but of anonymous and long-dead pastors," Searle aptly commented:

> The Fathers and the moralists may have had negative views of sexuality and marriage; the assembled families may have had very specific economic goals or social ambitions in mind in marrying off their children. In their presence, and before this young, barely pubescent couple, what was a man of faith to say? Liturgy is always a moment of decision, when the theorizing has to end and the ideal has to yield to the practical: something has to be said and something has to be done. These documents witness to what nameless believers have found to say about marriage in the concrete, about the life and relationship that is opening up before this couple, and about the *sacramentum*. The *sacramentum* of matrimony—using the term in a broader sense than Augustine—is what holds the order of faith and the order of experience together. It is not an ideal, but a given reality.

As testaments to such "given reality," Searle explained, these documents of the marriage liturgy are a valid source of theological reflection on Christian marriage. While this perspective was consistent with mainstream liturgical scholarship that viewed the liturgy and its texts as a form of "primary" theology on which "secondary" theological reflection could be based, Mark Searle was one of the first to apply this perspective to the rites of marriage. Looking out over the landscape of theological writings on marriage, he commented that the documents of the marriage liturgy have "rarely served as anything more than a useful source of quotations in treatises on the theology of marriage, or as evidence of the development of canonical legislation on marriage." Culling through these rites from various places and times, Searle found that they "show, more than the writings of the theologians, and more than those who romanticize the erotic, a balanced and forward-looking vision of how the mystery of marriage can be understood and lived." The themes that he distilled from the marriage rites in the second half of this essay certainly expanded the theological vocabulary and range of motifs that were commonly associated with marriage.

The first half of the essay offers one of the best and most concise histories of Christian marriage available. Those looking for greater historical scope and detail would need to consult other resources such as Kenneth Stevenson's two books from the previous decade (*Nuptial Blessing: A Study of Christian Marriage Rites* [New York: Oxford University Press, 1983] and *To Join Together: The Rite of Marriage* [New York: Pueblo Publishing Co., 1987]), but Mark Searle's self-described "sketch of the development of Christian thinking about marriage" still serves as an excellent introduction to the array of practices and thinking that has come under the heading of Christian marriage over the course of two thousand years. Particularly noteworthy is his outline of three traditions of Christian marriage in the West and his warning that a theology of marriage based on just one of these traditions is limited at best. It was against the backdrop of these three traditional sources that Searle proposed the documents of the marriage liturgy as an essential source for a Catholic theology of marriage.

Searle's historical overview also helped to locate various negative attitudes toward sexuality in Church documents and teaching from late antiquity and the Middle Ages. Particularly interesting are his comments about the parallels between the nuptial blessings and the prayers for the consecration of virgins in Roman documents from late antiquity, his note that "the amount written on marriage in the patristic period is miniscule compared with the amount written in praise of virginity," and his observation that couples who actually followed medieval Church injunctions against marital intercourse for extended periods of time were hardly the norm, but rather "were often considered candidates for canonization." By looking at the texts of marriage rites from various eras, Searle was able to provide some background for the negative attitudes associated with Church teaching on sexuality, thereby contributing to the development, that was well underway in the late twentieth century, of a more positive view in the Church of marital sexuality.

Pastorally, Mark Searle's attention to marriage rites as documents of faith contributed to a growing awareness that the *Rite of Marriage* was a valuable source of reflection for both engaged and married couples. Assisted by resources such as Austin Fleming's *Prayerbook for Engaged Couples* (Chicago: Liturgy Training Publications, 1990), astute pastoral ministers introduced engaged couples to the Scripture and prayer texts of the marriage rite as sources of prayer and reflection for their formation for the sacrament of marriage. Similarly, the largely untapped arena of pastoral care with recently married couples could find in the texts and ritual actions of the wedding liturgy excellent fodder for mystagogical reflection on the lived reality of Christian marriage. This type of incorporation of the marriage rites into pastoral ministry with engaged and married couples would, as Searle indicated, "work to counter an excessive psychologization of the married relationship, restore a sense of marriage as a vocation to be followed in faith and fidelity, and thus propose a view of marriage as a salvific reality, a participation in the dying and rising of Christ."

Paul Covino is associate chaplain and director of liturgy at the College of the Holy Cross, Worcester, Massachusetts, and program coordinator (adjunct) for the Georgetown Center for Liturgy, Washington, D.C.

Marriage Rites as Documents of Faith: Notes for a Theology of Marriage[*]

Whether or not the marriage of Christians be considered a sacrament in the strict sense of the term, however that be defined, it is rarely understood as a simply secular undertaking. Because it is lived by two baptized people and constitutes their common life, it cannot but be the form in which their Christian vocation and their engagement in the mystery of salvation is lived out. But for many, especially for those who belong to the Catholic and Orthodox Churches, marriage between two baptized people is considered a visible sign of the unfolding of the hidden mystery of God in this world and thus significant not only for the couple themselves, but for the wider community to which they belong. Precisely because marriage is understood as an integral part of the whole economy of grace, itself conceived in sacramental-incarnational terms, this understanding of marriage has to be integrated into any adequate and coherent theology. And this presents particular problems, for while sacramentality, by definition, means the intersecting of two worlds of reality—the divine and the human, the invisible and the visible—the relation of these two orders in marriage is not particularly easy to identify. Marriage has always existed and continues to exist without being a sacrament: not every marriage is sacramental. A marriage between two non-believers is not regarded by the Church as sacramental, nor is a marriage between a baptized and an unbaptized person. The status of marriages contracted by baptized persons who lack faith continues to be disputed, though in law they are treated as sacramental marriages. A further problem relates to what it is precisely that constitutes the sacrament, a problem that continues to vex the

---

* This article first appeared in Mark Searle and Kenneth W. Stevenson, *Documents of the Marriage Liturgy*, Collegeville: Liturgical Press, 1992. Editors' note: The texts of the marriage rites referenced herein are not included in this volume but may be found in *Documents of the Marriage Liturgy*.

Catholic Church in particular.[1] This is not the place to rehearse the canonical issue, but a sketch of the development of Christian thinking about marriage will help situate the texts of this collection and underline their significance.

I. Christian Marriage in History

Marriage in the Early Christian Centuries

It is important to realize from the outset that marriage was originally considered a "Christian marriage," or a marriage contracted and lived "in the Lord" (1 Cor 7:39), because it was a marriage between two baptized believers in Christ. In other words, the sacramentality of the marriage as a *state* depended not on a wedding rite but on the baptismal identity of the couple. Their life together was a form of the Christian life, a form which, in the mutual love and reciprocal service for which marriage afforded occasion, was capable of iconicizing the mutual relationship between Christ and the Church (Eph 5:21-33).

In the early centuries, the way Christians contracted marriage differed little, if at all, from the way non-Christians got married, viz., through the customary domestic rites of betrothal, the handing-over of the bride, and the celebration of cohabitation, as these were done in different societies. It did not exclude marriage by cohabitation alone, where this was a socially acceptable way of marrying as, for example, among the lower classes. Nor did it fear to recognize marriages which the state would not recognize, as when the Roman Church recognized as marriage the permanent relationship between a free woman and a slave. The arranging, celebrating, and consummating of these marriages were matters, usually, for the families concerned, though it appears that in the East the local bishop did on occasion take an active role in finding suitable spouses for orphaned or abandoned children. Marriage was a domestic matter in all societies, being arranged by the two families and celebrated in the two households. Christians seem to have taken this entirely for granted although, as was only to be expected, their faith prompted them, on the one hand to suppress or adapt the religious (i.e., "pagan") dimensions of the inherited customs, and on the other to invite the bishop or priest, as leader of the faith community, to pronounce a blessing on the couple as they began their life together.

For many centuries, the presence of the clergy and the giving of the nuptial blessing seems to have been something rather like the blessing of a house today: a privilege sought by the devout rather than an obligation incumbent upon all. In fact, it only began to be urged upon couples who were marrying if the bridegroom was a member of the clergy. From the late fourth century, clerics who married were expected to seek the blessing of the bishop upon their marriage and to dispense with the traditional raucous and often rather ribald custom of the *domum-ductio* (procession to the groom's house). The fact that the traditional Roman Rite, as found in the Verona, Gelasian, and Gregorian sacramentaries, consisted of a Nuptial Mass and blessing, without any exchange of vows, reflects this non-involvement of the Church in the actual arrangement and conduct of the betrothal and wedding (texts 4, 5, and 6). In the East, however, in the fourth to seventh centuries, matters took a different direction, and the clergy became closely involved in both the rites of betrothal (which, in the solemn form involving the *arrhas*, were considered binding and virtually irrevocable) and in the rites associated with the beginning of married life. This seems to have happened in part because the need for the Church to regulate marriages seems to have asserted itself earlier in the East than in the West, and in part because of a rather vivid sense of identity of the Church itself as the Bride of Christ. Whatever the reasons, we find, beginning in Armenia in the late fourth century and spreading to the rest of the Eastern empire in the centuries following, that the priest or bishop is coming to assume a central role in the conduct of the marriage ceremonies. Central to these ceremonies from ancient times were the rites of the joining of the couple's hands, the handing over the bride to her husband, and the crowning of the couple with garlands. These came to constitute the central elements of what quickly emerged as a specifically Christian wedding liturgy, and the last of them came to lend its name (*stephanoma*: "crowning") to the whole liturgy (see texts 7 and 8). Sometimes this rite took place on the same day as the secular or domestic aspects of the celebration, sometimes the day before. Even so, it was not until the late ninth century that Constantinople ruled that this marriage liturgy, conducted by the clergy, would henceforth become the *only* way of marrying recognized by the Church as valid.

If the Eastern Church had a strong sense of the community of believers as constituting the Bride of Christ, that awareness in the West became somewhat obscured by the writings of Tertullian (d. ca. 220) and Cyprian (martyred 258) in North Africa. Responding perhaps to the fact that women considerably outnumbered men in North Africa, they both encouraged young women to dedicate themselves to a life of virginity by applying to the individual woman who so dedicated herself the title that had previously and properly belonged to the whole community: bride of Christ. In the late fourth century, we find Ambrose of Milan talking about a public ceremony in which women were dedicated to God, a ceremony called "the veiling of virgins." The veil in question was the orange-colored *flammeum*, customarily worn by the Roman bride on her wedding day: if the virgin was to be the bride of Christ, she should be publicly espoused to Christ and given the veil.

Although this whole history of the development of the "veiling of virgins" and its connection with the developing Christian marriage rite at Rome remains obscure, it is certain that there was some connection. In the *Verona Sacramentary*, the marriage rite is called "the nuptial veiling"; in the *Gregorian* it is "the veiling of brides." In pre-Christian Roman tradition, however, the veiling of the bride was not part of the ceremonies: when she appeared for her wedding, she was already dressed and veiled. There is reason, however, to think that, in the late fourth and early fifth centuries, the newly developed rite for the consecration of a virgin (the so-called *velatio virginum*) began to influence Christian marriage rites at Rome and lead to the introduction of a ceremony of "nuptial veiling" of the bride, comparable to the public veiling of the woman in the rite for the consecration of virgins. In both instances, the underlying motif would be that of the dedication of the young woman as "bride of Christ," in the one case through a life of virginity, in the other through married life. Nevertheless, there are several difficulties with this hypothesis: it is hard to see how the priest or bishop could actually give the veil (did the bride appear in public bareheaded?); there are no extant rubrics or descriptions to indicate how it was done; later medieval sources, like the *Liber Ordinum*, refer to a veiling of *both* husband and wife; there is no mention in the prayers of any veil or act of veiling. In support of the hypothesis, on the other hand, is the whole tenor of the nuptial blessing and of most of the Mass prayers in the sacramentaries, which pray almost exclusively for the bride, and constitute a sort of consecration of the woman to married life. Certainly the very close parallel between the nuptial blessings and the prayers for the consecration of virgins in these Roman documents from late antiquity is unmistakable and has often been commented on.[2]

Whatever the truth of the matter concerning the origins and inspiration of the Roman nuptial blessing, the fact is that the role of the clergy, and thus the liturgical celebration of marriage, did not usually include, in the West, their involvement in the arrangement of the dowry and the contract of betrothal, nor in the handing over the bride to her husband's family, nor in the joining of hands, nor in the customs associated with the bringing of the bride to her new home. The only exception might have been the marriage of orphans who were under episcopal protection or, as we see with Paulinus of Nola's marriage ode (text 3), the marriage of clergy. But the mindset revealed in the ode also shows that the clergy wanted to keep a clear distance between the marriage liturgy and whatever else popular custom might require.

Here we catch a glimpse of another, more problematic dimension of the parallel established in Christian antiquity, especially in the West, between the life of marriage and the life of virginity. The preference for virginity had already been unequivocally expressed by St. Paul in 1 Corinthians 7: "he who marries his betrothed does well; and he who refrains from marriage will do better." But, whereas Paul, in expressing a personal preference for virginity, particularly in view of the imminent end of the world ("the appointed time has grown very short"), also took pains to insist that marriage was not sinful, there was always a strong dualistic strain of Christianity which thought otherwise. In this Gnostic tradition, later taken up by the Manichees, all matter is evil and all involvement with the life of the flesh, as in marriage, is sinful. Now, while the leaders of the Church defended the legitimacy and even the sanctity of marriage, they could not quite get over a deep-rooted cultural suspicion of sexuality, so tied up did it seem with the world that was passing away, with mortality and corruption, with passions that threatened to cloud the rational mind and thereby possibly to shipwreck the soul on its journey to salvation. It thus came to be the common opinion of teachers and theologians in the West that while marriage was a legitimate way of life for Christian people, sexual pleasure was always sinful and sexual intercourse could only excuse such pleasure (reducing it to a minor sin) when it was undertaken exclusively for the purpose of conceiving a child. For this reason, perhaps, the amount written on marriage in the patristic period is miniscule compared with the amount written in praise of virginity.

Marriage in the Middle Ages

The Middle Ages begin when the Roman Empire is replaced in the West by a new civilization, bringing together the old Roman peoples in Italy, Spain, and Gaul with the new peoples who had migrated West in waves from Eastern Europe, the steppes of central Asia, and ultimately from Mongolia. The Vandals, the Goths, the Franks and others burst through the defenses of the Roman Empire along the Rhine and Danube, and came to settle in what is now Western Europe, bringing with them their own languages, their own laws, and their own customs. In what concerned marriage these Germanic peoples shared one thing in common that differentiated them from their new Roman neighbors: for them marriage rested not upon consent of the couple, but upon cohabitation. The bride was treated pretty much as a family asset, which might be lost to another family by elopement or capture perhaps, but was preferably transferred in orderly fashion and to the satisfaction of both families by purchase agreement. This agreement involved drawing up a contract between the heads of the respective families which stipulated the dowry the girl might bring to the marriage and the compensation to be given the girl's family for the loss of her. This agreement constituted a betrothal, and penalties were reckoned if one of the families reneged on the agreement and failed to go through with the marriage. Sometime after this betrothal, at a time and place stipulated in the agreement, the girl would be handed over to the authority of her husband's family and the couple would then be married. The Gallican and Celtic traditions of the blessing of the marriage chamber, with or without the blessing of the food and drink and the rings, reflects this Germanic tradition and the domestic setting in which it was celebrated (texts 9 and 10).

A tension thus arose between Roman practice based on consent and Germanic practice based on the bride price and cohabitation, between negative patristic views of sexuality and Germanic understandings of marriage which defined it almost exclusively in terms of sexual relations. From this tension arose juridical conflicts that were not resolved for several centuries, while from the unsettled social conditions of the so-called "Dark Ages" sprang the problems of widespread infidelity, divorce, abuse of women, disinheritance of lawful heirs, and so on, that so taxed serious-minded churchmen of the time. The compromise eventually arrived at, beginning with Hincmar of Rheims in the ninth century, was to define an indissoluble marriage as one that was both *ratum* and *consummatum*, i.e., freely and lawfully entered into and then consummated by sexual intercourse. This canonical combination of both the Roman and the Germanic definitions of marriage was the reason, it has been suggested, why marriages in the later Middle Ages were commonly celebrated at dusk![3] The combination is seen in our texts, however, in the Anglo-Norman synthesis represented by the *Benedictional of*

Archbishop Robert (11), and especially by *Bury St Edmunds* (18) and *Barbeau* (19), which lead through *Sarum* (20) to the modern rites.

Nonetheless, while such a solution may have satisfied the lawyers, it did little to resolve the conflict of mentalities. From the eleventh century, the Church began to assert its juridical authority over marriage in a series of reforming synods. From these synods emerged legislation affecting the public nature of marriage and intended to curb the worst abuses of clandestine marriages. But these synods, in attempting to reform marriage, also contributed to the denigration of marriage by imposing celibacy upon the higher clergy. Thus the reform movement perpetuated the negative attitudes towards sexuality found in Jerome and Augustine, suggesting that it was incompatible with service at the altar. Of course, most of the writers and reformers of the early Middle Ages were monks, who naturally tended to view women as a temptation and sexuality as the plaything of the devil. These attitudes seep over into preaching and into the exhortations that married people should abstain from sex during Lent, on the vigils of major feasts, on Sundays, and before approaching the Eucharist.[4] Such teaching derived from Paul's exhortation to couples not to refuse each other "except perhaps for a season, to devote yourselves to prayer," but succeeded in turning it into a prohibition of intercourse under pain of sin. The book of Tobit which, in its interpolated form, also played a crucial role as the model which had inspired the fourth-century *Statuta ecclesiae antiqua* to advocate continence on the first night of marriage "out of respect for the blessing," was now invoked to propose more extended periods of continence.

There is very little evidence, however, that such teaching was ever taken very seriously by most laypeople, who went on living and loving and lusting pretty much as people had always done. Certainly, historical research on the sex lives of medieval Christians suggests that fornication, adultery, prostitution, and concubinage all had their acknowledged place in medieval life and, apart from occasional outbursts of reform in response to zealous itinerant preachers, tended to be taken pretty much in stride by the local clergy.[5] But then local pastors tended to be closer to their flocks than reformist preachers and episcopal synods. When clerical marriage was outlawed, it was not infrequently replaced by clerical concubinage, especially in more remote areas. Those few couples who took the Church's teaching on married sexuality seriously and made a mutual vow of continence were often considered candidates for canonization.

Christian Marriage: Tradition or Traditions?

Although the rites of marriage documented in *Documents of the Marriage Liturgy* were increasingly shaped by the emerging canon law relating to marriage, they remain (until the sixteenth century) essentially anonymous creations, the work, presumably, of local pastors who were asked to "say something" at the marriage of members of their flocks. It is essential, then, to recognize that there are at least three traditions of Christian marriage in the West.

First, there is the doctrinal, moral, and canonical tradition developed and preserved in the teaching of the Fathers, and in the theological and canonical works of bishops and theologians. It is this that is the usual source for a Catholic "theology of marriage," but it is only one such source and cannot be safely used in isolation.

There is, second, the way Christian people through the centuries actually contracted their marriages and lived their married lives. For the most part, it must be said, history has not associated marrying with falling in love, but with doing one's duty as a son or daughter in a matter affecting the well-being of the family. Among the lower classes, it is quite likely that, at least up until the sixteenth-century Protestant and Catholic reforms, people frequently married without benefit of clergy. The canonical reforms of the eleventh century and the rites developed in response to them were primarily aimed at men of property and power, for the protection of their women and children. It did not prevent clandestine marriage or marriage by cohabitation, it merely delegitimized it; but that would not have had much effect on those who had neither name nor property worth speaking of to pass on to prospective heirs. Thus, while the lay tradition of marriage must be distinguished from the far better documented clerical tradition of marriage, within that lay tradition we need to distinguish marriage with the blessing of the Church from what one might call simply "marriage by cohabitation." Unfortunately, it is not possible at the present time to say with any confidence what percentage of the population of any given country at any given time used the rites presented in this collection.

Third, there is the romantic tradition which, historically, probably bore as little relation to most people's lived experience of marriage as did the theological tradition. It is represented by the much-discussed phenomenon of "courtly love" in the high Middle Ages, as reflected both in works of the creative imagination, such as the legend of Tristan and Isolde and the lays of the troubadours, and in the writings of mystical theologians.[6] Both in its medieval form and its reviviscence in nineteenth-century romanticism, and again in the twentieth-century idealization of "falling in love," it represents a drive to transcend the mundaneness of the institution of marriage in a *grand amour* for an idealized object, whether it be Christ, or the Virgin, *la belle dame sans merci* or some "dream woman." Paradoxically, under this heading have to be grouped two forms of other-worldliness: that which attempts to transcend the flesh in asceticism, and that which plunges into unbridled eroticism. Both are "otherworldly" from the perspective of marriage; both are romantic in their flight from the realities of mundane living and in their quest for an immediacy of experience of an ideal lover. What they have in common is their unwillingness to hold together the two dimensions of the *sacramentum*: the visible and the invisible, the tangible and the intangible, the sacred and the secular, the ecstatic and the mundane, the life of the Spirit and the life of the flesh. A theology of marriage will have to define itself, in part at least, in opposition to the romantic tradition, and not just as "better to marry than to burn," especially today when popular culture exalts immediacy of experience and romantic love to the detriment of marriage as an institution. In so doing, it will need to develop a positive understanding of asceticism and its role in transforming a Christian marriage into a credible sacrament of divine love in human form.

Finally, there are the documents of the marriage liturgy. They have rarely served as anything more than a useful source of quotations in treatises on the theology of marriage, or as evidence of the development of canonical legislation on marriage. But the importance of these marriage documents lies elsewhere. As was suggested above, most of the documents in this book were not the work of theologians or canonists, but of anonymous and long-dead pastors whose apt invocations in the context of marriage survived to accompany, interpret, and partially to transform the old, inherited ways of doing things. The Fathers and the moralists may have had negative views of sexuality and marriage; the assembled families may have had very specific economic goals or social ambitions in mind in marrying off their children. In their presence, and before this young, barely pubescent couple, what was a man of faith to say? Liturgy is always a moment of decision, when the theorizing has to end and the ideal has to yield to the practical: something has to be said and something has to be done. These documents witness to what nameless believers have found to say about marriage in the concrete, about the life and relationship that is opening up before this couple, and about the *sacramentum*. The *sacramentum* of matrimony—using the term in a broader sense than Augustine—is what holds the order of faith and the order of experience together. It is not an ideal, but a given reality. At a wedding it may be more or less clearly evoked, more or less overlaid by the social or even the erotic; but it is never moralizing. It is what it is. In the liturgy of marriage it draws the couple and the attendance—more or less wittingly, more or less willingly—into its ambit. Over against all forms of dualism, these texts bear witness to the struggle of Christians to hold the two dimensions of the Christian life together in all their wholeness. Holism is the heart of Catholicism. These documents of the marriage liturgy show, more than the writings of the theologians, and more than those who romanticize the erotic, a balanced and forward-looking vision of how the mystery of marriage can be understood and lived.

II. Motifs for a Theology of Marriage

A complete analysis of the theologies implicit in these documents of the marriage liturgy is beyond the scope of this essay. Instead it will suffice to draw attention to certain themes or motifs that recur in different ways in the different traditions, allowing the reader to explore the presence and form of these motifs in the texts themselves.

1.Anamnesis

While a sense of anticipation is perhaps the chief hallmark of modern weddings—anticipation of a life of love, of success, of children, etc.—these traditional rites are strongly marked by memory, or *anamnesis*. The meaning of this moment and of this transaction is assessed not so much in reference to the hopes of the couple, as to the memories of the community. Marriage in general, and now this marriage in particular, is contextualized in the economy of divine salvation, seen as a long, continuous history of God's presence and assistance as generation after generation of believers have tried to live in marriage a life of faith.

This anamnesis has the effect of relating the present couple to the ancestors: to Adam and Eve, Abraham and Sarah, Isaac and Rebeccah, Jacob and Rachel, Tobit and Sarah, Joachim and Anna, Zachary and Elizabeth, and the anonymous couple at Cana. Thus each new couple takes its place in the succession of generations, hopeful of doing its duty by God's grace, and of being blessed with children and an old age in which they see the succession continued in their children's children, before they pass to their reward. Even more than that, the whole succession of generations is somehow summed up in this bridal pair: in a certain sense, they *become* Adam and Eve, Abraham and Sarah, and the rest. They become more than themselves, assuming a role which transcends their individual lives and loves and faith: they become Everyman and Everywoman, the archetypal Man and Woman, king and queen,[7] icons of the holy nation (text 2) wedded to its God.

In Christian usage, the image of the couple representing Israel yields, of course, to the image of the couple as living icons of Christ and the Church, based on Ephesians 5.[8] The importance of this for a theology of Christian marriage has already been discussed, but it is in the Byzantine and Coptic liturgies that this making of the couple into icons of Christ and his Church reaches full bloom. Properly understood, this could provide a starting point for a theology of the household as a domestic church constituted by marriage.

The divine sanction on marriage in general and on this marriage in particular is constantly recalled. Marriage is the first, original blessing conferred by God on humankind, a blessing that has survived the fall and the vicissitudes of history (and one might add, though the texts do not, a negative theological press in Christian history). In marrying before God, the couple take up what is their divine vocation, a way of life ordained by God and sanctified by its submission to God's plan for his creation. And the presence of Christ at the marriage feast of Cana, while simply the context for the first "epiphany" of Christ's glory in John's Gospel, has been seen in the ritual tradition as indicating the assumption of marriage into Christ's work of redemption. There, still, the Lord may manifest his glory in those who invite his presence in their lives.

In short, the role of remembering or anamnesis is to situate this marriage in a larger context of God's creative and redemptive work, to identify these two people with the couples who flit across the history of that work as recorded in the Scriptures, and to turn them into icons of the redeeming Christ and redeemed humanity. The couple do not merely minister the sacrament to each other: they become sacrament in assuming, fully, consciously, and actively, the sacramental role or vocation that the liturgy celebrates.

2. Invocation

Although the Jewish wedding liturgy maintains a mood of unqualified joy, content simply to bless God for the blessings of marriage, in all Christian traditions such a high vision of the married life evokes a corresponding call for divine assistance in living out this vocation. Out of anamnesis flows intercession, as the memory of God's economy prompts the request for help on behalf of those who are to be participant in it.

This pattern is common enough, but in the solemn blessings of the Roman Rite—the blessing of the font, the prayer of ordination, the eucharistic prayer—the first and chief blessing that is invoked is the descent of the Holy Spirit upon the action of the Church, to ensure that the sacramental sign be capable of effecting what it signifies. The nuptial blessing is the equivalent prayer of the marriage rite and becomes the central element in the nuptial liturgies of the West. Yet, for all its similarities to the other solemn prayers, it passes directly from anamnesis to intercession without an epiclesis invoking the Spirit. (The same is true in the rite for the consecration of virgins.) Can it be that the importance attached to the exchange of consent as constituting marriage (or to the intent to live a life of virginity, independent of any public ceremony of consecration), was such that the nuptial blessing was simply that: a blessing on a marriage that was already in place? If so, it is remarkable that later, when the marriage rite came to include the exchange of vows at the door of the church, no prayer for divine assistance was insinuated at that point.

The rest of the blessings prayed for inevitably reflect the social and cultural conditions of each liturgy and deserve closer comparison than can be undertaken here.

a. The *Roman* texts (4–6) tend to speak rather generically about God's lending assistance to the institutions he has ordained, but then become much more specific in the nuptial blessing. Here we have the mold, as it were, for the features of the ideal wife in late antiquity. She is to be, first and foremost, a lady: faithful, serious, modest, "a person of integrity and innocence," wise, and above suspicion. In her marriage "she devoutly serves the living God"; marriage is not so much for "lawful pleasures" as it is for fidelity both to God and to her husband. A contemporary theological note creeps in with the assertion, first found in an anonymous late fourth-century Roman writer, that woman is (morally) weaker than man, because her likeness to God is one step removed: God made man in his own image, but he made woman like man![9] Hence the prayer for grace to protect her against her own weakness, and to enable her to live a life of religious discipline. These prayers doubtless survived in the marriage rite less because they bore any direct relation to normal human experience (which would suggest, if anything, that it has usually been men rather than women who need such discipline), than because they matched the negative picture of woman fostered early by ascetics, cultivated by monks, and promoted by the clergy. While the anamnetic sections of the Roman prayers have some positive things to say about the divine institution of marriage and its procreative purpose in God's plan, their brevity, their focus on the woman, and their endorsement of the cultural stereotype of the wife-as-matron make them rather poor sources for a theology of marriage.

b. The Gallican tradition is that of the non-Roman West, though it came to be compromised early on by Roman influence and was eventually suppressed in favor of Roman Rites. Nonetheless, the conquest was not complete, for Gallican prayers and rites have continued to appear in Western marriage rites to the present day. They are represented in our collection by *Bobbio* (8) and *Egbert* (10), with their characteristic blessing of the couple in the nuptial chamber. In *Bobbio* the prayer is chiefly for those graces that make marriage companionable: peace of mind, oneness of heart, charity. In *Egbert* there is more of a sense of what might be called the religious dimension of marriage: "holiness, chastity, meekness, fulfillment of the law and obedience to God." But it is not purely moralizing, like the Roman prayers. The *sacramentum* is not overlooked: "may [the Holy Trinity] preserve your body, save your soul, shine in your heart, guide your senses, and lead you to everlasting life." But just as *Bobbio* asks for the graces of friendship, so *Egbert* is not ashamed to ask for long life. Both ask for the blessing of children, but neither seems defensive about sex or worried about the possibility of infidelity, though hints of this appear in the later Gallican documents, from Canterbury and northern Italy (12 and 13).

c. In the Visigothic or old Spanish tradition, the most characteristic prayer is perhaps that for "united hearts" and "virtuous children." They are not afraid to ask for the material security which makes a happy marriage possible, as well as for appropriate spiritual gifts, but there is an edge of anxiety creeping in from time to time that the goods of this world, including the joys of the marriage bed, might be a cause of their spiritual undoing. All in all, though, these Spanish prayers are for the couple that they may enjoy all blessings of body, heart, and mind.

d. The Eastern texts pray repeatedly for blessings that are poured out, pressed down, and running over, but like the Visigothic texts, they pray for material as well as spiritual, temporal as well as eternal goods. In the Byzantine liturgy, we see this overflowing to the benefit of others:

Fill their houses with wheat, grain and oil
and with every good thing,
so that they may give in turn to those in need.

The Coptic liturgy is similar, except that here the joy of the day and its promises are edged with the recognition of danger. Like the Byzantine liturgy, it asks God to strengthen the promises the couple have made to each other and to keep them united, but it adds "Save them from the wiles of the evil one, and from all diabolical temptation" and characterizes the anointing as "protection against evil spirits."

e. The later medieval rites are largely a synthesis of the earlier Western traditions, both Roman and non-Roman. *Sarum* (20), for example, adds little to those earlier traditions in terms of blessings prayed for. With the medieval Western rites, as with the Eastern rites, one gets the impression that a general, elaborate, and repeated request for God's blessing outweighs much attention to specifics, though the ancient Roman blessing continues to present its profile of the ideal bride of late antiquity and the Gallican prayers qualify the austerity of the Roman texts with their mutuality and homeliness.

f. The modern rites, those of the Reformation era and later, are different again. The *Roman Missal* (21) is content to reproduce the Mass prayers of the Gregorian sacramentary, but to set them in the context of chants based on Tobit and thus redolent of the whole medieval tradition. The final blessing of the couple is an ancient Gallican prayer asking for children, long life in this world and eternal life in the world to come. The *Roman Ritual* (22), as we noted in the introduction to the text, is less a liturgy than a canonical formula. It has only two brief prayers: one, for the blessing of the ring, asks that the woman remain faithful to her husband and to God's law; the other, at the end, asks God to keep together those whom he has joined together.

Curiously, the rites of the Churches of the Reformation—apart from Cranmer's *Book of Common Prayer* (25) which retains much of the

Sarum rite—tend to be long on exhortation and short on prayer. Luther (24), for example, has only one prayer, asking that

thou wouldst not permit this
thy creation, ordinance and blessing,
to be disturbed or destroyed . . .

John Knox (26) has merely a blessing at the end, in which the minister prays that God will enable the couple to please him and to live together in holy love to their lives' end.

The *Ritual of Coutances* (23) on the other hand is remarkable not only for the sober and exalted view of marriage it proposes, but also for the prayers for protection against, or deliverance from, the evil eye, which was thought to be responsible for infertility and impotence in marriage.

3. Marriage as a Way to Salvation

Thus, in sundry and diverse ways, these documents testify to an acknowledgment of the light and the dark of marriage, and such a double dimension deserves to be retained even if the way in which it is expressed is thought to be archaic. It deserves to be retained as underlining a conviction running all through the prayers: namely, that marriage, for all its splendor as established by God and blessed by God, is a venture that can go astray. It is this realization that prompts prayer in the first place, of course, but it also points to a recognition that in marriage Christians have to work out their salvation in a life of faithful obedience to God. Marriage creates its own exigencies, as Luther indicates in speaking of the Cross as well as the joy that God has given to married people. Prayers for peace, for singleness of heart, for obedience and mutual love make sense because marriage is potentially a cauldron of conflict, a battleground of conflicting needs and demands. Prayers for chastity and fidelity recognize the temptation to seek a way out, to avoid the discomfort, to seek to assuage one's hurts and one's unsatisfied desires elsewhere.

That is why marriage is spoken of as a bond, a law, an institution: what Martin d'Arcy called, in a felicitous phrase, "a quiet ordered love."[10] That order is not something the couple create for themselves, but something established by God and blessed by Christ and sanctified by generations of faithful couples for them to enter into. The crowning of the couple in the Byzantine rite captures this well. There are not the crowns of arrogance, or of make-believe princes and princesses, but the crown of martyrs, suggesting that married couples, too, faithful unto death, witness to Christ and make up what is to be made up in his sufferings. In other words, marriage is a pathway to salvation, a crucible for the transformation of faithful souls, a way to eternal life.

One thing all the texts pray for, but which we deliberately omitted from our brief survey of the nuptial epiclesis, is that the couple now being married may come at last to life everlasting. None of the rites pray that the couple may be happily married: they all pray that the couple may be found worthy to enter into eternal life. *Bury St Edmunds* (18), for example, prays God to bless the couple so that

. . . cleansed of all sin
the love of your love may grow in their hearts
which will please you on the dread judgement day . . .

On removing the crowns from the bridal pair, the priest prays in the Byzantine rite:

Receive their crowns into thy kingdom
preserving them spotless, blameless and without reproach
unto ages of ages.

In this way, a certain eschatological note enters into the marriage liturgy and qualifies the joy of the occasion by subordinating it to the final goal and purpose of human life: eternal life with God in the kingdom of heaven. Though the couple may still be young, the rites look beyond the hoped for years to come to the frontier of death. In the words of the old Gallican prayer retained at the end of the Nuptial Mass in the Roman Missal:

May you see your children's children
even to the third and fourth generation
and afterwards may you enjoy
eternal life without end.

Conclusion

Between the preoccupations of the families and the negativity of theologians, pastors, it seems, still found positive vision of marriage to present to believers on the occasion of their betrothal and their wedding. It is unclear to what extent their practice can serve as a model for renewing Christian marriage today, but the vision preserved in their prayers and blessings can continue to inspire.

It has been argued, for example, that a return to the practice of marrying in stages might be helpful in today's de-Christianized world, because it would help raise the consciousness of Christians about the splendor and seriousness of marrying "in Christ." Whether separate rites of betrothal or blessings for the beginning of married life could usefully surround and protract the celebration of the wedding is uncertain. It may well help the faithful, but it may do little for those whose faith is little more than notional. Among such people the most common pastoral problem today seems to be not only that they have no inkling of what a sacramental marriage might mean, but that they are often already living together or intend to do so with or without the blessing of the Church, which then appears as a more or less dispensable ceremony for helping them celebrate their relationship. In the Catholic Church, at least, the most pressing problem to be decided is whether marriage between two baptized but only nominal Christians is always and ipso facto an indissoluble and sacramental marriage. Unless it is decided that two baptized but practically unchurched Christians can be validly but nonsacramentally married, there seems little hope of being able to differentiate between those who are ready to celebrate a sacramental marriage and those who are not.

Once the possibility of full, conscious, and active participation in a sacramental marriage is established, then the kind of vision offered by these rites comes into play. They offer, we have tried to suggest, elements for a theology of marriage in which the validity of the experience of married people is fully accepted and provides a context of faith by which to interpret such experience. In doing so, they provide a timely reminder of the objectivity of the married state, work to counter an excessive psychologization of the married relationship, restore a sense of marriage as a vocation to be followed in faith and fidelity, and thus propose a view of marriage as a salvific reality, a participation in the dying and rising of Christ.

One final thought. The axiom upon which the whole Roman theology of marriage, and the whole jurisprudence of marriage in the West, has come to be built is that marriage is made by consent. This has led to the view that it is the couple themselves who are the ministers of the sacrament to each other. It is to be noted, however, that this is a legal axiom and relates primarily to the sine qua non of freedom as a condition for entering the married state.

The Eastern tradition makes the presiding priest the minister of the sacrament, because he represents Christ joining the couple together, just as when he is baptizing, it is not he who baptizes, but Christ the Lord. This takes the experience of the liturgy of marriage as its starting point, instead of the legislation governing marriage as a contract. And here it must be said, too, that in the West the dramatic iconography of the rite is the same: Christ presides over the wedding in the person of his priest. Liturgically, the priest is more than just the official witness to the marriage. According to the Liturgy Constitution no. 7, Christ is present in the person of the priest-presider and he is "present by his power in the sacrament, so that when a man baptizes it is really Christ himself who baptizes." Of course, in marriage Christ is also represented by the couple as icon of Christ and the Church, but they are constituted as such an icon by the liturgy, celebrated "in the sight of God and this congregation," over which the priest presides in the name of Christ the Head. This is not to suggest that the Western conception of the sacramentality of marriage is wrong, but only that, for a catechesis based on the actual rite of marriage, it needs to be complemented by the Eastern view.

But perhaps the one thing that these marriage rites call us most urgently to consider is the loss and gain involved in the gradual removal of Christian marriage celebrations out of the domestic sphere into the church. The result was not a sacralization of marriage, for marriage "in Christ" was always sacred, but a split between the "church marriage" and the "secular celebration," which led to the secularization of the domestic and its alienation from the realm of the sacred, now identified with the Church. It was part of the same development which led to the imposition of clerical celibacy and is intelligible in a so-called Christian world. When all the world is Christian, the sacred-profane dichotomy will run through the Church, instead of between the Church and the as yet unredeemed world. But in a post-Christian world, the divine has to be redrawn and the unity of the holy Church, composed of all baptized believers, can be re-asserted over against the purely secular life of the world, which Christians are to redeem. The renewal of Christian marriage, then, would seem to be inseparable, finally, from the renewal of baptismal consciousness and from the profound consequences that will flow therefrom not only for the life of the family, but for the structures of the Church itself. Thus we shall have come full circle, back to the baptismal foundations" of "marriage in Christ" with which the Church's theology of marriage began.

---

[1] See Theodore Mackin, S.J., *What Is Marriage?* (New York: Paulist Press, 1982).

[2] See P. d'Izany, "Mariage et consécration virginale au 4e siècle," *La vie spirituelle: Supplément* 24 (1953) 92–118. J. P. de Jong, "Brautsegen und Jungfrauweihe: Eine Rekonstruktion des altrömischen Trauungsritus als Basis für theologische Besinnung," *Zeitschrift für Theologie und Kirche*, 84 (1962) 300–2. R. Metz, *La consécration des vièrges dans l'Eglise romaine.* Paris: Presses universitaires de France, 1954.

[3] James A. Brundage. *Law, Sex and Christian Society in Medieval Europe* (Chicago: University of Chicago Press, 1987) 136.

[4] Conversely, the newly married could be barred from attending church. So Gregory I to Augustine of Canterbury: "It has always been the custom of the Romans from olden times that [a married man] should seek purification and reverently abstain awhile from entering the church after intercourse with his wife. In holding this view, we do not mean that the couple are at fault. It is just that marital intercourse cannot take place without the desire of the flesh and so they should stay away from entering the sacred place because such desire can never be aroused without sin" (PL 72:89). See Gel, 6. "Infra actionem for the thirtieth day after marriage, or for the anniversary."

[5] See Jean-Louis Flandrin, "Sex in married life in the early Middle Ages: the Church's teaching and behavioural reality," in Philippe Ariès and Andre Bejin, *Western Sexuality. Practice and Precept in Past and Present Times.* (Oxford: Basil Blackwell, 1985) 114–29. Also, Jacques Rossiaud, "Prostitution, sex and society in French towns in the fifteenth century," ibid., 76–94.

[6] Denis de Rougemont, *Love in the Western World*, 1940, 1956. Martin d'Arcy, *The Mind and Heart of Love*, 1947, 1956. C. S. Lewis, *The Allegory of Love*. Georges Duby, *The Knight, the Lady and the Priest. The Making of Modern Marriage in Medieval France*, 1983. Jean Leclercq, *Monks on Marriage. A Twelfth-Century View*, 1982.

[7] So the Coptic liturgy:
Crown them with glory and honor.
The Father blesses,
the Son crowns,
the Holy Spirit sanctifies and makes perfect . . .

[8] Curiously, the image of the wedding feast of the Church and the Lamb in Revelation (Rev 19 and 21, passim) seems to have found no echo in our texts.

[9] Ambrosiaster, *In Epistolam I ad Corinthios*, 11:3-25 (PL 17:252-254).

[10] D'Arcy, *The Mind and Heart of Love*, 48.

Mark Searle (1941–1992)

Chronology

9-19-41	Born to Paul Stanley Searle and Eileen O'Keeffe Searle in Bristol, England, the first of eleven children.
10-12-41	Baptism into Christ, Parish Church of St. Bonaventure, Bristol, England
1941–1944	Father overseas during World War II, Hospital Ship, Army Medical Corps
1946–1951	Primary School at St. Bonaventure Parish, Bristol, England
1947	First Eucharist, St. Bonaventure's
1951	Confirmation, St. Bonaventure's
1951–1958	Secondary School at St. Brendan's College, Clifton, England O-Levels in English, French, Latin, Art A-Levels in English Literature, Latin
1958–1959	Chilworth, England Novitiate, English Province of the Order of Friars Minor
1959, 1962	Simple Profession; Solemn Profession as Friar Minor
1959–1965	St. Mary's Friary, East Bergholt, England Theologate of the English Province of the Order of Friars Minor, Undergraduate studies in Philosophy, Graduate studies in Theology
1965	Ordination to the Presbyterate
1965–1966	Pontificio Ateneo di S. Antonio, Rome, Italy S.T.L. in Systematic Theology
1966–1969	Theologische Fakultaet, Trier, Germany Dr. Theol. under Balthasar Fischer
1966–1967	Chaplain to U.S. Army Base, Bitburg, Germany

1968–1969	Institut Supérieur de Liturgie, Paris, France Auditeur
1969	Liturgisches Institut, Trier, Germany Diploma in Liturgical Studies
1969–1977	Franciscan Studies Center, Canterbury, England Lecturer in Liturgy and Sacramental Theology
1969–1975	Vicar of Formation Community and Master of Post-Novitiate Formation, Order of Friars Minor
1972	Liturgical Training Course for native catechists, Prefecture Apostolic of Volkrust, South Africa
1972–1975	Provincial Counselor, Order of Friars Minor
1975–1976	Sabbatical Year: University of Notre Dame Visiting Instructor, Department of Theology, Consultant, Notre Dame Center for Pastoral Liturgy (then The Murphy Center for Liturgical Research)
1977–1978	University of Notre Dame, Department of Theology Visiting Assistant Professor
1978	Resignation from Active Ministry
1978–1983	University of Notre Dame, Department of Theology, Concurrent Assistant Professor and Associate Director of the Notre Dame Center for Pastoral Liturgy
1978–1983	Editor of *Assembly*, publication of the Notre Dame Center for Pastoral Liturgy
1979–1992	Consultant to the International Commission on English in the Liturgy
1980	Marriage to Barbara Schmich
1981, 1983, 1985	Births of Anna Clare, Matthew Thomas and Justin Francis Searle
1982–1983	Vice-President and President of the North American Academy of Liturgy
1983	St. John's University, Collegeville, Minnesota Visiting Professor, Summer Session, School of Theology
1983–1992	Tenured Associate Professor, Department of Theology
1983–1988	Director of M.A. Program in Theology, University of Notre Dame

1983–1986	Associate Director for Liturgy, Notre Dame Study of Catholic Parish Life
1983–1985 and 1987–1991	Coordinator, Graduate Program in Liturgical Studies
1988–1989	Sabbatical Year: Theologische Fakulteit, Catholic University of Brabant, Tilburg, The Netherlands, with Gerard Lukken and Semanet, an interfaculty group of theologians and semioticians
1989–1991	Return to full time teaching, Department of Theology
Summer 1990	Six-week lecture tour of Australia and New Zealand
Summer 1991	Diagnosed with Cancer
1991–1992	Anointed with the Oil of the Sick
Summer 1992	Taught Final Class: Ritual Studies
8-16-92	Death in Christ, Family Home
8-17 and 8-18, 1992	Wake and Prayer Vigil, St. John of Damascus Church, South Bend, Indiana
8-19-92	Funeral Liturgy Sacred Heart Church, University of Notre Dame
	Rite of Committal Riverview Cemetery, South Bend, Indiana

Mark Searle (1966–1995)

Bibliography

1966

"The Sacraments of Initiation in the Catechesis of St. Cyril of Jerusalem,"
    Thesina ad gradum licentiatus consequendum, Pontificum Athanaeum
    Antonianum, Facultas Sacrae Theologiae, Rome.

1968

"An Alternative Order for the Holy Communion in the Church of England
    (1967): Arbeit zum Erwerb des Diploms am Liturgischen Institut," Trier.
"The Communion Service of the Church of England, with particular reference
    to the experimental Order for Holy Communion, 1967: a study in 'compre-
    hensive liturgy.' A dissertation submitted to the Theological Faculty of
    Trier for the Doctorate in Sacred Theology," Trier.

1969

Review of *The Church is Mission*, by Enda McDonagh et al. *Clergy Review* 54:12,
    992–994.

1970

"The Eucharistic Prayers," *The Way* (supp. n. 11) 89–92.
Review of *We Who Serve: A Basic Council Theme and Its Biblical Foundations*, by
    Augustine Cardinal Bea. *Clergy Review* 55:5, 405–407.

1972

"The Word in the World," *Life and Worship* 41:1, 1–8.
"Liturgy for Holidaymakers," *Christian Celebration* (Summer) 14–16.

1973

"History of Penance." In *Three Talks on Liturgy*. Ed. Harold Winstone. London:
    Thomas More Center.
"What Is the Point of Liturgy?" *Christian Celebration* (Summer) 26–27.
"An End of Retreat Service," *Christian Celebration* (Autumn) 18–24.
"General Absolution," *Christian Celebration* (Winter) 27–29.

1974

Stations of the Cross. Bristol, England: Clifton Cathedral.

Eight Talks on Liturgy (Private circulation).

"The Church Celebrates Her Faith," *Life and Worship* 43:3, 3–12.

1975

"Penance." In *Pastoral Liturgy*. Ed. Harold Winstone, 189–213. London: Collins.

"Penance Today." In *Penance: A Pastoral Presentation*, 3–11. London: Catholic Truth Society.

"The New Rite of Penance: A Report by John Robson and Mark Searle." *Southwark Liturgy Bulletin*, no. 17, 11–18.

1977

"Eucharist and Renewal through History," *Liturgy* 1:3, 4–19.

"The Mass as a Living Tradition." *Southwark Liturgy Bulletin*, no. 24, 15–23.

1978

Christening: The Making of Christians. Southend-on-Sea, England: Kevin Mayhew.

In *Assembly*

"The Act of Communion: A Commentary," 4:4, 6–7.

"The Washing of the Feet," 4:5, 14–16.

"Sunday: Noblesse Oblige (Editorial), 5:2, 25.

"The Day of Rest in a Changing Church," 5:2, 30–32.

"The Cup of His Blood" (Editorial), 5:3, 33.

"The Tradition We Have Received," 5:3, 38–40.

1979

"Prayer: Alone or with Others?" *Centerlines* 1:5, 19–20.

In *Assembly*

"The Word of the Lord" (Editorial), 5:4, 41.

"On Death and Dying" (Editorial), 5:5, 49.

"The Sacraments of Faith," 5:5, 54–55.

"Liturgy and Social Action" (Editorial), 6:1, 57.

"Contributing to the Collection," 6:1, 62–64.

"Active Participation" (Editorial), 6:2, 65, 72.

"Liturgical Gestures" (Editorial), 6:3, 73, 80.

"Genuflecting," 6:3, 74.

"Kneeling," 6:3, 74.

"Sign of the Cross," 6:3, 75.

"Keeping Silence," 6:3, 76.

"Communing," 6:3, 79.

"Bowing," 6:3, 79.

1980

"Serving the Lord with Justice." In *Liturgy and Social Justice*. Ed. Mark Searle, 13–35. Collegeville: The Liturgical Press.

Christening: The Making of Christians, rev. ed. Collegeville: The Liturgical Press.

Ministry and Celebration. La Crosse, Wis.: Diocesan Liturgical Office.

Basic Liturgy (Four Talks). Kansas City, Kans.: NCR Cassettes (Oral version of *Liturgy Made Simple*. Collegeville: The Liturgical Press, 1981).

"The Journey of Conversion," *Worship* 54:1, 35–55.

"The Christian Community, Evangelized and Evangelizing," *Emmanuel* 86:10, 556–562; 86:11, 609–618.

In *Assembly*

"The Three Days of Easter" (Editorial), 6:4, 81.

"Holy Thursday: Opening of the Paschal Feast," 6:4, 82–83, 88.

"Parish: Place for Worship" (Editorial), 6:5, 89.

"Advent" (Editorial), 7:1, 97.

"The Spirit of Advent," 7:1, 100–101.

"The Homily" (Editorial), 7:2, 105.

"Below the Pulpit: The Lay Contribution to the Homily," 7:2, 110–112.

1981

Liturgy Made Simple. Collegeville: The Liturgical Press.

"Introduction," *Parish: A Place for Worship*. Ed. Mark Searle, 5–10. Collegeville: The Liturgical Press.

"Liturgy as Metaphor," *Worship* 55:2, 98–120. (Reprinted in *Notre Dame English Journal* 13:4, 185–206).

"The Pedagogical Function of the Liturgy," *Worship* 55:4, 332–359.

"Diaconate and Diakonia: Crisis in the Contemporary Church," *Diaconal Quarterly* 7:4, 16–31 (Reprinted in *A Diaconal Reader*. Washington, D.C.: National Conference of Catholic Bishops [1985] 93–107).

"Conversion and Initiation into Faith Growth," *Christian Initiation Resources*. Vol. 1, *Precatechumenate*, 65–74. New York: Sadlier.

"Attending [to] the Liturgy," *New Catholic World* 224:1342, 156–160.

In *Assembly*

"Ritual Dialogue (Editorial)," 7:3, 113, 120.

"Lord, Have Mercy," 7:3, 114.

"May the Lord Accept the Sacrifice . . . ," 7:3, 116.

"Peace Be With You," 7:3, 118.

"(Inter)communion," 7:4, 121–122, 128.

"Rites of Communion," 7:4, 126–127.

"Keeping Sunday" (Editorial), 7:5, 129.

"Sunday Observed: Vignettes from the Tradition," 7:5, 130–131, 136.

"Liturgical Objects" (Editorial), 8:1, 137, 144.

"Bell," 8:1, 138.

"Chair," 8:1, 139.

"Oil and Chrism," 8:1, 141.

"Bread and Wine," 8:1, 143.

"The Saints" (Editorial), 8:2, 145.

"The Saints in the Liturgy," 8:2, 150–152.

1982

"Introduction" and "The Shape of the Future: A Liturgist's Vision." In *Sunday Morning:A Time for Worship*. Ed. Mark Searle, 7–9 and 129–153. Collegeville: The Liturgical Press.

"Reflections on Liturgical Reform," *Worship* 56:5, 411–430.

"The Narrative Quality of Christian Liturgy," *Chicago Studies* 21:1, 73–84.

"On the Art of Lifting Up the Heart: Liturgical Prayer Today," *Studies in Formative Spirituality* 3:3, 399–410.

"On Gesture," *Liturgy 80*, 13:1, 3–7 (Reprinted in *Worship and Ministry* 82:2, 10–17 and *Liturgy* 7:2 [1985] 49–59).

"Welcome Your Children Newborn of Water . . ." *Pastoral Music* 6:4, 16–19 (Reprinted in *Pastoral Music in Practice*, vol. 3, *Initiation and Its Seasons*. Ed. Virgil Funk, 3–9. Washington D.C.: The Pastoral Press).

"The R.C.I.A. and Infant Baptism: A Response to Ray Kemp," *Worship* 56:4, 327–332.

In *Assembly*

"The Joy of Lent" (Editorial), 8:3, 153.

"The Spirit of Lent," 8:3, 158–159.

"Mary" (Editorial), 8:4, 161.

"Mary, Seat of Wisdom," 8:4, 166–168.

"Households of Faith" (Editorial), 8:5, 169.

"Silence" (Editorial), 9:1, 177, 184.

"The Child and the Liturgy" (Editorial), 9:2, 185

"Childhood and the Reign of God: Reflections on Infant Baptism," 9:2, 186–187, 192.

1983

"Liturgy: Function and Goal in Christianity." In *Spirituality and Prayer: Jewish and Christian Understanding*. Eds. L. Klenicki and G. Huck, 82–105. New York: Paulist Press.

"Liturgy as a Pastoral Hermeneutic." In Theological Education Key Resources, vol. 4, *Pastoral Theology and Ministry*. Eds. D. F. Beisswenger and D. C. McCarthy, 140–150. Association for Theological Field Education.

"Symbol: A Bibliography." With John A. Melloh. In *Symbol: The Language of Liturgy*. Ed. John B. Ryan, 70–72. Washington, D.C.: Federation of Diocesan Liturgical Commissions.

"New Tasks, New Methods: The Emergence of Pastoral Liturgical Studies," *Worship* 57:4, 291–308.

Confirmation: The State of the Question," *Hosanna* 1:2, 4–11 (Reprinted in *Church* 1:4 [1985] 15–22).

"Assembly: Remembering the People of God," *Pastoral Music* 7:6, 14–19
   (Reprinted in *Pastoral Music in Practice*, vol. 6, *The Singing Assembly*. Ed.
   Virgil Funk, 3–16. Washington, D.C.: The Pastoral Press).
"The Liturgy of the Cantor." *Liturgy 80* 14:3, 2–5; 14:4, 5–7.
In *Assembly*
   "The Days of Pentecost" (Editorial), 9:3, 193.
   "Mystagogy: Reflecting on the Easter Experience," 9:3, 196–198.
   "Of Pasch and Pentecost" 9:3, 199–200.
   "Marriage" (Editorial), 9:4, 201.
   "Marriage: Sacrament of Faith," 9:4, 202–203, 208.
   "Liturgical Renewal" (Editorial), 9:5, 209.
   "Reconciliation" (Editorial), 10:1, 217.
   "A Time for Repentance," 10:1, 222–224.
   "Church Building" (Editorial), 10:2, 225.
   "Sacred Places,"10:2, 226–228.

1984
"Sunday: The Heart of the Liturgical Year." In *The Church
   Gives Thanks and Praise*. Ed. L. J. Johnson. Collegeville: The Liturgical Press,
   13–36.
"Faith and Sacraments in the Conversion Process: A Theological Approach." In
   Conversion and the Catechumenate. Ed. Robert D. Duggan. New York: Paulist
   Press, 64–84.
"Images and Worship," *The Way* 24:2, 103–114.
"The Ministry of the Word" (Parts I and II). In *Proceedings of the 1984
   Clergy Convention* by the Archdiocese of Portland, Oregon, 3–14.
"The Uses of Liturgical Language," *Liturgy* 4:4, 15–19 (Reprinted in *The Land-
   scape of Praise: Readings in Liturgical Renewal*. Ed. Blair Meeks. Harrisburg,
   Pa.: Trinity Press International, 1996).
"The RCIA in the United States," *Southwark Liturgy Bulletin*, no. 49, 11–18.
"A Sermon for Epiphany," *Worship* 58:342–345.
"Christian Liturgy and Communications Theory," *Media Development* 31:3, 4–6.
In *Assembly*
   "The Rites of Death" (Editorial), 10:3, 233
   "Sacrifice" (Editorial), 10:4: 241
   "Liturgy and Religious Education" (Editorial), 10:5, 249
   "Perspectives on Liturgy and Religious Education," 10:5, 250–252.
   "The Introductory Rites" (Editorial), 11:1, 257.
   "Collecting and Recollecting," 11:1, 258–259.
Review of *Nuptial Blessings: A Study of Christian Marriage Rites,* by Kenneth
   Stevenson. *Worship* 58:1, 72–75.
Review of *Unsearchable Riches: The Symbolic Nature of the Liturgy*, by David
   Power. *Worship* 58:5, 451–453.

1985

The Celebration of Liturgy in the Parishes. With David C. Leege. Notre Dame
Study of Catholic Parish Life, n. 5. Notre Dame, Ind.: The University of
Notre Dame.

Of Piety and Planning: Liturgy. the Parishioners and the Professionals. With David C.
Leege. Notre Dame Study of Catholic Parish Life, n. 6. Notre Dame, Ind.:
The University of Notre Dame.

"Observations on Parish Liturgy," *New Catholic World* (November/December)
258–263.

In *Assembly*

"The Kiss of Peace: Ritual Act and Image of the Kingdom,"11:3, 276–280.

". . . at whose command we celebrate this Eucharist . . ." 11:4, 284.

". . . He showed the depth of his love . . ." 11:4, 285.

". . . Lord, may this sacrifice advance the peace of the whole world . . ."
11:4, 287.

"A Place in the Tradition," 12:1, 301–303.

"A Meditation on All Saints and All Souls," 12:2, 308–309.

"Ritual and Music: A Theory of Liturgy and Implications for Music," 12:3,
314–317 (Reprinted in *Church* 2:3 [1986] 48–52; Reprinted in *Pastoral
Music* 11:3 [1987] 13–18).

1986

"The Parish at Worship." In *The Parish in Transition*. Ed. David Byers, 73–88;
panel discussion, 88–96. Washington, D.C.: United States Catholic
Conference.

"The Notre Dame Study of Catholic Parish Life," *Worship* 60:4, 312–333.

"Issues in Christian Initiation: The Uses and Abuses of the R.C.I.A.," *Living
Light* 22:3, 199–214.

"The Mass in the Parish," *The Furrow* 37:10, 615–622.

"Growing Through Celebration." *Music and Liturgy* 12:4, 110–118.

"Participation and Prayer," *Music and Liturgy* 12:5, 145–154.

"Not the Final Word," *Pastoral Music* 10:6, 44–45.

In *Assembly*

"Liturgical Language," 13:1, 337.

"The Feast of the Holy Family: Toward a Paschal Celebration," 13:2, 348–349.

1987

"Infant Baptism Reconsidered." In *Alternative Futures for Worship*, vol. 2, *Baptism
and Confirmation*. Ed. Mark Searle, 15–54. Collegeville: The Liturgical Press,
192 pp. (Reprinted in *Living Water, Sealing Spirit: Readings on Christian
Initiation*. Ed. Maxwell E. Johnson, 365–409. Collegeville: The Liturgical Press,
1995).

"Rites of Christian Initiation." In *Betwixt and Between. Masculine and Feminine Patterns of Initiation*. Eds. Louise C. Mahdi et al., 457–470. LaSalle, Ill.: Open Court.

"Initiation and the Liturgical Year," *Catechumenate* 9:5, 13–19; 9:6, 13–19.

"Pastoral Liturgy," *Music and Liturgy* 13:1, 7–18.

In *Assembly*

"The Spirit of the Liturgy: A Workshop," 13:5, 372–373.

"Confirmation and the Church," 14:1, 377, 383–384.

Review of *Una liturgia per l'uomo: La liturgia pastorale e i suoi cómpiti*. *Worship* 61:6, 557–560.

1988

"Renewing the Liturgy—Again. 'A' for the Council, 'C' for the Church," *Commonweal* (November 18) 617–622.

"Forgotten Truths about Worship," *Celebration* 17:1, 5–10.

"For the Glory of God. The Scrutiny of the Fifth Sunday in Lent." *Catechumenate* 10:1, 40–47 (Reprinted in *Commentaries on the Rite for the Christian Initiation of Adults*. Ed. James W. Wilde, 61–72. Chicago: Liturgy Training Publications).

Review of *Beyond the Text: A Holistic Approach to Liturgy*, by Lawrence Hoffman. *Worship* 62:5, 472–475.

1990

"*Semper Reformanda*: The Opening and Concluding Rites of the Roman Mass." In *Shaping English Liturgy. Studies in Honor of Archbishop Denis Hurley*. Eds. Peter Finn and James Schellman, 53–92. Washington, D.C.: The Pastoral Press.

The Church Speaks About Sacraments With Children. Baptism, Confirmation, Eucharist, Penance. With commentary by Mark Searle. Chicago: Liturgy Training Publications.

"Private Religion, Individualistic Society, and Common Worship." In *Liturgy and Spirituality in Context. Perspectives on Prayer and Culture*. Ed. Eleanor Bernstein, 27-46. Collegeville: The Liturgical Press.

"A Priestly People (video)." In *The Dynamic Parish Series* by the Institute for Pastoral and Social Ministry. Notre Dame, Ind.: The University of Notre Dame.

"The Effects of Baptism," *Catechumenate* 12:4, 15–22.

"God Writes Straight in Crooked Lines: Part I. The Inner Process: Conversion," *Catechumenate* 12:6, 2–9.

1991

"Culture," in *Liturgy: Active Participation in the Divine Life*. Ed., James P. Moroney, 27–52. Collegeville: The Liturgical Press.

"Tussen enonce en enonciatie: naar een semiotik van gebedsteksten." In *'Gelukkig de mens' Opstellen over psalmen. Exegese en semiotik aangeboden aan*

Nico Tromp. Eds. P. Beentjes et al., 193–211. Kampen, The Netherlands: J. H. Kok (Trans. from the English, "Between Utterance and Enunciation: Toward a Semiotics of Prayer Texts," by Magda Misset-van de Weg).

"*Fons Vitae*: A Case Study of the Use of Liturgy as a Theological Source." In *Fountain of Life*. Ed. Gerard Austin, 217–242. Washington, D.C.: The Pastoral Press.

"Liturgy and Catholic Social Doctrine," In *The Future of the Catholic Church in America. Major Papers of the Virgil Michel Symposium*. Eds. John Roach et al., 43–73. Collegeville: The Liturgical Press.

"Two Liturgical Traditions: Looking to the Future." In *The Changing Face of Jewish and Christian Worship in North America*. Eds. Paul F. Bradshaw and Lawrence A. Hoffman, 221–243. Notre Dame, Ind.: University of Notre Dame Press.

"Liturgy and Social Ethics: An Annotated Bibliography," *Studia Liturgica* 21:2, 220–235.

"God Writes Straight in Crooked Lines, Part II. The Social Process: Initiation," *Catechumenate* 13:1, 2–12.

"God Writes Straight in Crooked Lines, Part III. The Ritual Process: Liturgies of the RCIA," *Catechumenate* 13:2, 11–20.

"Trust the Ritual or Face 'The Triumph of Bad Taste,'" *Pastoral Music* 15:6, 19–21.

Review of *Ritual Criticism*, by Ronald Grimes. *Worship* 65:4, 376–378.

1992

Documents of the Marriage Liturgy. With Kenneth W. Stevenson. Collegeville: Liturgical Press.

"Semiotic Analysis of Roman Eucharistic Prayer II." In *Gratias Agamus: Studien zum Eucharistichen Hochgebet für Balthasar Fischer*. Eds. Andreas Heinz and Heinrich Rennings, 469–487. Freiburg, Germany: Herder.

"Children in the Assembly of the Church." In *Children in the Assembly of the Church*. Eds. Eleanor Bernstein and John Brooks-Leonard, 30–50. Chicago: Liturgy Training Publications.

"Preface: The Religious Potential of the Church." In *The Religious Potential of the Child*. Ed. Sofia Cavalletti, 3–12. Chicago: Liturgy Training Publications.

"Ritual." In *The Study of Liturgy*, rev. ed. Eds. Cheslyn Jones et al., 51–58. London: SPCK.

Foreword to *A Place for Baptism* by Regina Kuehn, iv–vi. Chicago: Liturgy Training Publications.

"An Imperfect Step Forward: A Response to Lectionary-Based Catechesis. *Church* (Summer) 48–49.

Review of *The Monk's Tale. A Biography of Godfrey Diekmann OSB*, by H. Kathleen Hughes. *New Theology Review* 5:1, 112–114.

1993

Semiotics and Church Architecture. With Gerard Lukken. Kampen, The Netherlands: Kok Pharos Publishing House.

"From Gossips to Compadres: A Note on the Role of Godparents in the
Roman Rite for the Baptism of Children" *Studia Anselmiana* 110, 473–484.

1995

"Benediction," "Cabrol, Fernand, OSB," "Communion Service," "Elevation,"
"High Church," "International Commission on English in the Liturgy,"
"Liturgical Movement," "Low Church," "Neophyte," "Paraliturgy,"
"Paschal Candle," "Prime," "Rogation Days," "Sanctorale," "Temporale,"
and "Terce." In *The HarperCollins Encyclopedia of Catholicism.* Ed. Richard P.
McBrien. New York: HarperCollins.

The editors are grateful to Ann Moynihan of the Franciscan Study Centre,
Canterbury, England, for her assistance in providing citations and texts of
Mark Searle's graduate school writings and early articles published in Eng-
lish periodicals.

Index